T0038632

THE SPICE MUST FLOW

ALSO BY RYAN BRITT

Phasers on Stun!
How the Making (and Remaking) of Star Trek Changed the World

Luke Skywalker Can't Read: And Other Geeky Truths

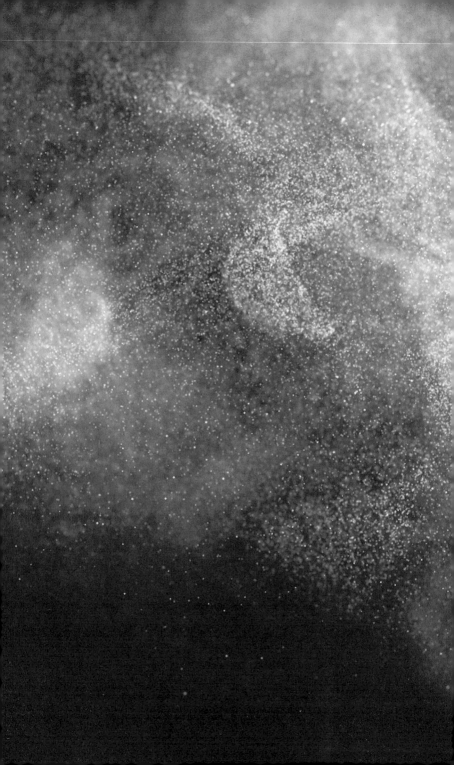

THE SPICE MUST FLOW

The Story of *Dune*, from Cult Novels to Visionary Sci-Fi Movies

Ryan Britt

PLUME

PLUME

An imprint of Penguin Random House LLC
penguinrandomhouse.com

Copyright © 2023 by Ryan Britt

Penguin Random House supports copyright. Copyright fuels creativity, encourages diverse voices, promotes free speech, and creates a vibrant culture. Thank you for buying an authorized edition of this book and for complying with copyright laws by not reproducing, scanning, or distributing any part of it in any form without permission. You are supporting writers and allowing Penguin Random House to continue to publish books for every reader.

PLUME and P colophon are registered trademarks
of Penguin Random House LLC.

Interior art: abstract black splatter background © Kitsana1980 / Shutterstock.com; gold particles wave © KanawatTH / Shutterstock.com; abstract sand cloud © piyaphong / Shutterstock.com

LIBRARY OF CONGRESS CATALOGING-IN-PUBLICATION DATA
has been applied for.

ISBN 9780593472996 (paperback)
ISBN 9780593472989 (ebook)

Printed in the United States of America
1st Printing

BOOK DESIGN BY LAURA K. CORLESS

While the author has made every effort to provide accurate telephone numbers, internet addresses, and other contact information at the time of publication, neither the publisher nor the author assumes any responsibility for errors or for changes that occur after publication. Further, the publisher does not have any control over and does not assume any responsibility for author or third-party websites or their content.

For Randell

CONTENTS

10

Twilight of the Emperor

11

Walk Without Rhythm

12

The Slow Blade Penetrates the Shield

13

The Sleeper Must Awaken

EPILOGUE

Spice Up Your Life . . . 239

Chronicling the real-life history of *Dune* isn't easy. In writing and researching this book, I learned that much that has been written about *Dune* is either highly specialized, maximalist, or both. In other words, because *Dune* is so vast and cool, there's a tendency either to focus on one aspect or, in focusing on multiple aspects, to document every grain of sand. So, in writing *The Spice Must Flow*, I took the opposite approach: to create a book that took a generous, and generalist's, view of *Dune*. Learning about the history of *Dune* should be hard work for me to research, but it shouldn't be hard work to read.

What I hope lifelong fans get from this book is a larger view of the sweep of the *Dune* phenomenon and how its journey is as improbable as it is amazing. I hope, by experiencing the real-life story of *Dune*, you fall in love with the science fiction world of the novels, films, and TV versions all over again.

The narrative here is the story of *Dune*, not just the story of Frank Herbert. To tell it, I have used a combination of primary and secondary sources, original interviews, conducted by me, with people including, but not limited to, Kyle MacLachlan; Rebecca Ferguson; Denis Villeneuve; Frank Herbert's widow, Theresa Shackleford; Timothée Chalamet; and Alicia Witt, as well as several scholars and experts writing about *Dune* today. I have also extensively researched various magazine articles, recordings, commentaries, newspapers, scholarly texts, letters, and much more. I wrote, researched, and edited the bulk of this book from December 2021 to February 2023, though some interviews predate that process. Although my 2021 interviews with various cast and crew from *Dune: Part One* (2021) do appear throughout this book, *Dune: Part Two* was filming and/or in post-production as I wrote this book, while the HBO series *Dune: The Sisterhood* was still in development. *Dune* is always changing, which is part of the fun.

I have had *The Spice Must Flow* fact-checked by independent expert sources and cross-referenced my research as much as possible. That said, if there are factual errors, objective or otherwise, those faults are mine and mine alone. Still, I am a pop culture critic as much as I am a science fiction historian, so there is a degree of subjectivity to this book, which I'd like to think is in the spirit of the metafictional books that Princess Irulan wrote about Muad'Dib.

For newer *Dune* fans, I want this to be clear: This book is very much for you, too. For decades, the nature of *Dune*'s fandom and cult status made it seem like getting into *Dune* was hard, that the books were challenging, or that the various film versions couldn't connect to a huge audience. Or, worse still, that somehow you had to be super well versed in the entire history of science fiction to "get it." But *Dune* is for everyone, and it always has been. In reading *The Spice Must Flow*, I hope you find that to be true, now more than ever.

Walk without rhythm!

RYAN BRITT
Portland, Maine
February 2023

Use the Voice, Paul

Timothée Chalamet's laugh is a sneak attack, a self-effacing weapon masquerading as a nervous tic. The Chalamet laugh deftly undercuts heavy subjects and briefly makes it seem like everything in the world is silly, even though he is the prince of the universe. His voice, his mannerisms, and his affect all conspire not only to make you believe in his sincerity but also to consider that he might be kidding around, too. It works like this: Chalamet wryly tells me that he's not really worried about the reception of the first *Dune* film, nor is he stressed about doing an adaptation of a book that has already been adapted twice. "That's something I learned from Greta Gerwig on *Little Women;* nobody minds another good adaptation of a good book." And then he laughs like you're college roommates and you've just snuck into a party without paying the cover charge. You laugh with him, because the laugh is infectious, and before you know it, he pivots right back to talking about something serious, profound, and complex. "But I think the projection of the future that *Dune* presents is much bigger, more urgent, than any one version of it."

Timothée Chalamet clearly gets *Dune*. But it's more than that. Timothée Chalamet is *Dune*.

The first public glimpse of *Dune*—published as a serial in the December 1963 issue of the magazine *Analog*—begins with young royal heir Paul Atreides undergoing a dreadful test and, briefly, getting manipulated by the power of "the Voice," wielded by the amoral and duplicitous Reverend Mother Gaius Helen Mohiam. In this fictional world, "the Voice" is a pseudo-hypnotic superpower that one person can use to make other people do whatever they want. In the *Star Wars* mythos, it's called a "Jedi mind trick," and it's powered by space magic. In Frank Herbert's universe, "the Voice" works through speculative science. As outlined in *The Dune Encyclopedia* in 1984, the Voice is an "extra perceptual auditory stimuli" that "only the Bene Gesserit were able to exploit for practical purposes." Paul's mom, the Lady Jessica, is a member of the Bene Gesserit, a secretive matriarchal sect who are not magical in any real way but are pejoratively called "witches" by both their friends and their enemies. In all versions of *Dune*, Jessica teaches her son to use the Voice to control the minds of others with minute inflections full of suggestive connotations. This is what Chalamet's laugh is like, and, correlatively, this notion represents what the *Dune* phenomenon is like for the entire world: You may not be aware it's changing your life, which is also true of how it was made. Frank Herbert wasn't setting out to change the nature of science fiction stories and conversations around ecology. But it happened anyway.

Chalamet was twenty-five years old when he perfectly and eerily personified the sixty-year-old beguiling science fiction phenomenon known as *Dune.* I interviewed him on July 27, 2021, three months before Denis Villeneuve's *Dune: Part One* was released into our world to (almost) universal acclaim. At this moment, Chalamet came across as deeply introspective, enigmatic, youthful, wise, and, crucially, goofy. Not goofy as in off-putting, but goofy as in charmingly unique. The word *special* is almost as overused as *amazing,* but the feeling of talking to Chalamet is both of those things: He's a special person who makes you feel amazing. "Sometimes he looks like he's fifteen years old," Villeneuve said in 2020, referencing Paul's age at the start of the novel. "Yet, he has the maturity of an adult. That's exactly what Paul Atreides is like, a teenager with an old soul."

To date, Timothée Chalamet is the most famous famous person I've ever interviewed at the time they were famous. But unlike about half the famous people I've interviewed, Chalamet is an artist first and a celebrity second. His answers are both polished and sloppy. He's down-to-earth and untouchable. An old soul indeed. As his costar Rebecca Ferguson told me, "Timmy brings the smaller to the grander."

In all of pop culture, the most popular supposedly unpopular thing ever is *Dune.* It's the grandest and yet smallest thing simultaneously. Like the giant sandworms that glide below the desert surface on the titular fictional planet, *Dune's* impact on our world is both immense and obscured. *Dune* is an indie band that never sold out but can still sell out Madison Square Garden. It's an underground, slow-burn novel with a sequel that became the first science fiction hardcover to top the *New York Times* bestseller list. It's a failed, unmade film in

1976, a bold and artistic box office flop in 1984, a pair of fan-loved made-for-cable miniseries in 2000 and 2003, and a mainstream critical hit in 2021 followed by a gargantuan sequel in 2023. It's also a story told in twenty-two unique novels, of which only six were written by its original creator. No other film, band, pop star, book series, album, TV show, game, or media franchise is more paradoxical in both reputation and content than the bewitching saga of the Atreides family and the famous desert planet known as Arrakis. But why? How can something be mainstream and underground simultaneously? How did *Dune* become the Timothée Chalamet of science fiction? Why do famous things that are also unknowable command so much power?

Some might say there's an easy explanation for the psychological impact and pop culture persistence of *Dune*. "It's a coming-of-age story," lifelong *Dune*-head Stephen Colbert said in 2020. "Not just for Paul Atreides but for all humanity." This explanation feels close and is certainly the beginning of the answer. As Frank Herbert's friend and collaborator Bill Ransom points out, Herbert very much had "Jungian training," which clearly informed his writing and brought some monomyth and hero-archetype baggage in *Dune*. So if you squint, the story told in Frank Herbert's first *Dune* novel is a classic hero's journey and coming-of-age story, albeit a very long one. John Campbell, the famous (and infamous) *Analog* editor who first bought it for publication in 1963, loved publishing stories about heroes and refused to print stories about what he called "anti-heroes." He enthusiastically labeled *Dune* as "just the kind of swashbuckler" he wanted to publish.

But there's one problem. *Dune*'s not only a coming-of-age story and its scope extends well beyond the hero's journey parameters. "The difference between a hero and an anti-hero is where you stop the story," Frank Herbert said in 1969. Meaning, if you think *Dune* works because it's an old-school gee-whiz space adventure with a coming-of-age story resulting in a hero's ascension, that assessment is a little like saying Timothée Chalamet is a good actor because he has nice hair. *Dune* isn't a classic hero's journey at all and contains very little straightforward swashbuckling. As twentieth-century science fiction gadfly Harlan Ellison wrote for *USA Today* in 1984, "*Dune* has no Rocky or *Chariots of Fire* sprinters to root for."

In 2021, director Denis Villeneuve tells me, earnestly, "I think Herbert wrote it as a warning, [against] leaders that pretend to know what will happen, who pretend to know the truth, who might be lacking humility."

Essentially, whatever you think *Dune* looks like, according to an astounding collection of smart people, isn't really what it is. *Dune* is a sheep in wolf's clothing, a philosopher disguised as a swordsman, a story about environmentalism and ecology masquerading as a religious tale. *Dune* won the American science fiction award the Nebula in the award's inaugural year, and it also won the older, international science fiction award the Hugo the same year. Novels rarely win both awards in the same year, and because *Dune* won the first Nebula ever, it literally set the standard for American science fiction. And yet, despite this, *Dune* is also, apparently, a science fiction classic just perfect for people who don't like science fiction.

"I'm not crazy about science fiction and I'd never read

Dune before I accepted this film," David Lynch said in 1984. "But when I finally got around to it, I was just knocked out. . . . In a lot of ways, this novel is the antithesis of the usual ray gun and spaceship science fiction I'm used to seeing."

It's a brilliant observation by one of the greatest cinematic artists of our time. But, with all due respect to Lynch, it should also be noted that people in *Dune* fly in all kinds of spaceships, that space travel is central to the economics and overall thrust of the story, and plenty of people who aren't our heroes do fire ray guns, which are just called "lasguns."

Assurances from countless fans all drive home one point: *Dune* only seems dorky and needlessly complicated. But once you get to know it, it's deep as hell. All of that zany stuff is just the trappings. *Dune* is not really a story about a hero, is not actually a fairy tale set in the far future—populated by a sword master named Duncan Idaho or a princess named Irulan or a wicked baron named Vladimir Harkonnen. This isn't frivolous fantasy stuff! Its strength and artistic endurance exist because it subverts all of those things, despite spending a lot of time on said things. It's the first science fiction novel to get serious about ecology and make direct comments on specific religious movements, and it is very much a story for adult fans of science fiction. It's also a story that makes sure you know that the smartest and coolest people in the novel are high as fuck. In 2022, at an independent bookstore in Portland, Maine, I noticed one member of the staff had picked the novel as her staff recommendation, with the following hastily scrawled write-up: "Started reading it; thought it was dumb. Kept reading, realized it was fun."

Dune's fun-ness is somewhat obvious to its faithful fans, but its broader mainstream reputation is sneakier and filled with contradictions. When it comes to the ill-defined double-headed monster of science fiction and fantasy, classifying *Dune* as one kind of thing is a mistake. Its contradictions are in fact what makes it so singular. In season 1 of *Russian Doll*, Natasha Lyonne's character Nadia uses the password "Jodorowsky's *Dune*" to gain access to a secret speakeasy-like back room. This joke works because referencing a version of *Dune* that was never filmed tips a snarky hat at nerdy esoterica. But, notice, this joke also exists in a very mainstream, and very popular, Netflix series. For millions, *Dune* is a secret password, and yet, it's a secret that's out in the open. You can't spoil the plot of *Dune* because it's been around for sixty years. Still, it's always surprising us, educating us, confusing us, and scaring us. As if by magic, aspects of *Dune* are just intuitively understood, even if you've never seen any of the filmed versions or read one word of the books.

"It's a story we all kind of know instinctively," director John Harrison tells me in 2022. In the year 2000, Harrison directed the Sci Fi Channel* miniseries *Frank Herbert's Dune*, and then, in 2003, he wrote and produced its miniseries sequel, *Frank Herbert's Children of Dune*. The former starred

---

*On the internet, there's a certain amount of pressure to refer to this as the SyFy Channel, and that's because in 2009, the Sci Fi Channel rebranded as SyFy, which has a retroactive effect on how Sci Fi Channel TV shows and movies are discussed. But because in the early 2000s, it was still the Sci Fi Channel, that's what we'll call it here.

William Hurt as Duke Leto, and the latter Susan Sarandon as Princess Wensicia. Harrison tells me neither of these very famous people would have done *Dune* without already being fans of it first. "The reason we got Bill is because he loved the book," Harrison tells me, and then reveals that Susan Sarandon basically cast herself, after producer Richard Rubinstein heard her casually mention that she "loved" a float during a Pride parade in New York City because it "looked like the sandworms from *Dune*."

And then there's the first cinematic Paul Atreides, Kyle MacLachlan. Just as Paul leaves his watery planet of Caladan for the desert of Arrakis, at twenty-four years old, MacLachlan, who had never once been in a movie, left his home of Seattle for the desert of Los Angeles and, eventually, Mexico City. But he'd been prepared for this process by Frank Herbert. MacLachlan was at that time the biggest *Dune* fan on the planet. In fact, MacLachlan was such a big fan of *Dune* that he was initially "disappointed" in the script for the David Lynch film version, because he felt it didn't fully do justice to the novel. "I'm an old friend of Paul's," he said in 1984. "I feel like I know him. In a sense I am Paul."

In 2023's *Dune: Part Two*, the role of the emperor of the universe is played by Christopher Walken, an actor known for countless brilliant roles, but in a Fatboy Slim music video directed by Spike Jonze, he flew through the air jamming to the 2000 dance hit "Weapon of Choice." The lyrics of that song go like this: *Don't be shocked by the tone of my voice / Check out my new weapon, weapon of choice, yeah.*

And in case you're confused about the reference, the rest

of the lyrics remind you to "walk without rhythm and it won't attract the worm," a direct reference to how the Fremen of Arrakis avoid getting eaten up by the sandworms.

Throughout the *Dune* novels, the power of prescience drives the story forward. This idea of seeing the future isn't just limited to a scrappy sci-fi novel. The truth of *Dune*'s longevity and its profound importance to the world is riddled with contradictions. Appropriately, those contradictions are connected to real-life paradoxes. Frank Herbert loved Zen riddles in real life. One of his favorites was the legend of a student coming to study with a Zen master. "Master, I have come to study with you, but I've brought nothing." And the master says, "Then set it down." And the confused student says: "But I have brought you nothing." And the master replies, "Then take it away with you." This is the type of paradox that typifies all the ways that the creation of *Dune* makes perfect sense and zero sense simultaneously. What came first, the *Dune* fan or *Dune* itself? Is each Paul Atreides—from Kyle MacLachlan to Alec Newman to Timothée Chalamet—perfectly cast? Or do none of them correctly capture the character?

The entire journey of *Dune* isn't just limited to the various machinations of a puckish, prolific author named Frank Herbert. It's not just controversial decisions made by movie studios and eccentric artists. It isn't just about awakening millions of readers to the realities of climate change. It's also not only about how weird it would be to ride a giant sandworm. The route *Dune* took to become itself is circuitous. MacLachlan's love of the book turned him into Paul, literally. Both William Hurt and Susan Sarandon basically cast themselves in the

Dune miniseries in 2000 and 2003. Jason Momoa and Oscar Isaac were huge fans before getting cast in the 2021 *Dune*. And thanks to a dance he performed twenty years prior, Christopher Walken assured himself a place on the throne of the universe in 2023's *Dune: Part Two*.

Dune's true meaning is a series of prescient moments and contradictions combined with the tension created by trying to unravel those contradictions through intellectual and artistic gymnastics. As Paul's father, Duke Leto, tells his son, there are always "plans within plans."

But perhaps the most compelling reason why *Dune* persists is the roundabout way it came to exist in the first place. *Dune* wasn't just created by one author or made popular by a handful of filmmakers and fans. Defying all reason, the true feature that makes *Dune* so fascinating is that it not only has ensured its own survival but also, perhaps, created itself.

Frank Herbert's Beard

The real-life origins of *Dune*.

To begin your study of the life of Muad'Dib, then, take care that you first place him in his time.

—Princess Irulan

Despite how many times Herbert has described his leap from nonfiction article pitch to epic science fiction novel, that pivot still seems bonkers. Imagine a struggling essayist—behind on IRS payments, in need of steady work—saying to themselves: "Oh, I couldn't sell this very specific newspaper article to anybody, and my agent hates it. Maybe I'll just turn it into the greatest sci-fi novel of all time instead."

Herbert didn't use those exact words, but that's effectively what happened. And, based on his history of making grandiose statements early in his life, you can almost imagine him saying something close to this ridiculous. On his eighth birthday, he told everyone he was going to be a writer, and by nineteen years old, he had landed a job as a journalist in

Southern California, working for *The Glendale Star*. The story of Frank Herbert's success is very much a study in "fake it till you make it," but it did take him a while to make it.

It's hard to pinpoint an exact moment when *Dune* began. Was it when Herbert was born? Was it at his eighth birthday party? Or was it, as many Herbert experts have claimed, when he met psychologists Ralph and Irene Slattery in 1949? These are the two people who introduced him to the work of Carl Jung and got him into Zen concepts. Without those two things, you don't have *Dune*, so really, they must be the most important people in his life, right? What about the moment he was discharged from the navy, early in 1941, for medical reasons? That's got to be it! Had Herbert served longer in the navy, everything would have been different!

Or maybe none of those things matter. If *Dune* does one thing remarkably well, it's that it makes the shape of our lives seem like the opposite of an accident. For all the prescient paradoxes that Paul finds himself in (am I remembering the future, living in the future, or just way too high?), the themes of *Dune* seem to prove that fate doesn't exist and that destiny is still a choice. At some point, Herbert decided he wanted to write about sand dunes. And that started in the summer of 1957, with Frank Herbert in the air.

Frank Herbert was flying high above the coastal town of Florence, Oregon, staring down at sand dunes, keenly interested in observing the crucial feature of these specific mounds of sand. Although their advance was glacially slow, these dunes were in fact moving. Like Paul Atreides riding in an ornithopter, surveying the desert of the planet Arrakis for the first time, Herbert wasn't the pilot of this aircraft, but rather, a passenger of a small Cessna. He'd chartered this plane for the specific purpose of observing these unique dunes because he planned on writing a sprawling nonfiction article about the phenomenon, titled "They Stopped the Moving Sands." This ambitious piece of journalism was destined to fail and be reborn as the greatest science fiction novel of all time. But as the thirty-six-year-old Herbert leaned out of the small plane, he couldn't know his future. All he could feel was the wind in his hair and bits of sand blowing through his beard.

Or maybe not. We don't know how much sand Herbert got in his beard that day, because we don't really know how big his beard was at that moment. In fact, he'd started wearing a beard less than a year prior. Today, Frank Herbert's beard is part of the defining image of the author, but it became his self-described "trademark" only much later. In 1957, it was a new part of his image, an intellectual affect he was trying out, partly to appease a German book publisher. Frank Herbert's agent, Lurton Blassingame, believed that "readers in Europe expected writers to have beards," and so, in 1956 Herbert grew a beard specifically for an author photograph on the German edition of his speculative submarine novel *The Dragon in the Sea*. Throughout his correspondence over his entire life, there are several instances of Herbert's complaining about intellectual and artistic "poseurs." Like Elvis wearing leather or MC Hammer pants, one part of Herbert's enduring image began as a pose. He didn't grow a beard because he was a beatnik intellectual at heart. He grew it because he wanted to seem that way. From beneath a famous mustache, Kurt Vonnegut once said, "We are what we pretend to be, so we must be careful about what we pretend to be."

Frank Herbert started pretending to be Frank Herbert right before he had the first imaginative spark that became the fire that lit up *Dune*. From the start of his professional fiction-writing career in 1945, with a short-story sale to *Esquire*, to 1963, when "Dune World" was first serialized in *Analog*, Herbert published over twenty stories and countless nonfiction articles and essays. According to most photographic evidence and eyewitness accounts, Frank Herbert did not spontaneously sprout his now-famous huge, bushy beard as soon as *Dune* was published in book form in 1965. Like those slowly advancing sand dunes, that huge beard became part of his legend gradually. By the 1970s, he was the messiah of *Dune*, but in 1957, he was an eccentric guy chartering a plane for a nonfiction article he hadn't even sold and would in fact never sell. When we think of Frank Herbert today, we think of a visionary novelist, not an absent-minded freelance essayist, willing to blow grocery money on an airplane rental to get a bird's-eye view of some sand and the plants with which it battled. Historically, the more heroic and professorial Herbert is the one that stuck: the jolly wizard, the man who created a specific blend of fictional spice that many of us crave, savor, and perhaps even need to survive.

In fairness, this retroactive visage of Herbert isn't a phenomenon limited just to him. When it comes to deceased white male novelists, these are the two types available: with facial hair and not. You don't see a lot of clean-shaven images of Charles Dickens, and the thought of Mark Twain (or Vonnegut) without a mustache feels somehow wrong, and maybe a tiny bit obscene. While some male authors remain slightly immune to this phenomenon, for the most part, if an author is a man, white, and dead, his facial hair becomes part of his immortal visage. In 1920, Herbert wasn't born with this beard, and in 1984, just two years before his death, he shaved it off completely. In between these moments are the deserts and oases that make up his entire life. He was a journalist, an inventor, a gardener, an ecologist, a political theorist, a lecturer, and a father. But for most humans, that multifaceted person doesn't really exist. It's hard to picture this energetic thirty-six-year-old guy leaning out of that plane in 1957. Envisioning the older Herbert, the thoughtful author, is easier. In terms of the never-ending retrospective of Herbert's lifework, that younger version of him isn't just unbearded; he's basically faceless. Frank Herbert's entire life can be reduced to one simple fact: He was the guy who wrote *Dune*.

The ghost of Frank Herbert is probably fine with this lack of nuance. After all, many authors are widely known by only one book, as though their entire lives were just a series of events manipulated by fate to get them to put those words on the page. We think of Herman Melville (another giant beard) as the person who wrote *Moby-Dick*, even though in his lifetime, nobody really liked that book. What makes Herbert's status as the real-life messiah of *Dune* singular is that he basically elucidated this exact kind of historical revisionism, step by step, in his *Dune* novels. "The man must recognize the myth he is living in," Herbert said in 1969. "One of the threads in the story is to trace a possible way a messiah is created in our society, and I hope I was successful in making it believable." For most critics, writers, artists, and fans, Herbert's entire life is just a way to talk about how he made *Dune*. And at some point, Herbert cultivated that perception, while his most famous books showed how the tricks of historical revisionism and reduction work.

The first *Dune* is remembered for many things, but its structure, in a sense, is a dual biography of a fictional messiah. On the one hand, the book takes us through a conventional third-person story about a fifteen-year-old named Paul Atreides, who, by the end of the novel (spoiler alert!), becomes emperor of the universe. But layered alongside the present-tense story are hints—mostly in the form of faux-historical epigraphs—of a distant future in which the truth of this tale will become scripture. As a biographer, Princess Irulan doesn't tell us that Paul will become the messiah; she assumes you already know.* This framing mechanism is uniquely brilliant because it allows Herbert to doubly immerse the reader in all sorts of narrative tricks. Just as Conan Doyle created Dr. Watson, a cipher through which we understand Sherlock Holmes, or Fitzgerald needed Nick to bring Jay Gatsby to life, Herbert crafted a future-tense religious status quo to make his science

---

*To be clear, *Dune* is obviously not narrated in the first person by Princess Irulan or anyone else. But these metafictional first-person books do exist, somewhere in the *Dune* universe. In other words, the first novel is not a sci-fi version of Nabokov's *The Real Life of Sebastian Knight*, but you are supposed to believe that books like that about Paul and various other characters, corrective texts that serve to tell "the real story," do exist. They're just exclusively read by fictional characters in the future.

fiction world seem more explicable.* This move also changed the way the reader glimpsed the adventure. Instead of wondering what was going to happen next, most of us, without even noticing, turned the pages of *Dune* to discover why things ended up the way they did.

And so, in charting the entire journey of *Dune*, from its origins in the mind of Frank Herbert to the most recent incarnations of this fictional universe in new novels, and on screens large and small, the myth of Frank Herbert can't be fully separated from the "truth" of his "real" life. Like Paul, Herbert was just too damn good at blending mundane truth and outlandish myth. We can try to pull apart the moments in the story that don't make sense, but the glue of Herbert's self-made myth is shockingly strong. A full biography of the man would perhaps be more accurate, but it would also distract us from the myth in which he lived: the idea that he was destined to become the bearded messiah who created *Dune*. In other words, we can't talk about the history of *Dune* by pretending like the myths of the present don't color our perception of the past. The existence of *Dune* seems to travel back in time to a point where Frank Herbert hadn't even created it yet. This isn't literally true, of course, but what's fascinating

---

*The future-tense moment in which we're supposed to believe these various historical texts were published is interestingly vague. Despite Frank Herbert's six books taking us through roughly more than twenty thousand years of future history, tragically, none of his sequels ever really give us the moment where we see Stilgar or Princess Irulan getting a book deal. However, in the film *Dune: Part Two* (2023), we do see Florence Pugh's Irulan recording notes in real time, a gesture at her future literary career.

about the life of Frank Herbert is that even before he wrote *Dune*, he was clearly getting ready to write *Dune*. Princess Irulan tells us that the reader should remember that although Paul was born and raised on Caladan, he's from the planet Arrakis. In all myths, there's a before and after. And knowing the after part almost certainly obscures our objectivity on the stuff that happened before.

"Six years of research had preceded the day I sat down to put the story together," Herbert said in 1984. "The interweaving of the many plot layers I had planned required a degree of concentration I had never before experienced." Objectively, six years feels roughly correct. However, in 1969, in one interview, Herbert claimed he'd been obsessed with sand dunes for "fifteen years," going back to "'53." If this is true, the earliest research for *Dune* would almost certainly involve an even younger, and almost certainly unbearded, Frank Herbert. But overall, his self-woven myth tends to stay consistent with 1957, because that's the point in time in which Herbert seriously researched what would become *Dune*. That's when he chartered that plane, and that's when he started asking his agent to help sell the article: six years before the first installment of "Dune World" was published in *Analog*. Frank Herbert may have become obsessed with sand dunes in 1953, but the legend of the creation of *Dune* begins in 1957.

"The idea came from an article—I was going to do an article, which I never did—about the control of sand dunes," Herbert explained in 1969. "What many people don't realize is that the United States has pioneered in this, how to control the flow of sand dunes, and it started up here at Florence,

Oregon. . . . I got fascinated by sand dunes, because I'm always fascinated by the idea of something that is either seen in miniature and then can be expanded to the macrocosm."

Soon Herbert turned that obsession, complete with its beautiful analogy, into a sales pitch. At the time, Herbert was entirely freelance and without a steady job. And, like many desperate writers trying to provide for their families, he was pitching wild, big ideas before he'd written anything. To his agent, he framed the possible nonfiction exposé as a human-interest story, chock-full of surprising earth science.

"The small Oregon coastal town of Florence is the scene of an unsung victory in the fight that men have been waging since before the dawn of recorded history," Herbert wrote to his agent on July 11, 1957. "The fight is with moving sand— with the dunes."

The concept, as Herbert saw it, was an untold journalistic tale of the triumph of science and human ingenuity in concert with a harmonious grasp of the natural world. Although the sand dunes were moving slowly, if left unchecked, over time these dunes would cause desolation, which, at the time, had been well documented in Asia and other parts of the world. Like climate change itself, you don't see the slow advance of one changing element causing damage and death. But it will happen eventually.

So the victory Herbert was referring to was that a research station run by the US Department of Agriculture had figured out how to prevent all this impending chaos: by literally halting the advance of sand dunes. Historically, this had never happened before. In the Sahara, and elsewhere, human life had a hard time surviving, in a traditional sense, because of the slow and deadly march of sand dunes. But what the dry-land ecologists of the USDA south of Florence had determined was exactly how to stop the dunes from moving, by planting a specific type of poverty grass, known as *Danthonia spicata*. This grass essentially fought the sand dunes and stopped those dunes in their tracks.

As his son Brian later pointed out, in 1957, Herbert's background in ecology was borderline nonexistent. Again, the myth of the writing of *Dune* has taught us that Frank Herbert was immersed in cutting-edge ecological theories, but the truth is, before this moment, he knew "comparatively little about the complex ecosystems of deserts." And his interest in the USDA project wasn't something he sought out on his own. Herbert was tipped off by a former colleague who had worked with him on a political campaign in Oregon. Just before fighting to write an article about grass beating back sand, Herbert had been a speechwriter for the Republican candidate Phil Hitchcock, a former member of the Oregon senate, who had run, unsuccessfully, in the 1956 primaries to become a US senator. Had Herbert's gig as a political speechwriter for Hitchcock continued, there's every reason to believe he would have never had the downtime or inclination to check out the USDA dune project. If Hitchcock had been elected to the US Senate, Herbert would have been retained as a speechwriter, since he would have been partially credited with making that election a victory.

Weirdly, Hitchcock was not the first Republican senator Herbert had worked for. In 1954, Herbert wrote speeches for Senator Guy Cordon, who was also a Republican. Thinking of

Frank Herbert as a mouthpiece for the Republican Party in the 1950s probably doesn't sit right with a lot of *Dune* fans. And yet, one reason why the *Dune* novels are such convincing political allegories is that we see, in great detail, how the words and speeches of political leaders can ensnare the public with half-truths and platitudes. Essentially, there's no reason to believe that Herbert bought into the beliefs of any one politician. Throughout his life, he used JFK as a negative example of how much power a charismatic politician can wield. "I think that John Kennedy was one of the most dangerous presidents this country ever had. People didn't question him." Conversely, and without any irony, he was also fond of saying that Richard Nixon was the "most valuable president of this century . . . because he taught us to distrust government and he did it by example."

Throughout his life, Herbert's politics weren't simply defined. From an environmentalist standpoint, he was what we might call liberal today, which was also true of his feminist views. And yet, when it came to government policies, Herbert at times came across as radically libertarian. In 1984, he told an interviewer that he would always "vote against whoever was in power." Still, if he were alive in the 2020s it seems impossible that he would support far-right Republicans. The paradigm of personality over policy is exactly what he criticized with the story of all six *Dune* novels. Herbert also supported a woman's right to choose, which would put him further away from today's conservative leanings. Again, Herbert wasn't a conservative, at least not in the way we would define a conservative today. But he did support the NRA at one point and grew up in a hunting family, in which his father taught him how to kill a deer with one bullet. As Herbert biographer William F. Touponce put it in 1988, "It is not easy to situate Herbert on the conventional political or ideological spectrum."

At the time, in the 1950s, science fiction in general could be described as having somewhat conservative leanings.* The publishing world of science fiction, and "men's fiction" of 1957, wasn't associated with left-leaning cautionary tales. Popular science fiction's reputation as a genre with a default mode of progressivism came later, thanks, in part, to *Dune*'s success.† By 1968, *Dune* was recommended by *The Whole Earth Catalog*, a counterculture publication devoted to ecology, which summed up the importance of *Dune* by saying "the metaphor is ecology, the theme is revolution." As Dr. Willis E. McNelly—a professor at California State University, Fullerton, and eventual author of *The Dune Encyclopedia*—pointed out, the entire story of *Dune* "is a thinly veiled allegory of our world's insatiable

---

*Herbert's own high-powered agent, Lurton Blassingame, had a much more famous client: Robert A. Heinlein, the most successful science fiction writer in the world in the 1950s and, basically, someone whom today we'd call a libertarian. Then again, Heinlein's politics were, like Herbert's, somewhat inscrutable. On the one hand, his novel *Starship Troopers* (1959) is often accused of being pro-fascist, while his other famous novel, *Stranger in a Strange Land* (1961), was labeled "the hippie bible."

†The notion that science fiction tended to be more progressive and anti-conservative was pretty much the norm by the 1970s thanks to the "New Wave" writers of science fiction literature. But, arguably, the seeds for this change—at least in mainstream perception—come from *Dune* and *Star Trek*, a TV series that Frank Herbert supported in its early days. Prompted by Harlan Ellison, Herbert even added his name to a petition to keep *Star Trek* on the air in 1966.

appetite for oil and other petroleum products." After *Dune* became successful, Herbert seemed to adopt many of the ecological interpretations of the first novel, even if those themes are somewhat submerged in the original text. To put it another way, when science fiction readers of *Analog* raved about the first three installments of *Dune* in serialized form, none of them mentioned ecology.

When Herbert was trying to pitch "They Stopped the Moving Sands," the real-life story wasn't about climate change at all, or really, anything about humans learning to respect nature more, or trying to save the world from pollution. Instead, in a way, as reported by Herbert, the story of "They Stopped the Moving Sands" was actually about how human beings could tame nature, a fact that, in Herbert's view, could be good or bad, depending on the people and, certainly, depending on the process. "It's been my belief for a long time that man inflicts himself on his environment. That is, Western man," Herbert said. "We tend to think that we can overcome nature by a mathematical means; we accumulate enough data and we subdue it." In "They Stopped the Moving Sands," mathematics resulted in nature's getting beat down by other kinds of nature. By exploiting the poverty grasses, scientists could manipulate another part of nature that was unappealing and dangerous for humans: the giant sand dunes.

What sets *Dune* apart from the bulk of science fiction from the same era is its organic texture. There are no robots or computers or artificial intelligence in the first *Dune* novel because centuries prior, a massive war called the Butlerian Jihad outlawed "thinking machines." The substance that allows space travel to be possible—the trippy drug known as the spice melange—isn't a technological achievement but, again, a naturally occurring resource, which has been harnessed by Guild navigators.

These navigators fold space to get various star travelers where they're going and use the prescience of the spice to help them navigate. Herbert's projection of a spacefaring future doesn't bother to marvel at the tech that got us there, but instead presupposes that the only things that will truly last tens of thousands of years from now are not only sustainable but, crucially, alive. In the first *Dune* novel, the ecologist Liet-Kynes wants to transform the desert planet Arrakis into a paradise. But this terraforming won't happen artificially; instead, as the Fremen leader Stilgar says, "[they] will trap the dunes beneath grass plantings . . . [they] will tie the water into the soil with trees and undergrowth." In the first novel, the goal of the people of *Dune* is to use organic means to achieve their organic ends. In Florence, Oregon, this happened on a relatively small scale, but on the planet Arrakis, the stakes are, obviously, much, much bigger.

But again, Herbert had not been hired by *National Geographic* to write this fascinating article on poverty grasses being used to control sand. And although he was a newspaper writer, holding various freelance and staff positions at papers ranging from the *San Francisco Examiner* to *The Oregon Statesman* and *The Oregon Journal*, he was not, in 1957, asked by any of those publications to write "They Stopped the Moving Sands." Instead, Herbert imagined the final product as a glossy magazine piece, a kind of prose version of an unwieldy Werner Herzog documentary.

His agent, Lurton Blassingame, pretty much hated it. Like many shrewd literary agents, Blassingame was concerned primarily about money. "Control of sand dunes may be a story, it is very limited in appeal," he wrote to Herbert on July 29, 1957. "This outline is so vague." And so Blassingame did his best to dissuade Herbert from pursuing the project any further. What happened next was almost certainly the most crucial moment in the history of science fiction literature.

Brian Herbert suggests that Frank Herbert became uninterested in a nonfiction version of "They Stopped the Moving Sands" after a period of "a couple of days." The dates on the letters between Herbert and Blassingame would seem to indicate a longer period of interest, but maybe the younger Herbert is right. Perhaps by the time the letter in which Blassingame kindly discouraged the entire pitch arrived, Frank Herbert had already decided to transform his entire vision. "Looking back on it, I realize I did the right thing instinctively," Herbert reflected in 1984. "You don't write for success."

Herbert's research on deserts and dunes also allowed him to make another crucial leap. Just as the grass could tie the dunes to a specific place, what tied Herbert's *Dune* together wasn't just a sci-fi story about ecology, but religion, too.

Dune is named for its setting, the desert planet Arrakis. But for Herbert, this setting was simply the beginning, or as he once said dismissively, "just the surface." The global obsession with *Dune*, now six decades old, isn't the result of a science fiction writer cleverly combining ecological speculation with critical commentary on religion. If the sustained adoration for *Dune* were the direct result of its environmental relevance and critical analysis of religious history, it may as well have remained nonfiction.

The power of *Dune* isn't just due to its topsy-turvy and utterly gutsy origins. The reason *Dune* endures is because of the incredible characters who populate this fictional desert planet. We may stay on Arrakis because of the ecological ruminations, but the reason we come back to *Dune* over and over again is because of its two protagonists: the tragic hero, Paul Atreides, and his mother, Lady Jessica. And to bring these stories to life, Frank Herbert needed help from one controversial editor named John Campbell. But, more crucially, the themes of *Dune* were shaped by another person who redefined his entire worldview—the real-life Lady Jessica, Beverly Herbert.

Fear Is the Mind-Killer

**How Beverly Herbert and the Bene Gesserit
saved *Dune* before it began.**

*She wanted to find what was good in everything and
everyone.* —Frank Herbert on Beverly Herbert

One of the quietest, most beautiful scenes in the first *Dune* novel is all about having a calm cup of coffee by yourself. While Paul is about to ride a sandworm for the first time, we find his mother, Jessica, in a private moment, thinking about wanting a cup of coffee, and then, silently, a cup appears, presented by a fellow Fremen. She hasn't used the Voice to make this happen, the Fremen are just good at taking care of each other. And, for Jessica, the best part is that she isn't hassled by the invisible Fremen barista, because the sietch community within the deep desert of Dune has "a natural regard for her privacy." Although Jessica's story in the first *Dune* has its ups and downs—she worries about her children, and her true love is killed by the Harkonnens—she is not a victim. Throughout *Dune*, Jessica usually gets what she wants, including a good cup of coffee, without having to resort to violence. Her story, and her cup of coffee, are just as important as Paul's story in the first *Dune* book, and that's because, even though the book has a reputation as a coming-of-age story about a young man, the truth is, the other main character of *Dune* is Lady Jessica.

For many historians of science fiction literature, the 1970s is when the field became more feminist. The decade that followed the publication of *Dune* saw the explosion of the literary-minded "New Wave" of science fiction and the time when feminism began as a serious force in SF and its related fields. But, as Kara Kennedy—a leading *Dune* scholar and author of two contemporary books on women's agency in *Dune*—points out, Frank Herbert's writing is just as relevant to the larger discussion about women's roles in SF literature, even if the first version was published in 1963, before the seventies began. "I have nothing against the seventies," Kennedy tells me in 2023. "But if we're going to give credit to these kinds of characteristics that are in feminist science fiction, why aren't we giving the same credit to *Dune*? Yes, it has a male author, but *Dune* was quite radical because there's a whole female organization [the Bene Gesserit] that has mind-body control and control over reproduction."

In crafting the 2021 film *Dune: Part One*, Denis Villeneuve and producer Mary Parent actively sought to crystallize and elevate the roles of the female characters, because, from their point of view, none of the male characters have nearly as much agency as the female characters. "[Women] really do have an impact on the evolution of [Paul's] journey," Tanya Lapointe, author of *The Art and Soul of Dune*—and longtime partner of Denis Villeneuve—said in 2021. "Starting with his mother, Lady Jessica."

This sensibility is extended to the music of the new *Dune* films, too. Composer Hans Zimmer thinks that the ultimate goal in crafting the unforgettable scores for *Dune: Part One* and *Dune: Part Two* was to reflect a feminist sensibility in the music itself. "Both Denis and I felt very strongly about the presence of female voices," Zimmer told me in 2021. "I think the underlying game Frank Herbert plays with us is that what drives the story forward is really the women. They're in charge, the Bene Gesserit. It's always a woman who seems to have the true strength in these stories."

If there is a twenty-first-century trend to reclaim *Dune* as a feminist text or to make sure new versions of *Dune* connect to women's issues, Kennedy doesn't think newer movie or TV adaptations of *Dune* need to work too hard. "You don't need to suddenly make *Dune* feminist," she tells me. "It's already feminist." In contrast with other, older science fiction—like Asimov or Heinlein novels—the story of the first *Dune* has always been powered by women, from the first line to the last line. Lady Jessica's mentor Reverend Mother Gaius Helen Mohiam tests Paul, and despite her anger with Jessica for having a boy instead of a girl, she still tells Jessica to train her son in the ways of the Voice. Essentially, the book opens with two women making decisions that will impact the rest of the book. Mohiam tells Jessica to "ignore the regular order of training" and make sure Paul knows how to use the Voice. This point is massive, because, as Kennedy points out, the Bene Gesserit aren't as unfeeling and witchlike as they are sometimes portrayed on-screen. On the page, the relationship between Jessica and Mohiam is more complicated.

"She tells Jessica to disobey!" Kennedy explains. "Mohiam obviously cares for Jessica. The last thing she does is tell her to train Paul in the Voice, and then we see her crying, which disturbs Jessica. The Bene Gesserit are complicated people."

Over the years, the women who have been involved in *Dune* adaptations have tended to agree with Kennedy. "I didn't have any perception that it was a male-dominated story at all," Alicia Witt tells me in 2023. At the age of seven, Witt was cast in the 1984 film version of *Dune*, playing Alia Atreides, sister of Paul, daughter of Jessica, who is "pre-born" with all the memories of her ancestors, including all the Bene Gesserit women who came before her. "I always thought the female characters were really strong. And of course, I was a female character, but I remember thinking about how strong Francesca Annis was as Lady Jessica. To me, she seemed to fully embody grace and strength, and I looked up to her."

Beginning its life as a failed piece of journalism, *Dune* later morphed into a series of adventure shorts in 1963, then became an environmental rallying cry in 1970, a cinematic artistic statement in the 1980s, an underground epic in the 1990s, and a mainstream shared mythology in the twenty-first century. But who is *Dune* for? Does it tell the story of all people, everywhere, or is it simply another science fiction story from the twentieth century created by a white man that attempts to unify various cultures and themes through appropriation?

And if the "Chosen Ones" of the books are often men, what does the saga of *Dune* really say about nonmale genders? Infamously, Duke Leto didn't marry his "concubine" Jessica so that the path to a political marriage would remain open. Ditto Paul, who marries Princess Irulan after the Fremen revolt against her father, Shaddam IV, all for the sake of universal unity, while keeping Chani as his one true love. In all versions of the book, the final line of the story concludes with Jessica commiserating with Chani about the fact that neither of them technically married the love of her life, but that's totally okay. "Think on it, Chani: that princess [Irulan] will have the name, yet she'll live as less than a concubine," Jessica says. "... While we, Chani, we who carry the name concubine—history will call us wives."

Read out of context and devoid of intent, the final line of the book could be very off-putting. Even the world's first *Dune* superfan, Dr. Willis McNelly, confronted Herbert in 1969 about this line, saying to him and Herbert's wife, Beverly, that he found the phrasing to be "overly dramatic," and needled Herbert to explain himself. "I said yech!" McNelly told Herbert in a recorded interview, regarding "history will call us wives." But Kara Kennedy thinks that if we look at the agency that Jessica, Chani, and the other women of *Dune* have, the final line of the first *Dune* novel is more layered than it might seem.

"I guess you could read it in a negative light," Kennedy tells me. "But if you read it in a positive light, what Jessica's saying is we are so influential and we are such forces in this world that we don't even need the institution of marriage to confer on us some kind of authority. It doesn't matter whether we're concubines or not. Leto relies on Jessica, and he dies. Jessica is the one that acts as a regent for Paul throughout the whole rest of the novel. The women are the survivors. They are in power."

In real life, the true power behind the empire of Frank Herbert was his second wife, Beverly Herbert. Although he had been married once before, to Flora Parkinson in 1941, she wrote him a letter saying she was leaving him just a year later, in 1942, while Herbert was serving in the navy. They divorced the following year, in 1943. In March 1946, after getting laid off from a newspaper job at the *Seattle Post-Intelligencer,* Herbert took a creative writing class and sat next to Beverly Stuart Forbes. The pair bonded over the fact that although they were in a creative writing class, both had been professionally published before. Secretly, at the age of seventeen, Herbert had written a western under a pseudonym and had had it accepted for publication by Street & Smith magazines in either 1937 or 1938.* In 1945, *Esquire* published one of Herbert's adventure stories, "Survival of the Cunning," and by the time he met Beverly in March 1946, the popular *Doc Savage* magazine had also accepted another of his adventure tales for the April 1946 issue. At this time, Beverly had sold a story to *Modern Romances* called "Corner Movie Girl." This pair of writers were married on June 23, 1946, just a few months after they

---

*Herbert kept the exact title and nom de plume for this western a secret. We only have his word on this sale.

met. And they remained married until Beverly's death on February 7, 1984.

Just as Lady Jessica quietly supported and controlled the fortunes of Duke Leto, the successes of Frank Herbert's career, and *Dune* specifically, are largely attributed to Beverly. According to Brian Herbert, his father was dependent on his mother, Beverly, describing him as "almost like a baby" without Beverly's support. Herbert described his early married life with Beverly as a kind of symbiotic writing relationship: "With two portable typewriters taking up considerable space on one table, we pretty well set the pattern of our life together: work to support music, writing and the other joys that living provides." For much of Herbert's writing career, there was inconsistency and failure. During the fifties and most of the sixties, Beverly supported the family, working as a wildly successful writer of advertisements. "She went out to the office and brought in a paycheck," Herbert said in 1981. "While I stayed home and did the cooking, laundry, and housekeeping, took care of the children, and worked on my writing." Eventually, in the late seventies, Herbert's *Dune* fortune was more than enough to provide for the family, but, crucially, that foundation came from Beverly. As Herbert wrote in 1985, "I was her bridge, and she was mine."

Beverly Herbert also had a hand in what went into all the *Dune* novels. In 1969, she pointed out that she had pushed Frank to include the profound and tragic reflections of the ecologist Liet-Kynes, saying that she felt it was extremely relevant for the reader to understand and feel the unique gravity of this moment. "A lot of the story swung around this,"

Beverly Herbert said in 1969. "I thought it was very important that the planet killed the ecologist. . . . I think it made it
more horrible, the fact that he completely understood [why]."
According to Brian Herbert, everything about *Dune* went
through Beverly first, with Frank reading passages aloud to
her. She encouraged him to follow a more literary and layered
prose style, a style that some fans might claim is mostly absent
from some of Herbert's previous, non-*Dune* novels. According
to Brian Herbert's biography of his father, Beverly told Frank
the "language was beautiful," but that's partly because she
helped make it that way.

Unquestionably, the origin of the Bene Gesserit comes
from Beverly, whom Frank Herbert considered to be a benevo-
lent "witch" who forecast his destiny through her interest in
horoscopes, tarot, and the I Ching. In every way that matters,
the original Bene Gesserit reverend mother was Beverly Herbert. And yet, there is an earlier version of *Dune* in which the
Bene Gesserit did not exist, Jessica was not a major character,
and the story was totally focused on the patriarch of all the
spice, the greatest space dad you've never heard of: Jesse
Linkam.

Cue record scratch. Jesse Linkam? Never heard of him!
This rough-draft version of Duke Leto would have been the
main character of a very different version of *Dune*, one that
thankfully was never completed. In the time after Frank Herbert quit the nonfiction article "They Stopped the Moving
Sands" in 1957, but before 1963, when he worked in earnest on
writing and publishing what became *Dune*, there was a very
different novel he outlined and never finished, called "Spice

Planet." When we leave Herbert's brain and focus on the spilled ink that created the *Dune* universe, the journey to *Dune* inauspiciously begins here: with space administrator Jesse overseeing a mining operation of a substance known as spice. In Herbert's outline of "Spice Planet"—some of which is typed, and some of which is scrawled out in pen—the first chapter opens as Linkam interacts with an early version of Gurney Halleck (picture Patrick Stewart or Josh Brolin) and is primarily concerned with motivating the workers to keep the spice flowing. Herbert's first written sentence in the "Spice Planet" outline is: "Linkam watches the last shuttle bring in the workers."

While some of these machinations about mining spice on a distant planet eventually appeared in *Dune*—specifically the thrilling scene in which Duke Leto (here, Linkam) slums it to rescue stranded workers himself—the characters, tone, and concept of "Spice Planet" aren't what *Dune* became. "Spice Planet" would have been a more compact science fiction novel, with inscrutable stakes and utterly unremarkable characters. The story concerned Linkam heading to "Duneworld" with his eight-year-old son, Barri, and his concubine, Dorothy Mapes. While these characters scan as rough drafts for fifteen-year-old Paul and the formidable Lady Jessica, it's clear that Herbert knew something was missing. And that's because the most damning difference is that in this version of "Duneworld," there was no Bene Gesserit, no Voice, no rejection of traditional power structures for women. This isn't to say Dorothy Mapes wasn't formidable, shrewd, and very helpful to Linkam, but this rough sketch of Lady Jessica did not possess her awesome abilities. Whereas Lady Jessica is a borderline superhero, Dorothy Mapes was an emancipated secretary.

To be fair, there is not a complete manuscript of "Spice Planet." The outline and various scraps of dialogue come from two safe-deposit boxes of files archived by Beverly, only opened decades after the author's death. Based on these notes, Herbert's son Brian and author Kevin J. Anderson wrote an approximate "full" version of "Spice Planet" and published their take on it as a kind of protracted deleted scene in the book *The Road to Dune* in 2005. It's a fascinating read for a hard-core fan, but also frustrating and more than a little bit boring. Unlike the provocative ending of *Dune*, Linkam and Dorothy formally get married. In the 2005 Brian Herbert and Kevin J. Anderson version of this, the last lines find her becoming "Lady Dorothy Linkam" because of the official marriage ceremony, not in spite of it. So, you know, the exact opposite message and tone of the ending of *Dune*. Yech?

That said, not everything about "Spice Planet" is bad. This is where it seems that Frank Herbert first conceived of this wonderful line: "Damn the spice . . . save the men!" Originally uttered by Linkam, this line would appear in a slightly different form in *Dune*, when Leto says, "Damn the spice! . . . We can always get more spice." According to Kevin J. Anderson and the junior Herbert, this specific line for "Spice Planet" was discovered on "a scrap of paper torn from a notepad," written in pencil. As Anderson and Brian Herbert point out, this single stray piece of dialogue is basically the "defining moment in the character of Duke Leto Atreides."

Although Herbert did eventually write other great fiction

beyond the *Dune* universe, his early efforts, including what we know of "Spice Planet," have a perfunctory feeling, as though he's rushing to get to his point. His only published novel in book form before *Dune*—*The Dragon in the Sea* (1956)*—is so chock-full of stock characters and cliché dialogue, it's a rough read today. Early in that novel, the character of Ramsey, a military psychologist, has this cringeworthy thought: "Great Grieving Freud! Am I going to be palmed off as a submariner!"

Luckily, Herbert's dude-heavy narratives—from unpublished westerns to *The Dragon in the Sea* (which has virtually zero female characters)—did not become his modus operandi for the final shape of *Dune*. Eventually, Linkam did morph into Duke Leto, which allowed Lady Jessica and Paul to become the real main characters of *Dune*, instead of the slightly boring dad who was the first hero of the story. And with the invention of the Bene Gesserit, Herbert gave us the beautiful and immortal internal character mantra of the Bene Gesserit Litany Against Fear, which begins with the chilling affirmation "Fear is the mind-killer," a catchphrase that is certainly cooler than "Great Grieving Freud!"

Throughout all six of Herbert's novels, spanning more than twenty thousand years of future history, various members of

---

*Not a book about dragons. This is a near-future submarine book. *The Dragon in the Sea* was tied for the International Fantasy Award in 1957 with William Golding's *Lord of the Flies*. Post-sixties editions of *The Dragon in the Sea* are titled *Under Pressure*. Weirdly, Herbert included the fact that *The Dragon in the Sea* "shared" an award with *Lord of the Flies* in his brief author bio in the first edition of *Dune*.

the Atreides family come and go, the universe is transformed, and even the titular planet is renamed, forgotten, and eventually destroyed. Throughout it all, the Bene Gesserit survive, not because they are all heroic and good, and not because they are evil and scheming. In the 2021 film *Dune: Part One*, Charlotte Rampling's version of Reverend Mother Gaius Helen Mohiam says, "Our plans are measured in centuries." It's not a line from the first novel, but it does perfectly represent the long game the Bene Gesserit are playing.

None of this means everything about the Bene Gesserit is a complete slam dunk for gender equality in science fiction or life. For longtime *Dune* scholar Emmet Asher-Perrin, Herbert was still trapped by the "gender binary," which means the women of *Dune* are still written in a way that doesn't sit right with everyone. "Herbert may not have believed that women were less," they tell me in 2023. "But he certainly believed women were different. It's a problem that we find in fiction even to this day, the acknowledgment that women are just as smart, as talented, as capable as the men around them, but still fundamentally other, separate, apart from them."

Still, the power of the Bene Gesserit is what sets the standard for strength in the *Dune* universe. Paul, as a man, is behind the eight ball because he's a man. "The risk of a boy child taking it [the Water of Life] is so great," Alicia Witt tells me. "Men are weaker than the Bene Gesserit. The reverend mothers, all of them, they are the ones who are able to take the Water of Life and survive."

Today, the Bene Gesserit Litany Against Fear may remind casual *Dune* fans of Yoda's infamous speech linking anger and fear from *Star Wars: Episode 1—The Phantom Menace* in 1999. For Nerdist, Matt Caron even made a deep-cut video demonstrating all of *Dune*'s cultural influences, highlighting the ways in which Yoda rips off the Bene Gesserit. But where Yoda is warning us that fear can turn us all into little Darth Vaders, the Bene Gesserit are giving great advice on how to face it. This philosophy of facing fear, accepting it, and allowing it to "pass over" and "through" us is mature, wise, and deceptively simple. The Bene Gesserit Litany Against Fear also seems uniquely connected to one of Beverly Herbert's personal credos. In the afterword to his final novel, *Chapterhouse: Dune*, Frank Herbert wrote that Beverly was known to say: "Revenge is for children. Only people who are basically immature want it." At their best, the Bene Gesserit teach all of us, of any gender, to rise above the petty, to face our fear, and to look at what remains when it passes: ourselves. Without this philosophy, without this religion of the mind, *Dune* wouldn't have worked. But in order for the world to benefit from the teachings of the Bene Gesserit, *Dune* had to get published first.

Magazine Worms

"Dune World" and the world's first glimpse of Arrakis.

They have prepared a way for us in the desert.

—The Lady Jessica Atreides

Frank Herbert's pre-*Dune* clunky prose is so uneven that had "Spice Planet" ended up being the book we got, there's every reason to believe it would have been just as forgotten as his other early work. While Herbert haters would say his prose isn't much better in *Dune*, either, there's a clear before and after, at least in how Herbert saw himself. This shift exists artificially through the lens of history because nobody interviews hacks when they're hacks. The world only starts to document these kinds of writers after they've ceased being hacks, which is why artistic revisionism is so rampant in every single conversation you'll have about pop culture in your entire life. Unlike someone like, say, Kurt Vonnegut, who sort of owned up to the crappiness of his earliest writing,

Herbert tended to repaint himself as a scholar who was just using science fiction as an outlet for his important philosophical musings. Post-1965, after *Dune*, Herbert liked to claim he was really "a journalist" who "just write[s] a bit of fiction."

Most biographies of Herbert support this claim for the simple reason that Herbert worked as a journalist from the 1940s well into the 1960s, even after *Dune* was published. And yet, Herbert was never able to support his family, nor his obligations to the IRS or his first wife, Flora, with his journalism. The proof? Beverly Herbert supported Frank and their two sons, Bruce and Brian. While Beverly and Frank were married, the family moved houses and cities well over twenty times, and in 1956, even fled to Mexico to avoid the IRS, blowing a good deal of book advance money from Herbert's sale of *The Dragon in the Sea*. Frank Herbert may have been a journalist by training, but he didn't straighten out his family life or his responsibilities until he became a successful fiction writer. Obviously, this sounds nuts. Most people don't become more stable and more responsible by working on fiction, but if we just chart the broad strokes of Herbert's life, that's the truth. He wasn't a journalist who wrote a bit of fiction. He was a fiction writer who needed to get away from journalism to become a stable person.

Herbert had been churning out science fiction stories for a variety of publications since 1952, when *Startling Stories* published his short story "Looking for Something?" Ten years later, by 1962, Herbert had published a total of twenty more science fiction stories and novellas in every leading SF magazine of the era, from *Amazing* to *If* to *Astounding Stories of*

Super-Science, the last of which would undergo a strange meta-morphosis to become *Analog*, the first home for *Dune*.

Before the first magazine publication of "Dune World" in 1963, Herbert wasn't exclusively researching religion, wandering the desert looking for inspiration; instead, in addition to flying over sand dunes in Oregon, he'd also been hustling as a professional fiction writer for over a decade. Despite his impressive, prolific output of fiction, and the plethora of imaginative concepts in those published stories, the bulk of that writing is simply not that great. Even stories that foretell the future themes of *Dune* are too on the nose. In "You Take the High Road" (later "The Godmakers"), Herbert plays with the idea that religion could be manufactured through sci-fi shenanigans, which results in a character named Orne thinking to himself, "Could this psi machine amplify the energy we call religion?" Technology plus telepathy equals robo-religion. Get it? One of the things that makes *Dune* great is that it doesn't insult the ability of the reader to discern the meaning.

So the primordial soup from which *Dune* came was swimming with science fiction writing clichés that looked backward stylistically rather than forward. And yet, all of Herbert's earlier (and inferior) science fiction writing gave him raw material he could harvest and then make more interesting in *Dune*.

In various retrospectives and biographies of Herbert, and from Herbert's own revisionism, the origin of and impetus for the writing of *Dune* is nearly always chalked up to his golden idea: combining his interest in desert environments and the history of various religions. In 1969, he told Willis

McNelly: "For a science fiction writer anyway, it was an easy step from that to think what if I had an entire planet that was a desert? And during my studies of deserts and my previous studies of religions, we all know that many religions began in a desert atmosphere. So, I decided to put the two together, because I don't think any one story should have any one thread."

Herbert claimed that his style of writing was about using a "layering technique," which is certainly not something a creative writing teacher could safely teach budding writers in any kind of class on the craft of writing. But according to Herbert's telling of the creation of *Dune*, he worked with ideas and nonfiction research way before he invented any characters. He repeated the story of studying deserts and religion before coming up with *Dune* many times, right up to 1984, when he told Denis Fischer: "I had to go into the history of desert cultures . . . approximately six years later, I was ready to write the book. You could see it as an adventure story, or a love story, plus there's political commentary and a metaphor for the things that are happening all around us."

This last statement vaguely checks out with the novel we got, but, hilariously, could also describe nearly every good novel ever written. No rational person would argue *Dune* isn't one of the most groundbreaking books from a metaphorical perspective, but Herbert's insistence on peddling it as thinly veiled nonfiction bizarrely undersells why the book is so good. Just like other bearded so-called geniuses, Frank Herbert is not the first person to be shortsighted about why their art is great, and as anyone knows, he's not the last. And yet, within this special group of out-of-touch smart people, he's the only one who created a science fiction novel that broke through to the mainstream. But—great grieving Freud!—to create realistic characters in fiction, you can't be thinking only about what eventual political point you're trying to make. This means Herbert's process must have been more than what he tended to describe. However, because we can't prove what Herbert was thinking about when he invented *Dune*—just listen to the retelling of his own myth—the paper trail of what he was specifically writing between 1957 and 1963 is the only real way to guess at how *Dune* was logistically formed. And in that era of Herbert writing, there are essentially three elements that mattered:

- The "god-making" concept from his linked short stories "You Take the High Road" (1958), "Missing Link" (1959), "Operation Haystack" (1959), and "The Priests of Psi" (1959), later republished as the novel *The Godmakers* (1972).

- An addictive natural resource called spice from the "Spice Planet" outline.

- The pseudo-terraforming notion of transforming sand dunes from the failed nonfiction piece "They Stopped the Moving Sands."

After 1959, Herbert had these three notions not just rolling around in his head, but also on paper. If we take Herbert at his word, once he realized he could combine a spicy desert planet with a cool sci-fi novel about a religion on said desert planet, then he was all set! The reason *Dune* is so great is because Herbert mixed ecology and religious critique. Of course! That's why people loved it and that's how he sold it . . . right? Let's imagine it: Herbert has this brain wave, writes a long letter to his agent, Lurton Blassingame, and explains that this new science fiction novel will combine world religions and stuff on a desert planet. Blassingame realizes this premise is pure gold, drinks two gin and tonics in celebration, and buys himself a new car that same day, all because he knows he and Herbert are going to be millionaires. The rest is history. Herbert is hailed as a hero and an ecological visionary and a brilliant religious scholar at the same time. Done and done!

Saying *Dune* was accepted for publication because one editor saw the brilliant collision of ecological and religious themes would be like saying Brian Epstein decided to manage the Beatles because he liked their politics. The themes of *Dune* mattered later, of course, but not at the beginning. What mattered was the characters. Damn the spice. Save the men.

Frank Herbert's personal mythmaking makes it seem like *Dune* was written as a complete masterpiece and that its length was determined by a tireless novelist pounding out his 188,000-word tome. The reality is, *Dune* was published piecemeal, written on demand, and workshopped and revised as it was being written. And just in case you're unclear as to what this means, let's break it down: Before *Dune* was a novel you could hold and buy, it was a serialized story, told in parts, published in installments in the pages of what had at one time been considered the *New Yorker* of science fiction,* John W. Campbell's *Analog*, which, perhaps more famously, had begun its life as *Astounding Stories of Super-Science* in 1930. Although basically unheard of in the twenty-first century, the idea that a novel would have been serialized and broken up in magazines before getting released in one volume was not only common, but that process describes the history of several famous novels, from Dickens to Hemingway. In the science fiction field, nearly every so-called classic released before the 1970s was initially published like this, too. Bradbury's *Fahrenheit 451* and *The Martian Chronicles* are both "fix-ups," novels that were really a combination of various short stories, compiled to make a book. Isaac Asimov's *Foundation* is another one, which, like "Dune World," was edited and published by Campbell as disparate, sometimes unrelated stories set in the same continuity, well before anyone (including Asimov) considered it to be one unified story. As pitched to Campbell, Herbert's vision for *Dune* wasn't as incongruous and seat-of-the-pants as Asimov's was with *Foundation*, but the process by which these texts were brought out into the world was similarly pseudo-collaborative.

But what made the pitch for "Dune World" stick out? Why

---

*When *Analog* published "Dune World," it was also owned by Condé Nast, and when you hold those issues, you can totally tell. The physical magazine doesn't have the pulplike quality of earlier iterations, and it's simply much bigger. By the time "The Prophet of Dune" was serialized in 1965, *Analog* would switch back to the smaller digest-sized issues, during the final two installments of that story.

did the infamously mercurial Campbell take it on? Scholarly revisionism tends to hop over the first published version of *Dune* and jump to the point where it was a complete novel in 1965. But that leaves out the most crucial step in the formation of *Dune:* the moment where somebody bought it. The most pivotal moment for *Dune's* birth is the crucial fact that one very specific and very infamous editor had a real thing for characters who could see the future.

When famous (and very controversial) science fiction editor John W. Campbell* wrote to Frank Herbert on June 3, 1963, telling him he was accepting the then-in-progress three-part story "Dune World" for serialized publication in *Analog*, he mentioned desert planets and religious studies exactly zero times. This is not a short letter. It's four pages long and is entirely focused on what Campbell correctly intuits is the broader allure of *Dune:* the fact that the story is about a teenager who has the power to see into the future.

"Dear Frank: Congratulations!" Campbell writes. "You are now the father of a 15-year-old superman! But I betcha you aren't gonna like it...."

Campbell then details what is both the greatest strength and greatest challenge of *Dune:* If Paul Atreides can accurately see the future, how does the rest of the story work? Isn't the tension removed if the main character is locked into a destiny

---

*John Campbell is frequently confused with Joseph Campbell, the scholar famous for *The Hero with a Thousand Faces* and one of the biggest influences on how everyone talks about mythical structure, storytelling, and yes, science fiction. Still, the two Campbells have nothing to do with each other.

he can't change? Campbell worried that Paul couldn't have "so much precognition that you can't build a workable plot for the next yarn. . . . If 'Dune' is to be the first of three,* and you're planning on using Paul in the future ones . . . oh, man! You've set yourself one hell of a problem!"

Keep in mind, this is an acceptance letter. Campbell calls "Dune World" a "grand yarn" and promises to "buy it," but his hands-on editing approach meant he wanted to make sure Herbert was focused on what Campbell considered to be the problems of the most important thing in the story—its main character. "Give your hero precognition *that works*," Campbell suggested, and in that suggestion the fate of Paul Atreides and all of *Dune* was pretty much sealed. By saying Paul needed precognition "that works," what Campbell meant was that there needed to be realistic consequences of Paul's prescient visions. Later, this conundrum occupies pretty much the entire last half of the first *Dune* novel and nearly all of its first two sequels, *Dune Messiah* (1969) and *Children of Dune* (1976). While it's unclear how much of Herbert's overall plan for *Dune* was altered by Campbell, one thing is for sure: The original *Dune* is the only one of the series that Campbell worked on. Campbell wasn't the Gordon Lish to Frank Herbert's Raymond Carver, but he had served that role with several pivotal science fiction writers before. Meaning, his influence on *Dune*

---

*What Campbell meant by "the first of three" results in the three parts of the first novel. At this stage, Campbell is discussing only the short novella "Dune World," which is essentially the first third of the published novel.

wasn't nothing. And the fact that Herbert wanted Campbell to buy, shape, and publish his masterpiece is revealing.

"[Campbell] was a very prescriptive editor," science fiction historian and Campbell expert Alec Nevala-Lee tells me. "He took a very firm hand with the kinds of things he wanted to see in the magazine in a way that I don't think editors these days can do." In *Astounding*, his nonfiction history book about the "Golden Age of Science Fiction," Nevala-Lee illuminates the specific ways in which Campbell's "firm hand" shaped and defined early stories from Isaac Asimov, specifically the idea that some of the big sci-fi ideas that we associate with Asimov—like the famous laws of robotics—actually came from Campbell first. Asimov later said that Campbell viewed all the authors he published as "extensions of himself": "We were his literary clones; each of us doing, in his or her own way, things Campbell felt needed doing."

While Nevala-Lee believes that Campbell probably didn't have the same kind of power over Herbert that he'd once had over his 1940s protégés, like Asimov, the fact remains that Herbert had been corresponding with Campbell since 1953 and had had stories published by Campbell in *Astounding* since 1954. So prior to the moment where Herbert pitched "Dune World," he'd had a working relationship with Campbell that had lasted nearly a decade, which indicates that at some point in time, Herbert must have either drunk the Campbell Kool-Aid a bit or pretended to enough to get his stuff published.

Just as the Fremen had been toiling in the desert for ages before Paul and Jessica arrived, the historical context of science fiction is important. Frank Herbert didn't revolutionize science fiction by inventing it. Instead, like the heroes and villains of *Dune*, he worked within existing systems and, in many cases, destroyed and pushed back against their rules. But how did it all come about? What kind of universe was Herbert entering when he was working on *Dune*?

Here's the brief history lesson: In 1926, Hugo Gernsback launched the pulp magazine *Amazing Stories*, which is commonly viewed as the first science fiction magazine. At the time, Gernsback preferred the term *scientification* and published short fiction in which the plausibility of fictional technology was central to the story. This may sound like a bad way to write stories—idea first, character second—but in the 1920s, the notion of demanding that fanciful narratives have more concrete science mixed in was fairly new. While certain very famous authors—like Mary Shelley, Arthur Conan Doyle, and H. G. Wells—were known to employ what was later called science fiction, it wasn't until the late 1920s that it became a codified genre, specifically within magazines. And while the term *science fiction* emerged from *Amazing*, it was popularized by one of its competitors: *Astounding*. That magazine began its life as *Astounding Stories of Super-Science* in 1930. In 1938, it was retitled *Astounding Science Fiction*. The editor who made this change was John W. Campbell. In 1960, he changed the name again, to *Analog Science Fact/Science Fiction*.

Now that we've done a history download, we must fast-forward to the future briefly and make it clear that Campbell's reputation today is beyond problematic. Like many great American institutions, the publication history of American science fiction has a few downright evil progenitors, even if some of their impacts were positive. Campbell may have codified the SF field as a strong-willed editor, but his failings weren't limited to just being pushy with some rewrites. He was a horrible racist who tried to "prove" nonwhites were inferior humans. He was sexist to the point of publishing very few women and was anti-Semitic enough to try to convince Isaac Asimov to use a pen name to hide the fact that Asimov was Jewish. Campbell was also heavily involved with L. Ron Hubbard, another science fiction writer he championed. Campbell didn't die a practicing Scientologist, but later in his life, his support of pseudoscience made him so polarizing and unlikable that science fiction authors like Robert A. Heinlein (a right-leaning libertarian!) disavowed any positive influence Campbell had on their careers. From the political right to the political left of science fiction, rational people all agree, Campbell was bad news, even if he did publish and edit a lot of great stories. In 2020, the Hugo Awards, which had previously given out the John W. Campbell Award for Best New Writer, changed the name of the award after author Jeannette Ng said in 2019 (while accepting the award): "John W. Campbell, for whom this award was named, was a fascist. Through his editorial control of *Astounding Science Fiction*, he is responsible for setting a tone of science fiction that still haunts the genre to this day."

The tone Ng refers to is essentially the one thing Campbell was obsessed with throughout his editorial stewardship of *Astounding* (and later *Analog*) and, briefly, a magazine called *Unknown*. Campbell believed in a strict adherence to various formulas that always demonstrated that a "super-man" or "super-human" would win the day by virtue of being a super-being. What Campbell either ignored about *Dune* or outright missed was that Frank Herbert's "super-being" wasn't set up as a positive thing. In the pages that Campbell edited and published for "Dune World," Paul's prescience about his messianic destiny fills him with a sense of "terrible purpose." This phrase, "terrible purpose," is repeated ten times in "Dune World." While some might say Herbert pulls his punches on being critical of Paul's role in the first novel, the story in no way suggests that Paul's ascendancy to false godhood is noble. On top of this, when Paul discovers he's the product of controlled breeding, he's disgusted and outraged, saying to himself, "I'm a monster! A freak!"

If Campbell harbored any notions that Frank Herbert would have been in support of systematic racism or eugenics, the feelings and beliefs of Herbert's protagonists suggest the opposite. While "Dune World" may have been written in the space opera, swashbuckling style that Campbell essentially invented, Herbert's actual dialogue in "Dune World" (which is what Campbell published) totally runs counter to the kind of diluted Great Man–theory propaganda Campbell was fond of. As Herbert has said many times, his goal with *Dune* was to say "cult leaders have feet of clay, if not worse. They lead their followers to the Coliseum, where they get to be eaten by lions." He could have been talking about L. Ron Hubbard or Campbell himself. Although Campbell gleefully published the three-part "Dune World," from December 1963 to February 1964, and then the five-part sequel "The Prophet of Dune" from January 1965 to May 1965, it's likely he missed the point.

Interestingly, Nevala-Lee asserts that the moment in which Campbell accepted "Dune World" for publication came at a time where Campbell's influence and the reputation of *Analog* weren't so hot. "The interesting thing here is that by this point, *Astounding* is kind of in decline," Nevala-Lee explains. "It's no longer the leading magazine in the market. It's been in decline since the Hubbard period in the 1950s." This viewpoint was backed up by Harlan Ellison in 1967, who wrote: "John Campbell . . . used to edit a magazine that ran science fiction called *Astounding* and now runs a magazine that runs a lot of schematic drawings called *Analog*." Burn!

Ellison was mostly referring to the 1960s revolution within printed science fiction that is now generally called the New Wave. This was a period of writers like Philip K. Dick, Ursula K. Le Guin, Samuel Delany, and many more, folks who (like Herbert) were more interested in saying something relevant than describing spaceships. More politically progressive, and more concerned with style than technical writing, the New Wave SF writers were decidedly anti-Campbellian. Frank Herbert and his "Dune World" weren't ever really considered part of the New Wave, mostly because the beginning of the saga was published by the old guard. And yet, because *Dune*'s backstory rejects computers and artificial intelligence while downplaying the specifics of space flight, Herbert was, in many ways, the most important New Wave science fiction writer of them all. He fooled Campbell into believing he was an old-school science fiction writer, when the truth was, he'd evolved into something new. The only thing he had left to do was to finish the story of Paul Atreides, whom "Dune World" left crying in a cave, finally mourning the loss of his father.

By January 1964, several readers of *Analog* were furious about this "ending." Although they had been promised a three-part serialized novel called "Dune World," the third and final installment, billed as the "conclusion," ended without resolution. After the Atreides are betrayed on Arrakis, and Paul and Lady Jessica escape into the desert, the story promptly stops and leaves the reader as Paul considers all the possible futures he might have. And that's when the tears come. If you squint, this ending—the first public ending of *Dune*—is a little like a much harsher version of the cliffhanger of Denis Villeneuve's *Dune: Part One*, but this time, the movie stops well before Jessica and Paul meet the Fremen, about an hour and a half in. Even for the most loyal *Dune* fan, reading the third part of "Dune World" and imagining it presented as the end of the story is ridiculous. One particularly annoyed reader, Mark L. Schibel, wrote to editor Campbell that "the conclusion was disappointing, to say the least," while another, P. M. Strain, complained that "Dune World" was "misrepresented as being a story with a beginning, middle and an end," and added that they couldn't "call it a novel; it was butchered too badly, either by you or by the author." But the common thread in all of the criticism of "Dune World" was clear: It wasn't that *Analog* readers thought the quality of the story or the writing was bad. Just the opposite; they loved it. Their anger came from feeling cheated. *Is this it? Really?*

Campbell forwarded these letters to Frank Herbert, who

dutifully informed his newfound fans that, yes, there was more to the story, and a serialized magazine sequel to "Dune World" was in the works. To P. M. Strain, Herbert wrote back: "That ending was put on it to 'tie it off' for serialization of the first third. John [Campbell] will publish the rest of the story later . . . and we hope to have a single-volume of the story out shortly afterward." By "we," Herbert meant himself and his agent, Lurton Blassingame. By "single-volume of the story," Herbert referred to what is commonly known as a book.

On September 7, 1964, in Oakland, California, "Dune World" was a big deal at the Hugo Awards. It had been nominated for best novel, even though everybody hated the ending, it had appeared only in magazine form, and it was, admittedly, unfinished. This moment may have been one of the earliest indications of the strange uniqueness of *Dune*; even before it was done, and even before anyone knew how the story ended, it was still being called a novel and getting nominated for awards. It didn't win, of course. Which makes sense. The version of *Dune* readers encountered first was incomplete and with a future only vaguely glimpsed by the prescience of both Paul Atreides and his creator. "Dune World" was a strange, inauspicious, and humble beginning for a novel that would soon conquer the world. The sleeper had yet to awaken fully, and Herbert was yet to publish the iconic scene in which Paul learns to ride a sandworm. And yet, by mastering *Analog* and controlling John Campbell, Frank Herbert had essentially done the same thing. A monster that had created the context for science fiction hadn't been tamed. But Herbert had ridden that monster and used it for his own purposes.

Novel Repair Manual

The publication of the first *Dune* novel.

It's so small.
But it has eighteen hundred pages.

—Paul Atreides and Dr. Yueh

f anyone has ever told you *Dune* is a "tough read," it would be interesting to see if that same person was able to read an eight-hundred-page Stephen King or Harry Potter novel. Although there are dozens and dozens of characters, and various layers of politics, religion, philosophy, and science fiction projections, if you're able to keep track of more than five seasons of whatever TV show is hot right now, the story of the first *Dune* novel is not that tough to follow. The actual cause and effect of the novel isn't subtle, even if Paul's clairvoyance is spotty. As longtime sci-fi journalist and *Dune* expert Paul M. Sammon noted in 2021, "a handy way to look at [*Dune*] is to think of *Game of Thrones* set on a desert planet. And instead of dragons think of giant sandworms, and instead of a battle for who will sit on the Iron Throne . . . think of a struggle of a young untested prince, who is unwitting and unwilling, at first, who winds up becoming, essentially, a religious messiah."

Not only is this analogy useful in tearing down funny biases a newcomer might have against *Dune*, but it also underscores the way in which decades-old talking points have a pervasive habit of sticking around, even if those talking points no longer apply to the culture at large. Haters like to say *Dune* is long and boring because people used to say *Dune* is long and boring. But that was decades before mainstream culture became obsessed with science fiction and fantasy. Readers and moviegoers in the twenty-first century are probably more primed to enjoy and "get" *Dune* for its plot alone than perhaps any other generation before. In 1965, mainstream culture wasn't inundated with complicated fantasy narratives.* But today, thanks to the bedrock of Tolkien, *Doctor Who, Star Trek, Star Wars*, anime, Marvel movies, and *Game of Thrones*, the average person—a phrase here that means "a person who has never gone to a comic-con of any kind and likely never will"—is more willing and able to follow intricate feudal fantasy plots than they were in the 1960s.† In other words, the next time you need a reason to say *Dune* was ahead of its time, you can just say it invented *Game of Thrones* before *Game of Thrones*, complete with the tedious descriptions of food.

---

*Sure, *The Lord of the Rings* was published in 1954 and 1955, and *The Hobbit* in 1937, but it's not like your grandma knew who Saruman was back then.

†Obviously, those of us who go to comic-cons have loved *Dune* forever. That's not the point. A sci-fi or fantasy thing is mainstream only when it's popular both inside and outside of "geek" circles.

The first *Dune* novel—eventually published as a hardcover book in August 1965—is a dense tome with a simple plot made complicated on purpose. It goes like this: In the distant future, Duke Leto Atreides is ordered by his emperor to pack up and leave the super-cozy oceanic planet Caladan and move to a desert-planet hellhole, Arrakis, nicknamed "Dune." The stated job is to take over the production of spice, a freakishly valuable natural resource that can only be mined on Arrakis, which is very tricky because the planet is an inhospitable wasteland crawling with giant sandworms. If there's one thing a non-*Dune* person knows about *Dune*, it's those sandworms, perhaps the most iconic space beasts in all fantastic literature. In 1978, for a special audio version of *Dune*, Herbert made his artistic intents with the sandworms clear:

"The concept behind the sandworms of *Dune* has attracted swarms of questions and speculation. The answer is that they are 'the mindless monster[s] from the depths.' At the same time, they are the guardians of 'the priceless treasure.' They are both the source of treasure [the spice] and the source of infinite danger. What is that, except the embodiment of all the unknowns which confront questing life, questing awareness."

Herbert's interest in Middle Eastern history was linked to his research about deserts and the overall history of world religion. And so this naturally led to a study of Arabic. Throughout *Dune*, Herbert transmogrified various Arabic words to describe the nomenclature of Arrakis. Karin Christina Ryding, a professor of Arabic at Georgetown University, points out that the Fremen word for the sandworms—*shai hulud*—is likely derived from Arabic. "If taken as written by Herbert, the term *shai hulud* could translate as 'immortal thing' or 'eternal thing' (*shay' khulūd*)," she writes. But Ryding also adds "fanciful speculation" that another reading could be interpreted as "old grandfather whale." In the 2021 movie, Paul says to himself, "I recognize your footsteps, old man," which references the fact that Paul has Gurney's walking pattern memorized, but also reminds us that the Fremen like to call the sandworm the "old man of the desert," which, again, is backed up by the Arabic references.

But old whalelike sandworms and scheming Harkonnens* be damned, the plot of the book begins as Leto moves his whole family and staff—including his son, Paul, and his bonded concubine Jessica—to the planet Arrakis. As we know, Jessica has trained her son, Paul, in the ways of the Bene Gesserit (including the Voice). For thousands of years, the Bene Gesserit have been trying to breed a super-being called the Kwisatz Haderach, and they believe Paul could be it. Meanwhile, the Fremen, the desert-dwelling people of Arrakis, also think Paul could be their messiah and lead them to freedom. Spoiler alert: Everyone is (kind of) right. With the help of the spice, and later, the Water of Life (sandworm bile!), Paul can see the future (inconsistently), which allows him to become the (convenient) messiah for the Fremen, if not quite the Kwisatz Haderach. After his father is killed in an almost instant Har-

---

* All these people are *Homo sapiens*, by the way. There are no space aliens in the *Dune* galaxy. There are shapeshifters called Face Dancers, pseudo-clones called gholas, mutated Guild navigators who look like fish in tanks, and, of course, giant alien sandworms, which are technically animals. But no actual aliens.

konnen invasion, Paul and his mother, Jessica—who is pregnant with Paul's baby sister, Alia—flee into the desert of Dune, where they meet up with the Fremen.

After a ritual knife fight and some spicy coffee, Jessica becomes the reverend mother for the Fremen, and Paul becomes the Fremen's messiah and learns to ride giant sandworms. Then, with the help of his Fremen lover (not wife!), Chani, and his baby sister, Alia—who is born with the memories of all her ancestors—Paul, the remaining members of House Atreides, and the Fremen ride those sandworms real hard, crush the Harkonnen forces, and conquer the galaxy. The first book ends with Paul's becoming the emperor as the underdogs of the universe become the top dogs.

Critically, none of this could have happened if *Dune* had remained a half-completed serial in a science fiction magazine with a circulation of one hundred thousand copies. Sure, one hundred thousand copies of a magazine seems like a lot, but magazines don't have the same kind of shelf life as books. Literally. Today, short stories in magazines might be available digitally after the issue is no longer on sale, but that technology obviously didn't exist in the 1960s. A series of linked short stories in a niche-interest magazine couldn't possibly hope to reach a massive audience. Books have the ability to travel into the future in a way that no other written medium does.

In 1963, Frank Herbert was paid three cents a word for "Dune World," which totaled $2,295. "Dune World" wasn't the only fiction he was publishing at that time, nor was a novel version of *Dune* the only book he was shopping around, either.

Still, despite not having found a publisher for *Dune* or a home for his other project, a novel called *The Santaroga Barrier*, Frank Herbert quit his day job at the *San Francisco Chronicle* in early 1965. This move was somewhat reckless, and by 1966, he'd already be working there again, only to quit again by 1969. Before *Dune* became a legit book, Herbert was gambling on future literary success,* which meant he needed a book deal, something he hadn't had at all since *The Dragon in the Sea* was first published by Doubleday in 1956.

The general sweep of Herbert's (few) biographies makes it seem like his agent submitted *Dune* to book publishers forever before getting a deal. And while it's true that Lurton Blassingame did shop one version of *Dune* to major book publishers in 1963 before landing an actual deal in 1965, this was not the version of *Dune* you think it was. In fact, in a letter dated April 5, 1963, Blassingame made it clear he was excited about the story, even though they both knew it wasn't done. As he wrote to Herbert: "I bow three times and hold out my hands for the rest of story."

Here's where the publication timeline gets confusing. In *Dune*, Paul's prescience bewilders him to the point where he can't discern whether he's remembering the future or the future has already passed. And because there are so many early formats for *Dune*, its path to becoming a novel you could hold

---

*In fairness, this gamble was based on some evidence. Lurton Blassingame was also Robert A. Heinlein's agent, which, in the late 1950s, was the science fiction version of having Ernest Hemingway's agent.

in your hands is equally bewildering. Because we know the endgame, there's a tendency to look at the process as inevitably leading to that result, even if there were a few dead ends and strokes of sheer luck along the way. So, in the interest of demystifying the road to the first *Dune*'s actual publication, here's the sequence of events, just in case the reader's own personal spice trance is too intense.

- 1957: Herbert pitches the nonfiction article "They Stopped the Moving Sands," which he later abandons.

- 1962: Herbert attempts an outline of a novel called "Spice Planet," which he also eventually abandons.

- 1963: Herbert completes "Dune World," the first third, or book 1, of *Dune*, according to Brian Herbert, "early" this year.

- April 1963: Lurton Blassingame tells Herbert he likes *Dune* and begins shopping book 1 around to publishers with the intention of this being a trilogy.

- May 1963: Blassingame contacts John Campbell at *Analog*, who purchased several of Herbert's stories before. Campbell expresses interest in book 1, which becomes "Dune World."

- June 1963: Campbell formally accepts "Dune World" for serialization in *Analog*. He initially asks Herbert to break the story into four parts but later decides that three parts is better. "Dune World" is scheduled for serialization from the December 1963 issue through the February 1964 issue.

- July 1963: Concurrently with all of this, Blassingame contacts Timothy Seldes at Doubleday, who says in his first letter, "I think I can offer a contract for DUNE by Frank Herbert if he is willing to do some work on it." To be clear, this *Dune* is merely book 1, or "Dune World."

- August 1963: Seldes softly rejects *Dune* and worries that the "problem lies in Mr. Herbert's thinking of the trilogy aspect." This "trilogy aspect" is what we now think of as the three sections of the first book. Herbert, at this point, thinks he can sell three novels instead of one.

- November 1963: According to Brian Herbert, Frank Herbert completes book 2 and book 3 of *Dune*, i.e., the rest of the novel. (This version is still not quite the final version, as we'll see.) "Dune World" is also the cover story for the December 1963 issue of *Analog*.

- December 1963: Campbell informs Blassingame that he wants to publish the remainder of the *Dune* story in five installments, to be determined at a later date. Campbell calls the new material a "gee-gorgeous hunk of stuff."

- Early 1964: Lurton Blassingame shops around at least two different versions of *Dune* to various publishers. In January, Seldes at Doubleday again passes on the manuscript.

- Summer 1964 to early 1965: Blassingame continues to receive various rejections for *Dune*, including from Scribner, New American Library, and others. In total, twenty-three publishers pass on *Dune*. Amid the negative feedback, Blassingame tells Herbert he is worried about the overall length of the text. In a strange contradiction, he also tells Herbert he doesn't think the concept of breaking up the novel into three books instead of one will work, either. Most publishers agree. As Brian Herbert later said, "[Those publishers] would not publish the material in any form, separately or combined."

- December 1964: "The Prophet of Dune"—part 1 of five installments—is the cover for the January 1965 issue of *Analog*. This serial runs until the May 1965 issue. For the final two issues of this serial, *Analog* changes format, going from a glossy "bedsheet"-size magazine back down to digest size.

- January 1965: Editor and science fiction author Sterling E. Lanier of Chilton Books—an automotive repair book publisher—contacts Blassingame and suggests that Chilton publish *Dune* as one volume in hardcover. He offers an advance of $7,500. Blassingame accepts the offer. The book was not submitted to Chilton. It was requested.

- Spring 1965: The fifth and final installment of "The Prophet of Dune" is published in the May 1965 issue of *Analog*.

- August 1965: *Dune* is published by Chilton Books.

If we zoom in on the period of 1964 to early 1965—when the second *Analog* serial is running to completion and the publisher rejections are piling up in Lurton Blassingame's mailbox—many accounts of *Dune*'s publication story gleefully focus on two details here. After those twenty-three book publishers rejected *Dune* eventually, only a publisher of car-repair manuals, Chilton Books, accepted it. Both things are true. But this simplistic telling of the story leaves out two super-important details: First, the *Analog* serialization was essential to the Chilton deal. Second, a *Lord of the Rings* megafan—Chilton's Sterling E. Lanier—was the real person responsible for *Dune*'s getting turned into a proper book, and is perhaps the most important person in *Dune* history. Without Lanier, we would be talking about a serialized magazine story here, not a book.

In January 1965, Lanier, a longtime reader of *Analog*, had a taste for what the rest of the story was going to look like. Keep in mind that as far as the insular science fiction readership of *Analog* was concerned, "Dune World" ended on a cliffhanger in 1964, and "The Prophet of Dune" was simply its sequel. In the final novel version, the text of "The Prophet of Dune" comprises book 2, "Muad'Dib," and book 3, "The Prophet," which in the first edition would be basically everything from page 161 to the end. In the contemporary mass-market paper-back version of the book, this would be everything from page 325 to the end. In the 2021 trade paperback edition, that's page 255 to the end. Great maker! Is *Dune* an eight-hundred-page book, a six-hundred-page book, or a four-hundred-page book? The answer is yes, there have been, and still are, a lot of different formats of *Dune*, and those varying page lengths can mostly be explained by typesetting in different formats. But because Frank Herbert didn't formalize any actual chapter numbers,* the different lengths of *Dune* easily explain why people can feel like they're getting sucked into the sands of Arrakis while wading through its pages.

Before we get freaked out by these contradictory page counts or start jumping to conclusions about alternate versions, let's just be clear on something: All single-volume† English versions of *Dune* in book form have the same words in them. And guess what? This also includes most of the serialized bit-by-bit versions published in *Analog*. That's right, if you read all eight *Analog* issues, you will only find minor differences between that text and the actual book. When you lay a *Dune* issue of *Analog* side by side with its corresponding prose in the book, you'll occasionally find some condensed character thoughts, or ideas slightly rearranged. But overall, reading the eight magazine installments of *Dune* back-to-back doesn't feel that different in terms of content. What does feel

---

*However, in the *Analog* versions, there is a roman numeral above each epigraph that begins each chapter. The chapters in the Kindle and Audible versions of *Dune* correspond with these numbers. But technically, no *Dune* novel has chapter numbers.

†I say "single-volume" because sometimes, when translated or republished, *Dune* was split up into two volumes. For example, the 1980 Michel Demuth French translation of *Dune*, from Presses Pocket, split the first book into two paperback volumes. These versions had unique cover illustrations from Wojciech Siudmak. In 2021, Denis Villeneuve told me these were the first versions of *Dune* he read, when he was just thirteen years old.

different is the fact that reading *Dune* piecemeal as a series of short stories in a magazine has the effect of recontextualizing the popular culture image of its being a massively long novel. *Dune* in magazine form is like imagining if Moses scribbled the commandments on some parchment paper before transferring the word of God to stone. When you read *Dune* in installments, it brings it down to earth, makes it feel less improbable, and instantly reverses its unwieldy reputation.

But beyond the vibes, what is specifically different about the words in the *Analog Dune* versus the words in the book? Luckily, the author himself laid it out exactly. In an exchange of letters between Herbert and Blassingame, between August 24 and August 27, 1965, Blassingame asks for the differences between the *Analog* version and the novel version for legal copyright purposes because he doesn't want "movie people quibbling." (Even in 1965, Herbert's agent sees the possibility of *Dune*'s getting optioned as a film!) This correspondence handily has Herbert elucidate the exact differences between the entire *Analog* run and the published novel:

"I wrote an extensive recapitulation for the beginning of Prophet which has been edited out of the Chilton book versions—about 5,000 words in all. . . . I also expanded the Fenring role and wrote several new chapter-precedes for the Chilton book—see page 84 of the book; also pgs. 163, 209, 210, 237, 271, 293. The map of course is new and the four appendices and the glossary . . . this rounds off at 15,300 words."

It sounds like a lot, but most of what is different is simply, as Herbert admits, the glossary and the appendices. The book has those, the magazine version didn't. The "recapitulation"

Herbert refers to is a recap that connected "Prophet of Dune" with the abrupt ending of "Dune World." In terms of story changes, "the Fenring role" refers to Count Fenring, a politician whose wife, Lady Margot Fenring (Léa Seydoux in 2023's *Dune: Part Two*), plays a specific role in both aiding Lady Jessica and, unrelatedly, furthering the Bene Gesserit breeding program. In the novel, Lady Fenring intentionally gets herself pregnant by the wicked Feyd-Rautha. Her child and the secret Bene Gesserit plan for the said child were not resolved by Frank Herbert. Meaning, a story detail that Herbert "expanded" for the novel was never addressed in future books written by Herbert. (Though some quasi-canonical books written by Brian Herbert and Kevin J. Anderson did pick up this thread.)

In 1966, Herbert defended his tendency to leave certain plot details in his books unresolved as purposeful. His son Brian Herbert asserted in 2003, "Dad intentionally sent his readers spinning out at the end of the book, with a fragment of it still clinging to them." In the junior Herbert's view, a Frank Herbert plot hole is really designed to "reflect the realities and uncertainties of life," and the degree to which you buy that may explain the entire longevity of not just *Dune* but perhaps all of science fiction, too. Either the plot holes are there on purpose, or we're all nuts.

Perhaps the most hilarious difference between the magazine version of *Dune* and the novel is the way various swear words are omitted in *Analog*. In the first chapter, as the reverend mother is stewing over the fact that Jessica had a son instead of a daughter, she says to herself, "Damn that Jessica!"

But in the 1963 "Dune World" version in *Analog*, she merely says, "That Jessica!" This was likely because, according to Alec Nevala-Lee, John Campbell's longtime copy editor Catherine Tarrant "occasionally took it on herself to remove bad language from stories."

Fascinatingly, one climactic and amazing plot detail that originated in the pages of *Analog* wasn't even Herbert's idea at all. In his original draft of the serialized "Prophet of Dune" (again, basically the last two-thirds of the novel), Alia, Paul's baby sister, who is "pre-born" with the memories of all her ancestors, dies before the end of the story. Foreshadowed by mentions of "Alia of the Knife" in various epigraphs earlier in the book, the notion that Alia originally died in Herbert's first take on *Dune* is somewhat shocking considering her hugely pivotal roles in the sequels *Dune Messiah* and *Children of Dune*. Editor John Campbell was the one to talk Herbert out of killing Alia, pleading with Herbert in a letter: "Sorry to see her go, by the way; did she have to be eliminated?"

Herbert agreed, and from that point on, Alia is the person who kills the evil Baron Harkonnen and lives to fight for several more days in the next two novels. There's a degree of strange irony in the fact that Campbell, a misogynist who rarely published women, ensured that one of the most complex female characters in the *Dune* mythos survived beyond her literal infancy. Broken clocks can be right twice a day, or, in the case of Campbell's asking for Alia to remain alive, right about one thing forever. If we view Herbert and *Dune* as having survived Campbell's overbearing editorial tendencies, the perpetuation of Alia as a character seems to be the one contradiction within that way of thinking. Herbert, like Duke Leto, may have had "plans within plans," but sometimes the plans of others ended up changing his writing for the better.

The idea that Herbert planned to kill Alia off in the first novel also calls into question his frequent assertions that aspects of the later books were in fact planned before the first one. If this were true on a granular level, and Herbert had plotted out *Dune Messiah* and *Children of Dune* prior to completing *Dune*, how would those books have worked with Alia dead? We'll never know. And the reason why we'll never know is the *Analog* ALIA LIVES! versions were the versions that sold the book.

Here's why this is such a big deal: At the point when twenty-three book publishers had passed on *Dune*, the only thing that turned it into an actual book was a fan who was already familiar with the story because of *Analog*. Sterling Lanier reached out to Blassingame, not the other way around. It's not like *Dune* had been rejected by twenty-three publishers and then Blassingame decided to roll the dice with a publisher of car-repair manuals. If Lanier hadn't been a fan and hadn't contacted Blassingame, none of this would have happened. "Dune World" and "The Prophet of Dune" would have been no less or more impactful on the world at large than any other interesting short stories in the pages of science fiction magazines largely forgotten by most of the world. The thing that made *Dune* grab hold of the culture and never let go was the fact that it became a real book. So this means that other than Frank Herbert, Sterling Lanier is the most foundational and influential figure in the entire story of *Dune*. If there's a true hero at this point in *Dune*'s journey, it's him.

Although Lanier was an editor at an automotive publisher in 1965, all photos of him make him look like a retired British naval officer, a monocle-wearing Colonel Mustard type, whom you can imagine owning a working cannon. Born in New York City in 1927, Lanier was just thirty-eight years old in 1965, seven years younger than Herbert, who was forty-five by this time. Like Herbert, Lanier was also largely self-taught. He said in 1969, "I've never had a writing course. Never had a course in sculpture. No one ever asked me to write. No one ever asked me to be a sculptor. I am a writer and a sculptor."

The fact Lanier was a sculptor holds an interesting place in history. In addition to making wild offers to publish *Dune* as Chilton's first fiction offering, in 1965, Lanier was also mailing handcrafted bronze *Lord of the Rings* figurines to J. R. R. Tolkien. Some people send fan letters, but in the case of Lanier, he sent the creator of Middle-earth bespoke sculptures made to represent characters from his favorite series of novels. These various figurine sets have surfaced over the years but were never released commercially. When Lanier died, his widow, Ann Lanier, said, "The characters in the 2001 movie bore a striking resemblance to the figures [he] created from his imagination."

Whether or not Sterling E. Lanier was directly responsible for the way Legolas looked in the 2001 film *The Fellowship of the Ring* is certainly up for debate and interpretation. But his correspondence with Tolkien was very real, beginning in 1951. This means by the time he decided to convince his colleagues at Chilton to publish *Dune*, Lanier was well entrenched in science fiction and fantasy literary circles. He had a short story published in *Analog* in 1961, and in 1964 was bickering in *Analog*'s letters column ("Brass Tacks") about the finer points of how to present zoology in science fiction stories. In short, Lanier was not only a science fiction and fantasy insider; he was one of a kind, a geek scholar, and a true fan. After securing the deal for *Dune*, Lanier sent a copy of the book to J. R. R. Tolkien, who was silent about his opinion on the novel for a year, but in 1966, when another fan named John Bush sent Tolkien another copy, he wrote, plainly, "I dislike *Dune* with some intensity."

The biggest Tolkien megafan in the 1960s was also the person who made *Dune* into a bona fide novel, even though Tolkien himself hated *Dune* and Herbert seemingly never said a word in public about Middle-earth one way or another. Legendary science fiction writer Arthur C. Clarke famously said of *Dune*, "I know of nothing comparable to it except *Lord of the Rings*," a statement Tolkien surely hated and Herbert probably didn't give a shit about. And yet, the fan, the reader, the true believer, Sterling E. Lanier, saw the connection. He felt *Dune*, like *The Lord of the Rings*, had the power to reach beyond just the readership of hard-core science fiction and fantasy folks. Lanier knew *Dune* could be a book for everyone. Brian Herbert also credits Lanier with being the final word on the actual title of the book. Instead of "Dune World," Lanier felt the one-word *Dune* was the way to go.

The first edition of *Dune*, published by Chilton Books in August 1965, is hands down the most beautiful version of the book ever. Chilton had never published fiction before, and the book looked nothing like anything else in their catalog. However, in 1966, they did publish a fantasy novel by James H. Schmitz, *The Witches of Karres*.

The way this first version of *Dune* looks is striking and unique. Even in her mostly negative review of the novel in the March 1966 issue of *Fantasy and Science Fiction*, Judith Merril calls it "a handsome volume," which is a massive understatement. The dust jacket presents a lush oil-painting illustration, mostly in deep greens and browns, of Paul and his mother, Jessica, traversing a canyon on Arrakis. This illustration comes from John Schoenherr and first appeared on the cover of the January 1965 issue of *Analog*, in which the first part of "The Prophet of Dune" was published. Schoenherr also illustrated the December 1963 *Analog* cover for the first installment of "Dune World"* and later gave the world the first color

---

* According to Campbell, he asked Schoenherr for six versions of this cover, until he was satisfied with the seventh attempt. In previous decades, Campbell often assigned science fiction stories based on the illustrations first, rather than the other way around. This practice was fictionalized in the 1998 *Star Trek: Deep Space Nine* episode "Far Beyond the Stars," in which a cipher for Campbell, Douglas Pabst (René Auberjonois), hands out sci-fi story assignments for his (fictional) 1950s magazine, *Incredible Tales of Scientific Wonder*, asking writers to write toward the illustration. Coincidentally or not, much of *Deep Space Nine*'s biggest character arc concerning Benjamin Sisko (Avery Brooks) has clear parallels to *Dune*.

illustration of a massive sandworm for the March 1965 issue.[*]
Schoenherr also provided a plethora of black-ink drawings
that illustrated every single installment of "Dune World" and
"The Prophet of Dune" in *Analog*. These illustrations depict
everything from the arrival of the Bene Gesserit reverend
mother in the opening pages of the story to Paul's battle with
the hunter-seeker, and, curiously, seem to depict Duke Leto
with what can only be described as a Mohawk. Herbert loved
all the illustrations, writing to Campbell, "Frequently, I have
to ask myself if the artist was actually illustrating the story his
work accompanied. Not so with John Schoenherr . . . [his art]
caught the tremendous power and beauty [of] the 'Dune
mood' I struggled so hard to create."

While the interior illustrations were never used again,
Lanier insisted on using the Schoenherr painting from *Analog*'s first "The Prophet of Dune" issue (January 1965) as the
cover of the novel. Again, say what you will about the other
covers of the book over the years, this cover is gorgeous.
But more important, the cover is genre neutral. It doesn't
scream science fiction, nor does it look particularly pulpy or
old-fashioned.

Contemporary science fiction book designer Lauren Panepinto said it best in 2020. In writing about the entire history

---

[*]This illustration is so iconic that it has appeared on the cover of various re-
prints of *Dune* in novel form and to this day remains perhaps the quintessen-
tial sandworm illustration.

of *Dune* cover art, she hit upon exactly what made the cover of the first edition of *Dune* not just special but also revolutionary:

"Notice that [Chilton] picked a piece of art with nary a sandworm in sight. . . . If you look at this cover without knowing anything about it, would you really know it was necessarily an alien planet? . . . They [Chilton] are deliberately trying to distance themselves from what the standard pulpy SFF covers looked like at the time. These are all decisions that say: 'take me more seriously than the disposable paperbacks you geeks have been reading' and it worked."

It didn't, however, work right away. The first edition of *Dune* cost $5.95, which, based on most inflation models, is like fifty bucks today. The first printing of the first edition of *Dune* was only 2,200 copies, which means that among rare and collectible books today, a *Dune* first edition can be worth anywhere between $1,000 and $25,000. And yet, at the end of 1965, this 412-page book, with a cool map on the back (hand-drawn by Herbert) and that moody cover, wasn't really selling. *Dune* was finally a book, and its destiny of becoming the most important science fiction novel of all time was sealed. And yet, for Frank Herbert, Lurton Blassingame, and Sterling Lanier, it didn't feel like that at all. As 1965 drew to a close, *Dune* was out in the world, waiting to consume us all like a giant sandworm.

At this time, Herbert had won both the coveted science fiction literary awards, the Nebula and the Hugo,* the first

---

*Hilariously, *Dune* tied for best novel at the 1966 Hugo Awards. The Best Novel was Roger Zelazny's *This Immortal*. It's an okay book, about a guy who lives novel ever to do so, and the first novel to win a Nebula, period, since those awards began in 1966. And yet, even within the community of science fiction writers, Herbert didn't feel entirely at home. He had conquered that subculture but still felt like an outsider. One of Herbert's collaborators, author and poet Bill Ransom, told me that while "Frank was more or less oblivious" to how other science fiction authors regarded him, he did think that "a lot of authors felt envy, which can be productive, but a fair number chose unforgivingly; jealousy." Ransom says, "I found it regrettable and small of the SFWA group [the Science Fiction Writers of America] to fail to name him a master when he was alive. There was a sense among some of our colleagues that neither of us had paid enough of the proper dues."

Indeed, although many SF publishing insiders, like Harlan Ellison, believed in the power of Frank Herbert, *Dune* is conspicuously omitted from several nonfiction SF surveys published before the late 1970s. The most glaring omission comes from Donald A. Wollheim's 1971 nonfiction book *The Universe Makers: Science Fiction Today*. Wollheim was a well-respected science fiction editor and historian in the field, and yet in 1971, six years after *Dune*'s publication and despite its award-winning status within the SF community, he declined to mention it even once in his otherwise comprehensive survey of the

---

forever, but to pretend it's on the same level as *Dune* is bonkers. Having *Dune* tie with *This Immortal* is like if *Titanic* had tied with *The Full Monty* for Best Picture at the 1998 Oscars.

genre up until that point. The same is true in another brilliant 1971 nonfiction book, called *Science Fiction: What It's All About*, by Sam J. Lundwall, which also doesn't mention Herbert or *Dune*, but does spend a decent amount of time on what was then the emerging New Wave of science fiction authors. In short, a huge majority of younger science fiction writers in the 1970s—like Harlan Ellison, Samuel R. Delany, Ursula K. Le Guin, and others—were grouped together as a new moment in SF literature because their writing tended to value literary artistry over technological stories about brave astronauts.

In this way, Frank Herbert was a bridge between the older traditions of science fiction writing and the so-called New Wave. *Dune* clearly used existing forms of narrative structure to tell a throwback-feeling hero's journey tale. But within that, Herbert subverted those tropes thanks to layered and realistic consequences. Some critics have labeled *Dune* a work of "soft" science fiction simply because even though Herbert presents a myriad of future technology and situations, he doesn't get into the nitty-gritty of how everything works and allows the reader to simply go with the spice flow. This technique is emblematic of many other New Wave writers, too, most notably Le Guin and Ellison.

The only real difference is that Herbert was older than many of the New Wavers, and *Dune* had immense popularity outside of science fiction circles in a way that most science fiction published in the early 1970s never did. That said, it's also possible that Herbert was isolated from the rest of the science fiction movements of the sixties, seventies, and eighties because he may not have cared much about the science fiction community itself. Herbert, like many great artists, was both an introvert and an extrovert simultaneously. He was happy for a seat at the science fiction table, but he wasn't going to always play by the current rules. Because if everyone thought they understood what *Dune* was about, Herbert's sequel novel was about to prove them all wrong.

5

My Own Private Duncan Idaho

Dune Messiah and the resurrection of *Dune*'s greatest hero.

> I think I tried to invent life, not realizing it had already been invented.
>
> —Paul to Chani

I f the 1969 novel *Dune Messiah* had been a contemporary romantic comedy set in an American city, it would end with Chani about to give birth and Paul frantically driving her to the hospital with his eyes closed. This would all be played for laughs, but the audience would be in on the joke: Paul can see the future, so, for him, driving blind is like a telepathic mash-up of Google Maps and autopilot. He always knows which way he's supposed to turn, because in his memory, he's already done it.

Although *Messiah* is not a *Dune* rom-com, Paul is blinded toward the end of the novel, and despite this, Chani lets him pilot an ornithopter from the palace to their former desert home in Sietch Tabr, where she'll give birth to their children,

Leto II and Ghanima. In passing, after they've arrived, we're told that "Eyeless, he [Paul] had guided the machine here. After that experience, she knew nothing he did could surprise her." It would be easy to say that Paul flying an ornithopter blind pushes the credulity of the *Dune* universe to the breaking point, but the truth is, by the time you get to the climax of this slim sequel, you've already invested so much that you're trapped by whatever Frank Herbert is going to throw at you. Like Chani, the reader is in the passenger seat; Herbert is driving. Is he flying blind? Do these narrative decisions make for a great book? The answers to these questions are slightly more complex than they seem, but after you read *Dune Messiah*, one thing is clear: Nothing Herbert does with the *Dune* saga can surprise you.

In 2021, Timothée Chalamet told me he found the 1969 novel *Dune Messiah* to be "more traditional" than the first novel, and in terms of cause and effect, and the book's overall length, he's not wrong. Whereas the first book slowly pushes readers into the expansive and ornate world of *Dune*, the sequel novel feels smaller by comparison. Part of this is because it's a hell of a lot shorter. *Messiah* is just over 72,000 words, making it a little less than half as long as *Dune*'s 188,000 words. In its first hardcover edition, it was 256 pages, as opposed to the 412 pages of the first hardcover *Dune*. In the easy-to-find mass-market paperback editions of *Messiah*, it's 336 pages, which is a stark contrast with its parent novel, which, as we know, comes close to 900 pages in that smaller paperback format. Remember when Herbert wanted to split the first *Dune* up into more than one book? With *Dune Messiah* (72,000 words) and the next book in the "trilogy," 1976's *Children of Dune* (140,000 words), he essentially got his way. If you combine *Messiah* and *Children*, you've basically got a megabook, only slightly longer than the first *Dune*. It's like Herbert knew topping the massive brilliance of *Dune* would be impossible, so he didn't even try.

Dune Messiah is nobody's favorite *Dune* book. Unlike other big fantasy or sci-fi franchises, in which there's some noticeably large debate between which installment or incarnation constitutes "the best," *Dune* is downright weird because there's an almost unanimous agreement that the first book owns all the others in nearly every way possible.* Average spice heads rarely say any of the other novels are better than the first. Self-described *Dune* megafan Kyle MacLachlan admits to having read only the first three books and personally ranks the first novel well above the others. MacLachlan has "love for *Dune*," while he "liked" *Dune Messiah* and considers *Children of Dune* just "okay," and noted in a 2022 Reddit AMA, "*Dune* [is] still the best."

"Anyone who is a fan of the series, of Herbert's books, will admit the longer the books go on, the less clear they are," Julie Cox said in 2003. Also a longtime fan of the books since she was very young, Cox played Princess Irulan in two Sci Fi Channel *Dune* miniseries. "The first *Dune* [novel] is absolutely

---

*Of course, there are fans out there on Reddit or wherever who say things don't really get good until the fourth book, *God Emperor of Dune*, but that's a little like kooky outlier Batman fans who claim Val Kilmer is somehow the best Bruce Wayne.

brilliant ... but by the third one, things become quite obscure."

The relationship the novel *Dune* has to the rest of the *Dune* book series requires you to imagine a strange alternate universe in which *The Hobbit* had somehow stayed much more popular than its sequels that comprise *The Lord of the Rings*. Julie Cox is essentially correct: None of the *Dune* book sequels can come close to the brilliance of the first book. And yet, the first two sequels, *Dune Messiah* and *Children of Dune*, are both surprisingly clarifying. Before Paul wandered into the desert at the end of *Dune Messiah*, it was possible and probable that many readers misunderstood the intended meaning of Paul's journey in the first book. But after *Dune Messiah* in 1969 (and certainly after *Children of Dune* in 1976), Herbert reduced the number of interpretations of the first novel dramatically. If *Dune*'s strength is its multilayered complexities, the strength of the first sequel is the opposite. The first *Dune* is a riddle wrapped in an enigma, slipped inside of a sandworm. *Dune Messiah* is just a giant blinking billboard flashing one message repeatedly: PAUL WAS WRONG. RELIGIOUS WARS ARE BAD.

From a structural standpoint, though, Chalamet is right: The book is straightforward. Other than its overarching and impossible-to-misunderstand thematic pronouncement, *Dune Messiah* is perhaps the most plot-heavy of all the *Dune* novels. It's less layered than the first book and has fewer digressions than all of its sequels. The book begins twelve years after the end of *Dune*, and the Imperium is now ruled by Paul, who has spread terror throughout the galaxy as the religious leader/ supreme dictator Muad'Dib. Chani, the love of his life, but technically not his wife, has been prevented from getting pregnant, because Princess Irulan, Paul's legal wife, is secretly poisoning her. Irulan is also part of a conspiracy involving Bene Gesserit reverend mother Gaius Helen Mohiam, members of the Spacing Guild, and the Bene Tleilax, a group of genetically altered humans who are capable of all sorts of feats, including (but not limited to) bringing people back from the dead as pseudo-clones called gholas, and have among their number a certain kind of human shapeshifter called a Face Dancer. Paul's prescient vision has made him aware of this conspiracy's endpoint, but at first he's fuzzy on the details.

Meanwhile, his sister, Alia, with her pre-born memories that include all of her and Paul's ancestors, is coming of age, and eventually, she falls in love with a very special someone: Duncan Idaho. That's right, in the sequel to *Dune*, Frank Herbert brought back the slickest swordsman in the universe, but this time as a slightly colder and enigmatic pseudo-clone (again, a ghola) with metallic eyes who goes by the name of Hayt (which is weirdly pronounced "hate"). According to Brian Herbert, his father resurrected Duncan because his readers loved the character, which is easily the best example of "fan service" impacting Frank Herbert's plotting of the six original *Dune* novels. The only character who consistently appears in a major way throughout all six books is Duncan. If you squint, this makes Duncan Idaho the true main character of the entire *Dune* saga, which is a bit like some bizarro version of *Star Wars* in which a clone of young Han Solo keeps popping up decades or centuries after his death.

In 2021, Denis Villeneuve told me he hoped to end his trilogy of *Dune* films with an adaptation of *Messiah*, saying, "I always thought doing *Messiah* would be a powerful movie. . . . I always saw it as a trilogy of movies, two movies for the first book and then *Messiah*." If and when *Messiah* becomes the capper for the Villeneuve *Dune* movie trilogy, it might be potentially the greatest sci-fi movie trilogy ending of all time. In the twisting climax of the book, it is the reborn Hayt/Duncan who saves the day. Even though he's been sent as a secret assassin, created by the Bene Tleilax to kill Paul, that plan backfires. Because Paul is totally hip to this scheme, he uses the power of love to summon the true private soul of Duncan Idaho buried within the ghola. The zombie Duncan that was designed by the conspirators to kill Paul becomes the salvation of the Atreides family. Villeneuve's scheme to end his cinematic *Dune* trilogy with *Messiah* is brilliant because so far, his adaptation of the first book is the only one that has correctly centered Duncan in that narrative as a major character. If you'd only ever seen the David Lynch version of *Dune* and never read any of the books, you'd probably barely remember Richard Jordan's Duncan. In each of the Sci Fi Channel miniseries adaptations, Duncan was played by a different actor. In the miniseries *Frank Herbert's Dune* (2000), James Watson played Duncan. But then in 2003's *Frank Herbert's Children of Dune** miniseries, Edward Atterton plays the ghola Duncan/

---

*The 2003 miniseries *Frank Herbert's Children of Dune* is three episodes long and adapts all of *Dune Messiah* in its first episode and the entirety of the third

Hayt. This recasting is funnily ironic, considering we're meant to believe this duplicate Duncan looks like the same person from the first series. By accident, the various adaptations of *Dune*, prior to 2021, all muddied the public perception of one of the most important characters in the saga. If you were only a casual fan of *Dune* before 2021, you might think Duncan was a slightly boring background character, that guy with the funny name who dies and comes back to life or something.

But the casting of Jason Momoa as Duncan Idaho changed all that. Since the release of the film *Dune: Part One* in 2021, thanks to Momoa's singular charisma and what Villeneuve calls his "bohemian quality," Duncan has rapidly, and correctly, become a prominent figure in the popular consciousness of what *Dune* is and what it represents. In the first wave of action figures from the 2021 *Dune*—which were released in 2020—the one that clearly kicks the most ass is the Duncan Idaho figure. Villeneuve filmed a scene for *Dune: Part One* in which Duncan Idaho heroically leaps from a spacecraft and skydives alone onto Arrakis as an advance scout. This deleted scene was the original opening of the movie, further proving how much Momoa's Duncan has taken over the focus of the new *Dune* movies, something that would have never happened if *Messiah* didn't exist. It makes sense Villeneuve cut this, because while it would have stuck with the chronology of what

---

novel, *Children of Dune*, in its second two episodes. So, that's three parts for two books. Not to be confused with Denis Villeneuve's plan, which also involves three parts for two books, but those books are *Dune* and *Dune Messiah*.

was happening in the book (things that have happened off-screen, so to speak), it wouldn't have scanned as faithful to the way we experience the events of the book. But it speaks to something bigger: Duncan looms large in our minds, even when he's not there. "I'm like the cool older brother," Momoa told me in 2022. "I'm the guy who tells you about cool music and how to dress. That's what I wanted to be for Timothée."

Thinking of Duncan Idaho as *Dune*'s resident "cool guy" is the correct way to view the character, but through his various ghola clones, he also has a fascinating character arc that spans all six of Herbert's original *Dune* books. Despite dying in the first book, Duncan Idaho survives for at least eighteen thousand years, as a "serial ghola." After *Dune Messiah*, other clones of Duncan appear, in each sequel and well into the estate-authorized continuation books written by Brian Herbert and Kevin J. Anderson.* Arguably, Duncan ultimately proves to be the most important person in the entire saga. Duncan Idaho is not only cool, he's cool forever. Although fans of the books have known this for a long time, it's hilarious that, upon the release of *Dune: Part One* in 2021, most mainstream press seemed unaware that the most tragic death in the film was one that will almost certainly be reversed.

---

*You've got far-future Duncans in the fourth book, *God Emperor of Dune* (set 3,500 years after *Children of Dune*), plus additional Duncans in *Heretics of Dune* (set 1,500 years after that) and *Chapterhouse: Dune*, which, overall, happens about 5,000 years after the first novel. This final ghola of Duncan also appears in the estate-authorized sequels *Hunters of Dune* and *Sandworms of Dune*. But then again, by that point, there are a lot of gholas of other classic characters running around, too, including gholas of Paul, Chani, and even Duke Leto!

In 2022, when GQ asked him if he could return for film sequels, Momoa replied, "Have you read the books? I mean the books are proof. . . . I'm not the one spoiling it here. You should continue reading." If the film version of *Messiah* ends the way the book ends, then that means this film trilogy will conclude with Jason Momoa's overcoming powerful brainwashing to save the lives of two babies: Leto II and Ghanima. Telling your friends that *Messiah* rocks because Hayt finally becomes loyal to House Atreides again is all well and good. Saying *Messiah* will bring tears to your eyes because Jason Momoa saves babies is money in the bank. When you strike Jason Momoa down, he becomes more powerful than ever.

But Duncan can't save everyone. Easily the saddest events of *Messiah* concern what happens to Chani, and how that impacts Paul and everyone else. Throughout the book, Paul has kept the knowledge of Chani's fated death to himself. He knows she'll die in childbirth, and she does. After this, Paul is exhausted by the existential nausea of always knowing the future and is doubly haunted by the guilt and shame of the massacres that have happened across the galaxy in his name. With the knowledge that his children are safe thanks to Duncan, Paul decides to walk into the desert alone. With Paul in depressed self-exile and Chani dead, *Messiah* ends with Alia, the reborn Duncan, Stilgar, and Irulan poised to look after these two babies, who may or may not be the salvation of the universe.*

Arrested Development Ron Howard voice: They're not.

These tragic events set the stage for *Children of Dune* but also elevate one of the most interesting secondary characters, Princess Irulan, into the foreground. By the end of *Messiah*, Irulan is no longer a political pawn used cruelly by Paul to gain power, Instead, in crafting *Messiah*, Herbert, almost casually, turns her into one of the more complicated characters in all of the books. Essentially a background character and quasi-narrator in the first novel, Princess Irulan realizes midway through the conspiracy (and offstage, so to speak) that she totally loves Paul and decides to become a loyal supporter of House Atreides, thus renouncing her previous connection to House Corrino and the Bene Gesserit. Irulan's offstage defection to the side of the protagonists is just as compelling and fascinating as Duncan's comeback from being dead, partly because it almost didn't happen.

In early drafts of *Messiah*, Frank Herbert initially planned on an ending in which Irulan is firmly still in service of the Bene Gesserit. In one discarded chapter, Irulan would have reported back to Reverend Mother Mohiam triumphantly, feeling as though the death of Chani meant she could have Paul for herself. Although this deleted scene from the novel would have given Irulan more "screen time," so to speak, it would have also made her into a petty and brutal character, which could have rendered her famous annotations and narrations of the first novel superfluous and, possibly, false. Instead, Herbert's final decision to bring Irulan over to the side of the Atreides and have her defect from the Bene Gesserit is both messy and wonderfully satisfying. And above all, this move preserves her status as the future-tense quasi-narrator of the first novel. As Alia puts it at the end of *Messiah*, "she reeks of trustworthiness!" We need to trust Irulan to make sure crucial epigraphs in the first *Dune* land. *Messiah* retroactively ensures this, and then, in *Children of Dune*, it could be argued Irulan is one of the only characters who doesn't have a double agenda and isn't lying to everyone all the time.

"Underneath all that there's this very sad person," Julie Cox explains. Although Virginia Madsen played Irulan in the 1984 *Dune* and Florence Pugh is Irulan in 2023's *Dune: Part Two*, Cox is the person who, as of this writing, has played Irulan for the longest and has taken the character further into her canonical journey than anyone else. Starring as Irulan in the two Sci Fi miniseries *Frank Herbert's Dune* (2000) and *Frank Herbert's Children of Dune* (2003), Cox took Irulan from a pawn in the schemes of House Corrino to a conspirator against Paul to the person who basically raises Paul's children after Chani's death. As Cox puts it, "she basically has to accept that she'll never be with the person she loves." As is true with almost all adaptations of *Dune*, certain characters become more interesting in the visual interpretations. In contrast to Duncan's getting pushed out of the zeitgeist by the various *Dune* movies prior to 2021, Irulan's presence always looms large. In the guise of Virginia Madsen in the 1984 film, Irulan made a big impression on our imaginations, mostly because she's the first face we see and she speaks directly to us. And with an expanded backstory created by John Harrison for the 2000 version, Cox's take on Irulan was even more complex than what Herbert wrote. All of this explains why Denis Villeneuve cast Florence Pugh as Irulan for *Dune: Part Two*. The character might be remembered as the faux narrator of the first book, but she's considerably more interesting and complex than simply the "storyteller."

But if such amazing things happen with underrated characters in *Dune Messiah*, why is it not more well loved? Well, while the plot result of *Dune Messiah* is an elevation of Duncan Idaho and Princess Irulan from secondary characters to saga-defining badasses, those journeys aren't exactly the point of the novel. Instead, what Herbert does with *Dune Messiah* is to take the perceived underdog triumph of the first novel and invert it.

In his 2008 foreword to *Dune Messiah*, Brian Herbert writes that this is "the most misunderstood" of his father's novels, noting that fans of the time generally disliked it, with even *National Lampoon* branding it the "disappointment of the year" in 1969. The thing is, with all due respect to Brian Herbert, any vitriol anyone hurled at *Dune Messiah* isn't because anyone has misunderstood it. The message of this book is impossible to misunderstand, because in it, Herbert makes his frequently stated thesis for *Dune* clear: "I wrote the *Dune* series because I had this idea that charismatic leaders ought to come with a warning label on their forehead: May be dangerous to your health." With the first book, readers could have it both ways: Herbert was critiquing the tropes of the hero's journey and white savior narratives, but as *Dune* expert Haris Durrani pointed out in 2021, this also means Herbert "reinscribes" those exact same tropes.

"If Frank Herbert was trying to criticize white savior narratives with [the first] *Dune*, he probably could have done a better job," science fiction historian Alec Nevala-Lee tells me in 2022. This statement is tough to refute, mostly because if you have a conversation with anyone about political interpretations of the first *Dune*, those interpretations are all over the place. But if you bring up *Dune Messiah*, it's a checkmate. Herbert isn't playing around by letting readers enjoy a hero's journey narrative that he also might be deconstructing. *Messiah* blatantly says that our obsession with the hero's journey might be horrible and is possibly destructive.

Appropriately, the proof that Herbert successfully made his point can be found in the vehement protests from the most infamous person who probably misread the first book, too: John W. Campbell. In 1968, Lurton Blassingame and Frank Herbert intended to do with *Dune Messiah* what they had done with "Dune World": get the entire thing serialized in *Analog* ahead of time. But Campbell hated this story.

On August 12, 1968, Campbell wrote directly to Herbert and complained about several nitty-gritty plot details that he felt were "full of loose ends" that "lead nowhere." He admitted that "in outline, it sounds like an Epic Tragedy" but disliked the style, structure, and tone so much that he compared *Messiah* to "one of those commercial crunchy dip things—Cheetos, Bugles ... It has flavor, bulk, texture ... and dissolves to a small, soggy mass in the mouth which leaves a somewhat unpleasant quasi-metallic aftertaste."

Clearly, Campbell misunderstood the intent of *Messiah*, but in that misunderstanding, he also seemed to choose the wrong snack analogy. *Messiah* isn't like a bag of Cheetos, it's more like a bag of Sour Patch Kids, which wasn't really a thing until 1985, but still, that's just more evidence this book was ahead of its time. It's supposed to taste like that, because that's what it is: mostly sour, with a little bit of sweet.

Obviously, *Dune Messiah's* publishing process was not going to play out with Campbell the same way the first book's had. This round of correspondence wasn't a blustering series of notes obscuring an acceptance letter. Campbell, eventually, refused to serialize any parts of the novel, even after Herbert gave him some light revisions. In the end, Campbell hated what *Dune Messiah* was about: It was a story that told the reader that heroes could turn into tragic figures, even if they were the heroes we loved the most. For Campbell, this wasn't just unappealing, it was basically against his own personal science fiction religion.

"The reactions of science-fictioneers . . . over the last few decades has persistently and quite explicitly been that they want *heroes*—not anti-heroes," Campbell wrote to Lurton Blassingame on October 15, 1968. "They want stories of strong men who exert themselves, inspire others, and make a monkey's uncle out of malign fates. . . . As Paul did in 'Dune'—not as he fails completely to do in 'The Messiah.'"

Analog didn't publish any version of *Dune Messiah* in magazine form; instead, it was accepted for serialization by Ejler Jakobsson, editor of *Analog's* biggest competition, *Galaxy* magazine. To be clear, it was very common for magazines in this genre to serialize books that would have a second life as a novel. That serialization ran in five parts, from July 1969 to November 1969. Right smack-dab in the middle of that run, the full novel was published by G. P. Putnam's Sons in hardcover. In 1969, Frank Herbert didn't need Campbell or

Analog. He'd had the book deal for *Messiah* for a while. But he did want the core readership of science fiction fans to be aware of the book, in order to boost sales of the actual hardcover. It didn't really work. The sales of *Dune Messiah* were sluggish and the reviews tepid. One review from Hugh Nations at *The Atlanta Constitution* gave a kind of backhanded compliment, saying "the deliberate obscurities evoke echoes of the metaphysical poets." Meanwhile, the *Pensacola News Journal* called it "a little far out for those who like their science fiction slightly more contemporary."

Neither these reviews, Campbell's rejection, or angry fans came from a place of confusion. All of the negative pushback against *Dune Messiah* proved that the book, and its stated thesis, worked. When longtime *Dune* scholar Willis E. McNelly confronted Herbert with the tin-ear ending line of the original *Dune*, in which Jessica says to Chani, "History will call us wives!," Herbert defended any questionable choices in that and other *Dune* books by saying the whole ending of *Dune* was written as "high camp." If we stick with the classic Susan Sontag definition of *camp*—that "the essence of Camp is its love of the unnatural, of artifice and exaggeration"—then suddenly everything about *Dune Messiah* starts to make more sense. Reading the entirety of the *Dune* saga through a camp lens might feel intellectually maddening to some. But Herbert did say aspects of the book were written in a camp style in 1969, the same year *Messiah* was published. With his first *Dune* novel, the various epigraphs (an artifice) constantly foreshadow plot details in future chapters, making the entire novel a clever spoiler for itself. This structure creates a sense of fatalism, which is doubled by Paul's emerging prescience. Not only does the first *Dune* know what is going to happen, the main character knows, too, and the book won't stop reminding you of both, which, if you throw in a giant sandworm that people have to ride, is more than a little campy. If Frank Herbert were a more whimsical artist, you could compare these narrative stylings to Kurt Vonnegut. Like Billy Pilgrim in *Slaughterhouse-Five*, Paul Atreides is basically unstuck in time; he doesn't just see the future, he remembers it and is trapped by it.

Herbert's version of this in *Dune Messiah* leans so hard into the paradox of prescience that in the hands of another author, the whole thing might be hilarious. *Dune Messiah* was the moment Frank Herbert revealed that *Dune* was playing a joke on you, and that if you didn't like the punch line, he didn't care. At the time, it wasn't clear if he would write a third novel to complete "the *Dune* trilogy." In 1969, *Dune Messiah* felt less like its own book and more like an extended epilogue for *Dune* itself. The sequel was still seven years away. In the meantime, the world had much bigger plans for the first book.

6

Golden Paths Not Taken

**The earliest visions for cinematic
Dune adaptations.**

Fortune passes everywhere.

—Farad'n to the Lady Jessica

n the 1970s, on the planet Arrakis, it was the best of times
and the worst of times. On one hand, 1976 saw the triumphant publication of *Children of Dune*; on the other, that
was also the year of the utter dissolution of Alejandro Jodorowsky's ambitious and troubled attempt to make the first
novel into a film. Although nearly every aspect of *Dune*'s existence contains fascinating contradictions, these two parallel
events take the spice cake. If you remain unconvinced that
Dune moves in mysterious ways, worming itself into all aspects of pop culture, then the *Dune* history of the seventies
should make the case clear. This is the decade when *Dune* was
bigger than ever and simultaneously, at least in the arena of
the movie business, became cursed. This was the decade when

Herbert wrote what is probably the very best *Dune* book sequel, while two major attempts to adapt the first book for the cinema began a trend that cast a superstitious shadow over *Dune* movies for years. And throughout all these conflicts and contradictions, several science fiction phenomena were created by accident. If it hadn't been for the topsy-turvy decade *Dune* had in the 1970s, the greatest sci-fi movie of 1979—*Alien*—would never have existed.

From 1971 to 1973, around the time that Herbert was trying to write this third *Dune* book, his first epic novel was in the process of getting turned into the next *Planet of the Apes*. Before Jodorowsky, before Lynch, the very first crysknife stab at turning *Dune* into a movie came from legendary producer Arthur P. Jacobs, who purchased the rights from Herbert in 1972, the same year the fourth *Planet of the Apes* film, *Conquest of the Planet of the Apes*, was released. The projected budget for the APJ *Dune* film was fifteen million dollars, and by August 1972, Jacobs had approached David Lean—world-famous director of *Bridge on the River Kwai* (1957) and *Lawrence of Arabia* (1962)—to direct *Dune*. While the *Lawrence of Arabia* connection to *Dune* seems obvious enough, there's an interesting roundabout David Lean connection to Arthur P. Jacobs, via *Planet of the Apes*. Lean's Oscar-winning *Bridge on the River Kwai* was based on the 1952 novel of the same name by French novelist Pierre Boulle. The other big book of Boulle's that was turned into a movie was his 1963 novel *La planète des singes*, known as *Monkey Planet* in the UK and *Planet of the Apes* in the United States. The fact that *La planète des singes* was published in 1963, the same year "Dune World" was first published in *Analog*, is also somewhat fitting. As novelists and prose stylists, Boulle and Herbert are pretty dissimilar. And yet, both *Dune* and *Planet of the Apes* spawned cult sci-fi followings, and both universes were created by authors capable of a variety of different literary ventures who later ultimately became known for only one novel. In the same way Herbert is forever remembered as the author of *Dune*, Boulle, to this day, is permanently associated with *Planet of the Apes*, even though several of his other books, including the collection *Time out of Mind*, are just as good.

Back in 1963, "Dune World" and *La planète des singes* both represented bold new archetypes of science fiction storytelling, the kinds of hyperbolic worlds in which the analogies and subtext of the works could be read as text, too. Fans love freaking out about apes on horseback and Fremen riding sandworms high on spice, but beyond that imagery, there's a lot more going on. As novels, *Dune* and *Planet of the Apes* feel related—distant cousins, perhaps, but books with similar vibes. And so it makes a lot of sense that the producer in charge of the *Apes* film franchise would attempt to make *Dune* into a movie, too. While the 1968 film *Planet of the Apes* took several liberties with the Boulle novel,* the core philosophy of the book remained, and arguably is why the first film, and several of its sequels, became cult classics.

---

* *Planet of the Apes* was directed by Franklin J. Schaffner with a screenplay from Michael Wilson and Rod Serling. The twist ending of the film is not like the book at all and is pure *Twilight Zone* Serling magic. That said, Boulle's novel does have two twist endings!

Although Herbert claimed that he had "no involvement at all with Arthur Jacob" in terms of developing the script, it's very possible that had it all coalesced, the APJ version of *Dune* might have transmuted the fictional world of spice and sandworms into a series of 1970s sci-fi romps in the style of *Planet of the Apes*. Early in 1972, APJ wanted Robert Bolt (who also wrote the script for *Lawrence of Arabia*) to adapt *Dune*, essentially re-creating the David Lean/Robert Bolt dream team. While Brian Herbert implies Bolt and Lean were legitimately part of the project at one point,* other anonymous sources I spoke to claim both Lean and Bolt turned Jacob down flat. If Bolt did write a screenplay for *Dune* in the early 1970s, it has been buried in the sand and swallowed by shai-hulud. But two other fascinating screen treatments were written, and both give a glimpse of how the very first *Dune* movie might have shaken out.

In March 1972, a partial screenplay and treatment by Joe Ford and Bob Greenhut was written for APJ.† In this thirty-eight-page document, the basic sweeps of the first *Dune* novel are condensed, though not significantly changed. As in the novel, Emperor Shaddam IV asks Duke Leto Atreides to take over the spice production on Arrakis at the beginning of the film, but does so in person, addressing Leto and Duncan Idaho

---

*Brian Herbert has really made it seem like he's seen some version of a script or screen treatment written by Robert Bolt. In 2019, he tweeted, "The Seydoux-Jodorowsky film would have been really good, but the Jacobs-Lean-Bolt version might have been superior."

†It appears that this treatment was written before APJ purchased the option to make *Dune* into a movie.

in a meeting at the top of the script. The fact that the emperor is conspiring with Baron Harkonnen is revealed quickly, and in this script, the Harkonnen heir, Feyd-Rautha, is the baron's son rather than his nephew. Although the overall plot of the novel is (mostly) retained, there are interesting changes. Alia appears nowhere in this script, meaning she doesn't kill the baron in this version. Rather, the baron is killed by a random Fremen agent of Paul's, which, in the script, simply sets the stage for Feyd's wanting to avenge the murder of his father. Although the original book introduced Feyd late in the game, this 1972 script makes his role much larger sooner, a tradition carried on in the 1984 David Lynch film and the 2000 John Harrison miniseries. The script also differs from the novel in its ending; here Paul initially resists becoming the emperor and worries that if he accepts his role as the Kwisatz Haderach, this will lead only to the downfall of the Fremen in the long run. The film would have ended on one of Paul's grim future visions, in which we see "the sand reclaiming the moist Fremen Basins. A Fremen body, like a drowning man, sinks into the sand, it is STILGAR . . . then [fade to] BLACK."

Like the pessimistic ending of *Planet of the Apes*, the ending of this 1972 *Dune* script would have been a kind of cautionary tale. Just as *Dune Messiah* ultimately finds Paul utterly disillusioned with everything he's done, the ending for this unmade movie version would have essentially teased the same outcome: Arrakis is doomed. The savior is not the savior.

While producing a musical version of *Huckleberry Finn*, Jacobs became unsatisfied with this script at some point and hired Rospo Pallenberg to take another crack. By January 23,

1973, Pallenberg crafted a fifty-two-page treatment that at times seems to dumb down the novel, and at other turns makes intelligent narrative decisions that could have made aspects of the original novel more explicable. For example, in Pallenberg's version of a *Dune* movie, the reason that the navigators need the spice melange would have been a mystery. Only at the very end of the movie, when Paul discovers his own prescience is boosted by the spice, does he connect the dots. "Mélange addiction gave them Prescience and a super-human understanding of the abstract forms of Space and Time," Pallenberg's treatment reveals. "Now that Paul has power over the Navigators, the Emperor abdicates. . . . The Fremen claim Paul the 'Emperor Mouse.'"

Pallenberg turned the spice into a kind of MacGuffin hiding in plain sight. Arguably, this kind of "mystery box" plot device could have worked if *Dune* were a different kind of novel. In the book, the only real mystery about the spice is its connection to the sandworms. In the Pallenberg version, we would have had a mystery at each end—the navigators and the spice, both shrouded in secrecy.

But while rendering the spice a double spoiler may have been clever, Pallenberg's other major change in his *Dune* screenplay treatment is the opposite of smart. Throughout his version, Pallenberg treats the language of *Dune* as something to be simplified and made infinitely more boring. Paul is never referred to as "Muad'Dib" in this script, but rather as "Emperor Mouse," which, yes, references the Fremen meaning of *Muad'Dib*, which is a desert mouse that Paul thinks is awesome, but doesn't let us feel the awesomeness. Similarly, the

Bene Gesserit sisterhood simply becomes "the Sisterhood" in Pallenberg's script, who aren't trying to create a super-being called the Kwisatz Haderach, but instead a "master race of noblemen." All of Herbert's carefully chosen words and memorable world-building are traded for the most generic nouns in the universe. If Pallenberg had been offered a chance to rewrite *Star Wars* a few years later, you can imagine him going in and changing "the Jedi" to just "the Knights" and renaming Obi-Wan Kenobi "Old Man Hero Robe." It's not that the Pallenberg screen treatment is bad per se, but the exclusion of the most *Dune*-ish words—including the fact that the name of the planet, Arrakis, appears nowhere in this document—is jarring. A *Dune* movie in which nobody says *Bene Gesserit* or *Arrakis* feels like it would have enraged hard-core fans and probably failed to capture new ones. In essence, Pallenberg missed that a big part of what makes *Dune* cool is its language.

With the Pallenberg script in hand in the spring of 1973, APJ intended to start filming *Dune* the following year. With David Lean out of the picture as the director, Jacobs wanted Terence Young—famous for directing the James Bond films *Dr. No* (1962), *From Russia with Love* (1963), and *Thunderball* (1965)—to helm the picture. But before that could happen, Arthur P. Jacobs had a heart attack on June 27, 1973. "He had the bad taste to die without consulting me," Herbert quipped. Because *Dune* was essentially Jacobs's personal passion project, his production company, Apjac International, let the option expire in 1974. In the larger story of *Dune*'s leap from the page to the screen, this moment may be more pivotal than fans have ever realized. Had Arthur P. Jacobs lived, it's very possible there could have been a *Dune* film out in theaters in 1975, a full two years ahead of *Star Wars*. Self-styled film geeks will tell you that this also almost happened with Alejandro Jodorowsky's *Dune*, which was the attempt immediately following APJ's. But when you think about how utterly mainstream the Jacobs version of *Dune* would have been (a Bond director!), and how effectively such a film would have been marketed, especially considering the widespread success of the *Planet of the Apes* franchise at the time, it's possible the most interesting and controversial lost *Dune* is this version—the one that borrowed from *Planet of the Apes*, James Bond, and *Lawrence of Arabia* as much as it did from Frank Herbert. Somewhere out there in the multiverse is a bizarro timeline of the 1970s in which Arthur P. Jacobs lived and this *Dune* was made. Would it have been good? A cult hit like the *Apes* franchise? It's tough to say. But because the 1970s were the decade in which the *Dune* novels became mega-popular, this unmade *Dune* movie certainly would have been remembered, regardless of quality.

Although the APJ failed attempt to make a *Dune* movie is tragically underdiscussed in the world of cinephiles who love discussing unmade movies, the other 1970s unmade *Dune* is perhaps the most famous unmade movie of all time. After the film option lapsed in 1974, it was immediately snatched up by French film producer Michel Seydoux* and his production

---

*Michel Seydoux is the granduncle of actress Léa Seydoux, who, in addition to being a world-famous film star in the twenty-first century, also stars as Lady Margot Fenring in Denis Villeneuve's 2023 film *Dune: Part Two*.

company Caméra One. There are conflicting reports as to whether or not Herbert was happy about this at first. Seydoux tapped experimental art-house auteur Alejandro Jodorowsky to make an epic film version of *Dune*. According to Seydoux, Herbert agreed to sell the rights only because of Jodorowsky's involvement. "Jodorowsky was not really well-known, but he was known by Frank Herbert's circle," Seydoux said in 2013. "They [Herbert's reps] believed in us, they believed in our folly, they believed in our fire . . . in our love for the book."

What happened next is unquestionably the most outlandish and spectacularly bizarre attempt to make a science fiction movie, ever. For decades after its failure, Jodorowsky's take on *Dune* became mythical and legendary in science fiction and cinema circles. After Jodorowsky's *Dune*, descriptions of subsequent *Dune* films were (and still are) often accompanied by a mention of this version, often in reverent or bemused tones. When the very first trailer for Denis Villeneuve's *Dune* was released on September 9, 2020, the action was set to a Hans Zimmer cover of Pink Floyd's 1973 song "Eclipse," a direct reference to the fact that Jodorowsky intended for Pink Floyd to compose the music for his *Dune* in 1975. Like the pre-born memories inside the minds of Alia, Ghanima, and Leto II, all of *Dune* cinema is haunted by the spirit of Jodorowsky's *Dune*.

But why? And is the obsession with this specific unmade *Dune* warranted?

Thanks to Frank Pavich's award-winning 2013 documentary *Jodorowsky's Dune*, this *Dune* has been dubbed "the greatest movie never made" and will likely never relinquish that crown, at least among certain folks who love director's commentaries and in-depth podcasts about movies. Pavich's documentary is so convincing that it's easy to overlook the most staggering aspect of what Seydoux and Jodorowsky set out to do: make a *Dune* movie that utterly changed not only the story of the book, but also its philosophical meaning. If the scripts crafted by Ford, Greenhut, and Pallenberg were straightforward attempts to condense or flatten *Dune* into a boring Hollywood movie, Jodorowsky's version intended to basically just write an entirely new story. Infamously, Jodorowsky admitted openly to the radical and drastic changes his version would have made to Herbert's first book. "It was my *Dune.* . . . I feel like a thief," Jodorowsky said in 2013. "The novel is one art . . . but picture [cinema] is another art . . . it's not the same."

Because it's impossible to surpass the sheer amount of information in Pavich's documentary, and also because countless thousands of words have been devoted to the Jodorowsky attempt, and because some versions of the script for this epic are longer than the book you're reading (Frank Herbert called this script a "phone book"), the only way to discuss Jodorowsky's *Dune* without losing your mind is to talk about three things that really matter about this unmade movie.

1. The movie would have drastically departed from the book.
2. The cinematic science fiction aesthetic of this unmade film created *Alien.*

3. Jodorowsky's controversial statements—about *Dune* and other matters—are probably enough to convince *Dune* fans this movie wouldn't have aged well.

The logistics of this *Dune* are flashy and unbelievable enough to quickly elucidate why the movie never got made. Mick Jagger was the first choice to play Feyd. The part of Emperor Shaddam IV was to be played by Salvador Dalí, for a salary of $100,000 an hour. To get around this budgetary problem, a robot puppet of Dalí was constructed, to be used in shots that didn't require Dalí to be present. Jodorowsky's own son, Brontis, who was thirteen years old at the time, was to play Paul. David Carradine, fresh from his success in the first kung fu TV series, was cast as Duke Leto. Orson Welles was apparently wooed to play Baron Harkonnen when Jodorowsky promised to get the chef from his favorite restaurant to cook for him every day. But the director of the documentary, Frank Pavich, didn't set out to chronicle the making of a disaster, instead to capture the pain *and* triumphs of Jodorowsky's take on *Dune*.

"When I was making the documentary, one of the things that Jodorowsky was really adamant about was that this was not a story of failure," Frank Pavich tells me in 2023. "This was not a sad story. This was a story of something great being accomplished, of all these interesting people coming together. And it didn't exactly work out, but look what did work out!"

Regardless of artistic merits, one thing Pavich's documentary reveals is that Jodorowsky's *Dune* would have been *ex-*

pensive as hell. Imagine if *Valerian and the City of a Thous-and Planets* had come out in 1997 instead of 2017 and starred Leonardo DiCaprio, and instead of that weird role for Ethan Hawke, Liam Gallagher was in the movie, and maybe Sean Connery, too. At a certain point, this unmade *Dune* becomes a monumental word salad of famous names, which, in terms of its legacy, isn't necessarily a good thing.

Although *Drive* director Nicolas Winding Refn says that this *Dune* would have been "awesome," the evidence suggests that there's not an alternate universe where this movie could have ever been completed, much less released. And even if there were, there's no universe where the movie would have made *Dune* fans happy. Of all the attempts to make *Dune* into a film, the Jodorowsky version is often regarded as a valiant and artistic failure because the movie was attempted by an art-house director fighting against the sensibilities of the American Hollywood system. And yet, at the risk of offending Jodorowsky fans, the script for this *Dune* is the least faithful to the novel by any metric.

"I want to create the prophet. To change the young mind[s] of all the world," Jodorowsky said. "For me, *Dune* will be the coming of a god. Artistically, [and] cinematographically, a god."

While it's tempting to say Jodorowsky understood that the message of *Dune* was ultimately against the mixture of reli-gion with politics, little about the ending of his script proves he grasped Herbert's intended irony. In Jodorowsky's script, after leading a Fremen crusade against his enemies, Paul is killed, but his spirit and consciousness immediately manifest in all his allies. From the super-baby Alia, to Stilgar, to Gurney, to Jessica and Chani, and all the Fremen, everyone begins to chant "I am Paul." At the same time, the entirety of the surface of Arrakis is instantly transformed into a water-rich paradise, and we learn the planet itself is also imbued with Paul's soul. Arrakis is now a "Blue Dune," a living planet, with a hive mind, and apparently, thanks to all the spice, possesses the ability to move through space on its own, sort of like if the Death Star were actually the "Life Star." The movie would have ended with this "Blue Dune" leaving the galaxy, presumably to spread the good word of Muad'Dib throughout the universe.

Now, imagine this idea came from Michael Bay and not Alejandro Jodorowsky. Is this still a good idea? Would it have worked? Maybe. Is this what *Dune* is about? Certainly not. Cinephiles tend to want to support the vision of an auteur, particularly one with as many trippy cult movies as Jodorowsky. But this ending feels a little corny, and not in the "high camp" way Herbert claimed to have intended.

Before he told producer Seydoux that he wanted to adapt *Dune*, Jodorowsky had not yet read the novel. "I didn't read *Dune*," he said. "But I have a friend who [said to me] it was fantastic. I don't know why I [said] '*Dune.*' I could have said '*Don Quixote*' or '*Hamlet.*' I don't know anything. I say '*Dune.*'" While it's clear (and has been confirmed by multiple sources) that Jodorowsky later did read the novel* and became enamored

---

*Many fans, including the person writing this sentence, were confused on this point, back in 2014, upon first viewing the documentary *Jodorowsky's Dune*. The question of Jodorowsky's having ever read the book can easily be missed while watching the documentary. Alejandro Jodorowsky makes this point a

of it ("I compare it to Proust in French literature"), this somewhat flippant regard for the source material extended to other aspects of the production. Specifically, artist Chris Foss—legendary science fiction cover artist, both then and now—admitted that he had "no idea what the actual story is . . . none whatsoever." As late as 2013, Foss said he "still hasn't" read the book and his entire perception of the story of *Dune* came from what Jodorowsky said. "As far as I'm concerned the story of *Dune* is what Alejandro told me it was."

Foss contributed extensive concept art for this project, and he's one-third of a triumvirate who worked on Jodorowsky's *Dune* and would go on to help craft an entirely different movie roughly three years after the Jodorowsky attempt failed—*Alien.* The other two pivotal figures who would cross over to work with Ridley Scott on *Alien* were special effects creator-turned–screenwriter Dan O'Bannon and outré artist H. R. Giger. Along with Jean Giraud (known as "Mœbius"), this creative team worked in Paris for well over a year in pre-production for Jodorowsky's *Dune.*

The result of this labor is mostly in the form of concept art, a few sculptures, a handful of costumes, and, most famously, at least ten massive hardbound books that outlined the entire movie in storyboard format. Today, these books are the holy grail of all *Dune* ephemera, with copies being valued at between $46,000 and $3 million. If Hollywood wanted to

---

bit obscure, but a close rewatch of the documentary (as well as checking with other sources) confirms that yes, he did end up reading it.

make another movie based on Jodorowsky's *Dune*, a heist movie in which criminals try to steal a copy of one of these storyboard books is probably the best bet. Can't you just picture Brad Pitt pulling one of these massive *Dune* books out of a safe while Matt Damon cracks wise about the spice?

Frank Pavich calls this book the "art bible" and tells me that it's important to remember that concept art, storyboards, and writing is all we have.

"They didn't shoot one frame of film," Pavich tells me. "There's nothing that exists that points to failure because there's not a day's worth of shooting. If there were raw footage, people could point and laugh, because raw footage always looks horrible. But it never even reached that point. It finished at the perfect moment of that art bible. There's truly no moment of failure."

As Pavich points out, everything bewitching and seductive about this film version of *Dune* comes from the art created by this group of four men. A chunk of this sci-fi concept art would be repurposed for other films, but perhaps the most recent homage to the artwork created for this *Dune* was found in Villeneuve's *Dune: Part One*, in which the Harkonnen stronghold of Giedi Prime is very reminiscent of Giger's concept art for a Harkonnen city that would have appeared in Jodorowsky's *Dune*.

There are several stated reasons the Jodorowsky movie never got made—personality conflicts, the inability of distributors to put faith into such an unwieldy project—but the notion of combined incompetence is seldom mentioned, even if it does seem to be the key factor. While everything about this production seems hilariously twee and outlandish in retro-spect, Frank Herbert was furious. Jodorowsky had blown two million dollars on pre-production and Herbert was also less than pleased about the idea of a twelve-to-fourteen-hour movie. The length of the film, including Herbert's reference to the "phone book" of the script, is often cited as the biggest reason why Jodorowsky's version was unfilmable. And yet, in 1984, in an interview for the French film magazine *L'écran fan-tastique*, Jodorowsky himself said that the super-long version of his *Dune* was not what he planned.

"When you say that my version could not have lasted less than ten hours on the screen . . . you show your ignorance of the project," Jodorowsky protested in a kind of open letter to Herbert. "I had signed a contract in which I promised to pro-vide a screenplay from which we could shoot a three-hour film and a six-part series for television. The version for the big screen would have lasted three hours, no more!"

Bizarrely, in the twenty-first century, and thanks to the documentary *Jodorowsky's Dune*, Jodorowsky himself has seemingly contradicted his own contradiction. The legend of the twelve-to-fourteen-hour *Dune* has grown so much that nobody, not even Jodorowsky, seems to remember the promise of a three-hour version of this movie. So which is it? Frank Pavich says that it sort of depends on if we're talking about the various screenplays *or* the complex storyboards.

"I've seen different versions of the screenplay," Pavich ex-plains. "Some that are like 150 to 200 pages. And that's a very long movie in itself. But then, after he wrote the screenplay and started doing the storyboards with Mœbius, that's when everything changed. They got even more creative. So there are wild scenes that weren't necessarily directly from script. When they finished storyboarding the entire film, far as I know, he didn't go back to rewrite the screenplay. And only through a screenplay can you really tell how long a film will be, and I think that he didn't care at that point."

So Jodorowsky's claim that one script was a reasonable length seems true. And the existence of the massively detailed storyboards suggests a bigger version. From Pavich's point of view, that's where the contradiction exists: script versus storyboards.

Either way, there was no love lost between the Herberts and Jodorowsky in the end, and after Frank and Beverly visited Paris in October 1976, the Jodorowsky production was shut down simply because it had run out of money. The distributors were spooked by the skyrocketing costs, and the option was about to expire anyway. Still, despite all of this, Pavich thinks the decision to stop production on Jodorowsky's *Dune* was more connected to the historical context combined with a lack of mainstream success from Jodorowsky, at least in the eyes of studio executives.

"I think the reason it didn't get completed, a large part is the time," Pavich tells me. "This was 1974 to 1976. So this is before *Star Wars*. Even when *Star Wars* was being made, the studios were going along with it. To them, George Lucas did a great job on *American Graffiti*, made them a lot of money, and they let him do his silly science fiction movie. But none of them got it. All the executives were like, they would watch test edits, and they were like, what the hell is this garbage? So once the movie was completed and released, it's obviously this cultural sensation. But nobody could have predicted that. Jodorowsky was working on *Dune* a little bit before any of that happened, and without something like *American Graffiti* behind him."

The attempt that was Jodorowsky's *Dune* is fascinating to think about but, for some critics and experts, feels like a moment where *Dune* fans collectively dodged a hunter-seeker. In his admission to changing the book radically, Jodorowsky joked, "I was raping Frank Herbert. But with love." Herbert clearly didn't feel the love.

Although not present in the 2013 documentary, noted science fiction critic Emmet Asher-Perrin pointed out in 2017 that Jodorowsky's very problematic use of the word *rape* is doubly problematic, because in 1972, in the book *El Topo: A Book of the Film*, Jodorowsky was quoted saying that he "really raped" his costar, Mara Lorenzio, in his film *El Topo*. Whether or not this statement was factual is not known, because Lorenzio never made a public statement about filming *El Topo*. But in the twenty-first century, Jodorowsky denies it, and instead has claimed his statement was one of intentional hyperbole.

In a 2019 statement to *Artforum*, Jodorowsky denied raping anyone while making his movies, saying that his previous statements were uttered *in character*, for publicity. "These words: 'I've raped my actress,' was said fifty years ago by El Topo, a bandit dressed in black leather that nobody knew. They were words, not facts; Surrealist publicity in order to enter the world of cinema from a position of obscurity. I do not condone the act of rape but exploited the shock value of the statement at the time." Previously on his Facebook account in 2017, Jodorowsky also denied actual rape, noting that the simple fact that so many people were present proves that he couldn't have done something like that, saying: "At the smallest hideout of royal violence, a group of men and women would throw themselves on me to immobilize me."

The truth can't be known, but the existence of the word *rape* in the documentary *Jodorowsky's Dune* exists, and Asher-Perrin's negative review of the documentary was a voice in the wilderness in 2017. But by 2019, they weren't alone. As Laura Jaramillo wrote in 2019, "New York's Museo del Barrio canceled a retrospective of the Chilean multimedia artist Alejandro Jodorowsky due to public protest over his claim that he raped the lead actress in his 1970 film *El Topo*."

From Jaramillo's point of view, the problem with Jodorowsky's cinematic style isn't only that he may or may not have committed a serious crime on the set of *El Topo*; it's that his treatment of women's bodies in his films created a permissive cult of personality around Jodorowsky. In her view, the art itself is problematic.

"For decades, Jodorowsky's film [*El Topo*] was synonymous with the cult spectatorship it inspired among its New York audiences, who attended screenings ritualistically," Jaramillo wrote in 2020. In essence, she argued that Jodorowsky's depiction of violence against women in his films was "central" to his cult following. Although Jodorowsky later claimed he made these statements on purpose, and that the sex scene in *El Topo* was consensual in real life, for feminist scholars like

Jaramillo, it doesn't really matter. And for Asher-Perrin, this connects to *Dune* because Jodorowsky's art lionized rape, and that feels incongruous with the sensibilities of Frank Herbert. "Frank worshipped women," Theresa Shackleford, Herbert's surviving widow, tells me. "Anyone who thinks he was a sexist is wrong. He thought women should be running everything."

As Asher-Perrin said, "It's no great tragedy that Jodorowsky's *Dune* never got made . . . we arguably got a better film out of it—because Dan O'Bannon, Mœbius, Chris Foss, and H. R. Giger all went on to create *Alien*."

They have a point. Because the real legacy of Jodorowsky's *Dune* is *Alien*. Although Jodorowsky recruited those four men, he obviously didn't intend for them to end up working together on another film. But after the dissolution of Jodorowsky's *Dune*, Dan O'Bannon was hospitalized for depression, and after writing over a dozen screenplays, he finally got one of those scripts green-lit, and that script became Ridley Scott's *Alien*. Foss, Mœbius, and Giger were brought on to the production team of *Alien*, and the rest is history.

The look and feel of that movie—from the design of the *Nostromo* to the hideously iconic xenomorph—both, in a roundabout way, owe a debt to Jodorowsky's *Dune*. This team of people would not have been brought together without Jodorowsky's pushing them into new spaces of creativity. Ridley Scott may be credited as the visionary who made *Alien* the indisputably classic film that it is. But the script couldn't have existed without Dan O'Bannon's long and winding road from *Dune*, and the iconic creature is all thanks to the twisted mind of H. R. Giger, primed to make sci-fi movies uniquely horrifying, all because of his work on *Dune*. In this way, it might be healthier for film historians to view Jodorowsky as a step-uncle to *Alien* rather than as an estranged *Dune* co-parent. All of this means that the sandworms of Jodorowsky are indirectly responsible for the literal birth of the chest bursters in *Alien*. In 2012, Chris Foss credited the genesis of chest bursters to a bout of horrible food poisoning Dan O'Bannon had had while in Paris, in preparation to shoot *Dune*. While in the hospital, O'Bannon felt like "there was a monster inside of him." Obviously, this later became one of the most famous scenes in horror movie and sci-fi movie history. But had O'Bannon not been in Paris and gotten sick at that exact time, could he have come up with *Alien*? Jodorowsky's attempt to make *Dune* put O'Bannon in the hospital, even if by accident.

As we know, there are zero space aliens—chest bursters or otherwise—in the *Dune*-iverse. But, in 1964, John Campbell had asked Herbert to cook up a *Dune* sequel that would have pitted Paul against a race of aggressive aliens. Herbert gave that suggestion a hard pass, and as such, prevented *Dune* from becoming the kind of science fiction he didn't want it to be.* And yet, without *Dune*, and without the failure of two *Dune* films, the greatest science fiction alien of them all could have

---

*To be clear, there are aliens in some of Herbert's other big science fiction novels. His ConSentiency universe features an entire intergalactic community of extraterrestrials. The most notable books in this series are *Whipping Star* (1970) and *The Dosadi Experiment* (1977). Herbert wrote a lot of SF novels, many of which were written and published in what we now see as "gaps" between *Dune* novels.

never existed. This means the degree of separation between the amazing film career of Sigourney Weaver and the writings of Frank Herbert is basically just two steps. If you take away the popularity of the *Dune* novel, you can't get Jodorowsky's attempt. And if Jodorowsky's failed attempt hadn't ever recruited the artists behind *Alien*, then the entire landscape of science fiction cinema after 1979 would have crumbled. Even though *Dune* didn't become a seventies movie, it accidentally gave birth to arguably the second (or third?) most important sci-fi movie of that decade. *Star Wars* (1977) is certainly the most influential sci-fi movie of the seventies, but this was also a big decade for sci-fi movies in general. Between *A Clockwork Orange* (1971), *Escape from the Planet of the Apes* (1971), *Logan's Run* (1976), and *Star Trek: The Motion Picture* (1979, the same year as *Alien*), it's tough to say which movie was the most important sci-fi movie (other than *Star Wars*) of that decade. Again, other than *Star Wars*, of all of those seventies sci-fi movies, *Alien* has probably aged the best, and because it spawned a franchise and helped solidify the careers of both Ridley Scott and, later, James Cameron (thanks to the 1986 sequel *Aliens*), its influence and larger cultural impact are massive.

The reception Jodorowsky's *Dune* would have received in the seventies from fans of *Dune* and, more generally, sci-fi fans is unknowable. True believers seem to think cinema would have pivoted around this one project, but it's also just as easy to argue that it would have been forgotten or misunderstood, like the 1974 sci-fi romp *Zardoz*, directed by another celebrated director, John Boorman. That film, which starred Sean Connery in a somewhat shocking diaper-ish outfit, complete with bandoliers and thigh-high boots, is, if you squint, not too far off from the concept art for some of the costumes for Jodorowsky's *Dune*. None of the same people worked on the two sci-fi projects, but the point is simple: Just because something was a science fiction movie, crafted by an auteur, and possessed striking (or goofy) production design does not mean that movie was good.

Had Jodorowsky's *Dune* been completed and released in the 1970s, it would have had stiff competition from movies that became bona fide classics. Many of those films, like *Star Wars* and *Alien*, couldn't have existed without Frank Herbert or Alejandro Jodorowsky. But *Dune*'s biggest triumph of the 1970s wasn't destined to happen in the movie theaters. Instead, Herbert was about to catapult the entire genre into an entirely new realm: the true mainstream.

I Am the Sandworm

Children of Dune changes the landscape of science fiction novels forever.

Grandmother, Ghanima is you!

—Leto II to the Lady Jessica

I n between the first hardcover of *Dune* in 1965 and *Children of Dune* in 1976, Frank Herbert published nine non-*Dune* novels.* This means counting 1969's *Dune Messiah*, Herbert published ten books before one of his *Dune* books, *Children of Dune*, became a runaway hit, in 1976. Some of these books, like *The Santaroga Barrier*, are among his most durable and

---

Destination: Void (1966), *The Green Brain* (1966), *The Eyes of Heisenberg* (1966), *The Santaroga Barrier* (1968), *The Heaven Makers* (1968), *Whipping Star* (1970), *The Godmakers* (1972), *Soul Catcher* (1972), and *Hellstrom's Hive* (1973). Of course, as a series of short stories, *The Godmakers* predates the first *Dune*, but it was published as a composite novel after the fact. (See chapter 3.)

wonderful non-*Dune* novels, ever. Others, like *Whipping Star*, feel perfunctory and rushed.

Either way, as *Dune* gradually began to overshadow the rest of his body of work, Herbert was building and rebuilding the mystery of his famous desert planet. By 1973, four years after the mixed reception of *Dune Messiah*, he staunchly proclaimed that he would make his third *Dune* novel the end point of the so-called trilogy. Before settling on the title *Children of Dune*, Herbert intended to call this conclusionary novel *Arrakis*, in honor of the formal name of the titular planet.* In 1973, Herbert told *Vertex* magazine, "I'm hard at work on the third and last one, which will probably turn out to be as long as *Dune*. How soon I can finish it, I don't know, because life and other immediate and urgent jobs keep intruding. But I'll get to it, and I'll get it out, probably this year."

Herbert had been researching and writing the third *Dune* sequel since early 1971. The stated goal was to make this novel more explicitly focused on ecology than the previous two installments, which was, according to Brian Herbert, a result of his father's acquiescing to the "desires of his fans and editors." In 1970, the public who loved *Dune* had made it clear to Herbert they viewed it as an environmental novel. After *Dune* was signal-boosted by *The Whole Earth Catalog*, Herbert spoke at the very first Earth Day and gained an entirely new readership, separate and apart from the insular readers of science

---

*No *Dune* book ever carried this title. In a sense, this is a tragedy. Can you imagine a *Star Wars* TV show called *Tatooine*? It just gives you chills.

fiction. And so, with the third book, Herbert, like Paul and Leto II, would give the people what they wanted, just not exactly in the way they wanted it. This isn't to say that Herbert hadn't always intended that *Dune* focus on themes of environmentalism. But a huge portion of the backstory of Liet-Kynes's father, Pardot Kynes, the first planetologist of Arrakis, wasn't part of the original version of "Dune World" and "The Prophet of Dune" in the *Analog* run. Herbert added those aspects to the book version, most notably the lengthy first appendix, "The Ecology of Dune."

But within its own boundaries and on its own terms, in 1976, the influence of *Dune* was expanding in the book world in a way it never had before and never would again. Herbert's publisher of the *Dune* novels at this time—the literary publisher Putnam—had given him a "small advance" for the third book, mostly because *Dune Messiah* had been a critical and financial disappointment. Though the book began somewhat humbly as a *Dune* novel that Herbert kept meaning to get back to, and a series that the publisher wasn't sure it wanted to support, the release of *Children of Dune* transformed the book industry forever.

Children of Dune picks up nine years after the ominous and cathartic ending of *Dune Messiah*. The planet Arrakis and the empire of the known universe are controlled by Paul's sister, Alia, who is now in her mid-twenties and constantly in touch with all the memories of her entire family line, ever. Like their aunt, Paul and Chani's children, the twins Leto II and Ghanima, are also coping with their pre-born memories, and despite being only nine years old, they behave, essentially, as adults. The planet Arrakis has been utterly transformed, now covered with more and more vegetation, meaning the dream of ecologist Liet-Kynes is coming to fruition. But there's a catch. This climate change has transformed Arrakis too quickly, and all the water on the planet threatens to drive the sandworms into extinction. Everyone is worried about this for two reasons: First, artificially induced climate change is bad for the literal health of the planet. Second, if the sandworms die, there's no spice, and therefore, Arrakis is no longer the most important planet in the universe. In a tragically misguided attempt to hang on to her power, Alia makes a deal with the conscience memory of her wicked grandfather, the evil Baron Harkonnen,* who, ironically, she herself killed when she was only a child. Quickly, the baron essentially takes over her body and is now ruling, through her. The greatest enemy of the Atreides somehow wins from beyond the grave.

While Jessica, Duncan, Gurney, Stilgar, and Irulan struggle to figure out what to do about Alia, Leto II decides that the only way to save all of humanity is for him to pursue a future vision he's had that he calls "the Golden Path." And in order

---

*The idea of a grandchild wanting to summon the spirit of their evil grandfather to gain more power is very reminiscent of Kylo Ren (Adam Driver) in *Star Wars: The Force Awakens* (2015), when he tries to speak to the spirit of his grandfather Darth Vader. Meanwhile, in *Star Wars: The Rise of Skywalker* (2019), Rey's (Daisy Ridley) learning her grandfather is Emperor Palpatine feels strikingly like Paul's learning that Baron Harkonnen is his (and Alia's) grandfather, too. In *Children of Dune*, when Alia turns to the Harkonnen side of the Force, this feels like what Palpatine hoped would happen with Rey in *Rise of Skywalker*.

to make this Golden Path happen, Leto must undergo an unprecedented metamorphosis and literally become one with the sandworms. After meeting with his father, Paul (who didn't die!), in the desert, Leto covers his flesh with sand trout (baby sandworms) and lets them convert his body. In the end, Leto becomes part man, part sandworm, and all messiah. Thanks to a future spice vision, he hopes to put humankind on this Golden Path, which will mostly involve his ruling as "the God Emperor," a giant man-worm who will control everything.

In the broadest sense, *Children of Dune* is the closest thing Herbert ever did to just remaking *Dune* itself. Although various twists and turns are different, the big stuff is essentially the same. In the first book, House Atreides struggles to control Arrakis, with interference from both House Corrino and House Harkonnen. Ditto *Children of Dune*, only now House Corrino isn't the ruling house anymore, and Baron Harkonnen's spirit possesses Alia to try to ruin House Atreides. Duncan Idaho dies in the first *Dune* protecting Paul and Jessica, and then in *Children of Dune*, the second Duncan dies as well, once again serving "the Atreides' interests even when the family itself was internally riven." Finally, both *Dune* and *Children of Dune* end with a bittersweet victory that is really a curse. Leto II becomes the new Paul of the story, struggling to control his prescience, and, like his father, is aware that his rule as emperor will not be a walk in the park for many, many people. Paul didn't literally fuse with a sandworm, of course, which makes *Children of Dune* the ultimate sequel that tries to top the original. Imagine if one of the *Jurassic Park* sequels ended with Jeff Goldblum transforming into a velociraptor and then ruling Isla Nublar and the world at large. That's how on the nose *Children of Dune* is. When it was published in 1976, fans loved it. And the reviews weren't bad, either.

In his review for the *St. Louis Post-Dispatch*, Robert La-Rouche pointed out the book was much more than a sequel in which a bunch of stuff happens. "Herbert does more than carry events forward: he deals with consequences. . . . As a work of ideas *Children of Dune* completes the trilogy's pattern but does not end it."

Bullitt Lowry of the *Denton Record-Chronicle*, who didn't think the book was perfect, nonetheless deemed it a comeback for Herbert, writing, "*Children of Dune* is far better than *Dune Messiah*."

John Campbell passed away in 1971, so in late 1975, when it came time to try to serialize *Children of Dune* in *Analog*, this homecoming was smooth sailing for Herbert. Following Campbell's death, *Analog* was edited by science fiction author Ben Bova, who enthusiastically published *Children of Dune* in four parts, starting with the January 1976 issue and continuing through the April 1976 issue. Because the cover date is always a month ahead for magazines, this means that from December 1975 through March 1976, newsstands couldn't keep the four-part serial in stock. *Analog* sold out of all newsstand editions that contained *Children of Dune* in serialization. The circulation of *Analog* in the early seventies was 100,000 copies, so when we consider that four issues would mean roughly 400,000 copies, that's a solid sign that *Dune* was in huge mainstream demand. Although this was the very last

Frank Herbert–penned *Dune* novel to be serialized in a science fiction magazine prior to book publication, this also all happened at the very end of the era in which *Analog* was still a Condé Nast publication. By 1977, Bova had quit, and by 1980, Condé Nast sold *Analog* to Davis Publications. But in 1976, having Condé Nast's random sci-fi magazine selling out on newsstands because of *Dune* was a massive deal. None of this was niche. All of it was mainstream.

Although Putnam had low-balled Herbert on the advance for *Children*, the successful run of serialization in *Analog* proved that there might be interest in the third sequel in a big way. As Brian Herbert put it, the *Analog* magazine sales gave Herbert's then-editor at Putnam, David Hartwell, "ammunition" to convince Putnam to change the publication plan for *Children of Dune*. The push to make *Children of Dune* into a massive event was similar to Peter Jackson's winning the Oscar for all three *Lord of the Rings* movies when he won for *Return of the King* in 2004: For Hartwell, this wasn't just about pushing the new *Dune* book, it was about reminding everyone of how great the first novel was, too. Although the first *Dune* was an underground hit by the 1970s, the book itself had never hit a formal bestseller list of the time, because of the slow-burn nature of its cult following.

A cherub-faced man known for wearing loud ties unironically and possessing one of the sweetest personalities in science fiction publishing, the late great David Hartwell understood that *Dune* appealed to "more than just science fiction fans." From 2010 to 2013, I personally worked with David Hartwell at the science fiction publishers Tor and Tor.com.

While there as a renegade twenty-nine-year-old blogger, I penned a column called "Genre in the Mainstream," in which I ignorantly tilted at windmills and hoped that various literary titles could be embraced by science fiction fans while various SF titles could be picked up by the mainstream. While some of it makes me cringe now, my heart was in the right place. But Hartwell, a legend in the SF publishing field, always encouraged this project. Before his death in 2016, around the early part of 2012, Hartwell leaned in the doorway of my cramped shared office on the top floor of the Flatiron Building,* rocking an analog film camera dangling around his neck. A group of us were heading to a book reading somewhere in the city, and Hartwell and I were chatting casually about how science fiction exists both in the public eye and in a private small fandom simultaneously. I was then, and still am, preoccupied with the reasons why niche science fiction narratives become mainstream obsessions, and why some very good sci-fi, for whatever reason, doesn't. And I'll never forget what he told me. "*Dune* proved science fiction could be mainstream."

David Hartwell was the person who made this happen. He pushed Putnam to print 75,000 copies, instead of the meager 7,500 copies that were planned. When *Children of Dune* hit bookstores in April 1976, it sold over 100,000 copies in the first two months. To support this huge success, Frank Herbert was

---

*I shared this office with two other people, Chris Lough and, yes, Emmet Asher-Perrin.

sent on his first-ever book tour, hitting twenty-one cities in just a month. By the time it was in paperback with Berkley Books in 1977, the first print run was 750,000. A science fiction hardcover had never been declared a *New York Times* bestseller before *Children of Dune*. Bill Erdman wrote for *The World* on May 28, 1976, "[The] third *Dune* book rings true," and that *Children of Dune* "redeems Herbert's reputation." On April 25, 1976, Ben Reuven in the *Los Angeles Times* wrote that *Children of Dune* "is a major event" and "serves to confirm the genre-shattering appeal of the *Dune* trilogy's ecological message."

The ecological message was there, of course. But notice that other phrase: *genre-shattering*. With 1976, the various versions of *Dune* weren't just science fiction stories. From the failed screenplays to the daring third novel, as 1977 unfolded, *Dune* was one of the most mainstream science fiction phenomena of all time. What could be more powerful than the spice and the Voice? In 1976, *Dune* ruled science fiction literary circles and mainstream literary circles. Now it just needed to conquer the movies. And no Force in the galaxy could stop it . . . yet.

8

Spice Wars

**Star Wars borrows the voice
and soul of Dune.**

**No, my father didn't fight in the wars, he was a navi-
gator on a spice freighter.**

—Luke Skywalker, *Star Wars* (1977)

T he greatest twentieth-century film version of *Dune*
was released in 1977, and it was called *Star Wars*. This
relationship isn't just a casual one. There is no way the
1977 *Star Wars* could have ever existed without *Dune* coming first. If there is a populist evolutionary chain of mainstream science fiction, and we consider *Star Wars* to be the
most "evolved" of the species because of its massive profits,
then *Dune* would be like the prehistoric *Homo heidelbergensis*,
and *Star Wars*, *Homo sapiens*.* This analogy isn't all that clean

---

*If we extend this analogy to the history of twenty-first-century science fic-
tion, this makes the 1950s space operas like E. E. "Doc" Smith's Lensman series

because *Dune* is more intelligent than *Star Wars*, even if it is less popular, or perhaps simply older. But still. *Dune* is the Elvis to the Beatles of *Star Wars*. And I'm not just saying that because a guy who played Elvis (Austin Butler) is also in a *Dune* movie.*

Back in 1977, fans of *Dune* noticed the striking visual similarities in *Star Wars* right away. "I must have been seventeen or eighteen, I remember seeing a couple of the scenes in the desert with R2-D2 and C-3PO and you see that crazy skeleton creature in the sand, and I said, 'Oh, that's sort of like *Dune.*'" The teenage *Dune* superfan who spotted the visual similarity was none other than Kyle MacLachlan. Ever since he was in junior high, when his friend Jim gave him the first Ace paperback edition of the novel, MacLachlan had been a big fan of the book. In 2022, after telling me about when he spotted *Dune* references in *Star Wars*, he added, "Everyone still pays homage to *Dune*," and pointed out that *Star Wars* has never stopped. "I still see it. I watch all those new shows—*The Mandalorian*, *Obi-Wan Kenobi*, *Andor*—and they're always referencing *Dune*. Spice is some kind of revered substance in *Star Wars*, and don't forget that thing in the desert that looks exactly like the mouth of the sandworm!"

Unsurprisingly, Kyle MacLachlan is right. The skeleton of

(made famous in the pages of John Campbell's *Amazing*) the extinct common ancestor of both *Dune* and *Star Wars*. In other words, in terms of evolutionary populism, E. E. "Doc" Smith and John Campbell are the Neanderthals of science fiction.

*Actually, that is kind of why I'm saying that.

a Krayt dragon, glimpsed in the first *Star Wars* film, later appeared as a flesh-and-blood sand monster in 2020, in the *Mandalorian* season 2 episode "The Marshal," and it really looked like a sandworm of Arrakis. The "thing in the desert" with the mouth of the sandworm is the Sarlacc on Tatooine, which first appeared in 1983's *Return of the Jedi*, one year before *Dune*, starring Kyle MacLachlan, hit theaters. Yes, the spice has been flowing through *Star Wars* for quite a while. Within the first five minutes of the original *Star Wars*, C-3PO worries about getting sent to "the spice mines of Kessel" if he and R2-D2 get caught. Han Solo moved spice illegally for Jabba the Hutt, and in 2019's *The Rise of Skywalker* we learned that Poe Dameron—played by Duke Leto Atreides himself, Oscar Isaac—was also a spice smuggler. Back in the 1990s, when *Star Wars* novels were all the rage, future *Dune* continuation novelist Kevin J. Anderson corresponded with George Lucas about the nature of the *Star Wars* version of spice, to make sure this was, indeed, some variety of space narcotic with mind-expanding properties. Although the editors of the *Star Wars* novels of the time wanted to tone down the druglike aspects of spice in *Star Wars*, Anderson claims that George Lucas told him, "Of course it's a drug." In that since-abandoned *Star Wars* continuity, some highly addictive forms of spice, called "glitterstim," are the byproduct of giant space spiders instead of sandworms.

Even as recently as 2022, the animated *Star Wars* series *Tales of the Jedi* revisited a planet called Raxus Secundus, which borrows its name from both the prison planet Salusa Secundus in *Dune* as well as "Rakis," the name by which Arrakis is known in the distant future, starting with Herbert's fourth *Dune* novel, 1981's *God Emperor of Dune*. In the second episode of the Disney+ series *Obi-Wan Kenobi*, the titular Jedi hero (played by Ewan McGregor) is offered street drugs right away by a young woman who says: "You want some spice, old man?" From the monsters they face, to the ground they walk on, to the spice they smuggle, the heroes and villains of George Lucas's famous faraway galaxy seemingly wouldn't have a galaxy to live in at all if *Star Wars* hadn't cribbed more than a little from *Dune*.

"*Star Wars* borrowed from *Dune* a lot," Frank Herbert told *Rolling Stone* in 1984, just months before David Lynch's *Dune* hit theaters. "I think they owe me at least a dinner." But did he always feel like this? And, more crucially, did *Star Wars* rip off *Dune* or merely pay homage?

Shortly after *Star Wars* hit theaters on May 25, 1977, it was Herbert's son Brian who alerted him via telephone, saying, "You better see it. The similarities are unbelievable." But by late August 1977, Herbert claimed he had still not seen *Star Wars*. When interviewed by the Associated Press* that month, he said he'd heard from friends and colleagues, and an editor at *The Village Voice*, that he might want to consider suing George Lucas. "I will try not to sue. I have no idea what book of mine it fits," Herbert said in August 1977. "I suspect it may be *Dune* since in that I had a Princess Alia and the movie has

---

*This article was widely syndicated in various Washington State newspapers with slightly different headlines, including "Is *Dune* a *Star Wars* Spinoff" (the *Daily News*, Port Angeles, Washington, August 19, 1977) and "Is *Dune* Trilogy *Star Wars* Basis?" (*The Columbian*, Vancouver, Washington, August 21, 1977).

a Princess Leia. And I hear there is a sandworm caucus* [*sic*] and hooded dwellers in the desert, just like in *Dune*."

This is amazing. By August 1977, *Star Wars* had been out for three months, and Frank Herbert just could not be bothered to see it. His supposed ignorance about which book of his other people thought *Star Wars* ripped off also scans as a bit much. Did Frank Herbert really think *Star Wars* could have ripped off *The Dragon in the Sea* or *The Santaroga Barrier*? Was he legitimately unaware or was he just being a snob? Based on what he said publicly, it's surprisingly tough to pin down what Herbert truly thought of the whole affair. Particularly throughout the back end of 1977, because he often seemed to take both sides. Either *Star Wars* totally ripped off *Dune* and Herbert wanted to sue, or Herbert didn't care and thought that *Star Wars* ripped off everybody. For what it's worth, George Lucas was also contacted by the Associated Press and basically said "no comment," without saying it. As the article states, "Lucas, who says he drew on many sources in preparing the *Star Wars* script, declines to say whether the *Dune* trilogy was among them."[†]

---

*All published versions of this news story quote Herbert saying "sandworm caucus," but surely he said/meant "sandworm carcass." Herbert was telepathically communicating with teenage Kyle MacLachlan, who saw that skeleton on Tatooine, right? Otherwise, we'd have to try to sort out what a "sandworm caucus" is and if there was one in *Star Wars*. Maybe when Emperor Palpatine dissolved the Imperial Senate (off-screen) in *Star Wars*, he convened a sandworm caucus first.

†In 1977, *Dune* was still a book "trilogy," because only the first three novels had been published at that time. Back then, it was common in interviews for Herbert to refer to the body of work as the "*Dune* trilogy."

On September 11, 1977, Herbert told *The Spokesman-Review* that he thought the idea that *Star Wars* was derived from *Dune* was "a lot of bull" and added, "There's probably a good number of similarities to the work of Isaac Asimov." *Spokesman-Review* staff writer Tom Sowa then paraphrased Herbert, claiming, "He is certainly not, however, interested in considering legal action about unlawful use of his property." Had Herbert still not seen *Star Wars* at this point, about a month after the previous interview? His quip about Asimov really makes you think he hadn't, simply because trying to find the work of Asimov in *Star Wars* is a stretch. Asimov in *Star Trek*, yes. But claiming Asimov influences in *Star Wars* feels superficial at best. Yes, Asimov wrote about a galactic empire, and sure, he had a few cutesy robots, but if Herbert had seen *Star Wars* when he said this, the Asimov thing makes it sound like he's sucking up to Asimov, which is just weird. Still, regardless of whether Herbert had or had not seen *Star Wars* yet in September of '77, at that point, he also claimed he didn't want to sue and seemed to try to distance himself from the conversation in general, mostly with the "a lot of bull" comment. It's almost like in downplaying this, Herbert was saying *Dune* couldn't have been ripped off, because *Star Wars* wasn't important enough to have ripped off *Dune*.

But then, by December 1977, Frank Herbert has seen *Star Wars*. And his tone changes. He mocks it outright, saying, "It is very shallow in the story and character development sense. [The movie] should have had balloons in there with 'Pow!' and 'Bang!'" And it's at this point that it seems like he's serious about suing.

On December 1, 1977, *The Register-Guard* (Eugene, Oregon) runs a story written by Fred Crafts with the headline: "Should Sci-Fi Author Sue? Writer of 'Dune' Says 'Star Wars' Used Elements of His Novel Without Permission." This article begins by calling Frank Herbert an "easy-going writer" with a "hearty laugh."* And at first it doubles down on the notion that Herbert doesn't want to talk about it. "I just hate getting into this damned thing. . . . I'm going to try very hard not to sue." But then Herbert goes on the attack and admits he's seen *Star Wars*, he thought it was "boring," and his wife, Beverly, fell asleep in the theater.† When asked directly if Herbert believes that George Lucas "plagiarized" *Dune*, Herbert replies, "I think there's reason to believe that he did." A far cry from "a lot of bull"!

Fascinatingly, within this same article, Herbert explains that while he's holding off on sending his loyal Fremen to destroy Lucas, he is suing Creed Taylor and CTI Records because of the release of the 1977 jazz album titled *Dune*. The article states that Herbert filed suit against the record company because the album was in "competition with Herbert's own reading of his own work on Caedmon records." This suit

---

*This is the only piece of journalism that attempted to paint Herbert as "easygoing." His son Brian revealed in the biography *Dreamer of Dune* that his father hooked him and his brother, Bruce, up to lie detectors when they were kids. Hardly easygoing!

†This is a weird flex from Herbert. Say what you will about *Star Wars*. But is that first 1977 movie "boring"? Sleep-inducing? This is a little like Sean Connery's James Bond implying the Beatles are horrible in *Goldfinger*.

failed. Today, you can easily get this album, which was re-corded and performed by a prominent pianist, David Mat-thews, who is not related at all to Dave Matthews of the Dave Matthews Band, because the world isn't ready for that musical take on *Dune*. This funky, fun jazz record is, as of this writing, readily available on Spotify and iTunes, and a copy on vinyl is easily the least expensive *Dune* collectible in the universe. Why Herbert believed this album was a threat to him is understandable at first, but upon closer inspection, it seems like he may not have done his homework before filing the lawsuit.

The first four tracks of David Matthews's *Dune* are very *Dune*-y. You've got "Arrakis," "Sandworms," "Song of the Bene Gesserit," and "Muad'dib." Then track five switches gears into . . . a cover of David Bowie's "Space Oddity." After that song (which includes the album's only vocal), you've got a jazzy version of the theme to *Silent Running*, followed by a funk version of "Princess Leia's Theme," capped off by, yes, a bizarrely underwhelming jazz version of "Main Theme from Star Wars." In terms of musical authorship, the only songs that David Matthews wrote for this album were the *Dune* tracks. The other half of the album is an easy-listening jazz sci-fi cover album that you can totally imagine playing in the background of deleted scenes in *Boogie Nights*. To top it all off, the cover of the album has the word *Dune* styled in what is clearly the yellow *Star Wars* font, set against a sea of stars, not a desert landscape.

Why was Herbert so mad about a jazz record? Here's one theory: Herbert loved jazz. In fact, he sometimes referred to conversations with fellow authors or readers as "jam sessions." The art of improvisation was deeply important to Herbert's thinking and writing, and he even considered certain conversations verbal "jazz performances." In the final Frank Herbert–penned *Dune* novel, *Chapterhouse: Dune* (1985), Darwi Odrade, Herbert's last great Bene Gesserit protagonist, is into jazz, and incorporates it into her philosophy, and thinks that conflicts can be resolved through the reactive qualities of jazz music, which is why Darwi Odrade says, "Feed us with jazz." Not the most famous *Dune* line! And yet, suddenly, when you realize how much Herbert liked jazz, you can see why a mostly corny jazz record with the word *Dune* on it might piss him off.

Herbert failed to shut down the funk of David Matthews's *Dune*, even though he tried. At the same time, he didn't even really try to take on George Lucas and instead joked about forming a club with other sci-fi writers called We're Too Big to Sue George Lucas. This joke and Herbert's posturing in interviews about whether *Star Wars* ripped him off reveals two things: First, that science fiction was changing rapidly in the 1970s, and second, that Herbert correctly intuited the real problem with *Star Wars*, at least relative to *Dune*. It wasn't a rip-off, but it was going to change the way the public perceived *Dune*, at least cinematically, forever.

"I mean, George Lucas took all the Bene Gesserit and turned them into men!" Kara Kennedy tells me in 2023. "The Jedi could not exist without the Bene Gesserit, and what Lucas did there is almost unforgivable."

Still, Herbert couldn't legally sue because Lucas didn't really rip him off. Homage and inspiration are not the same as plagiarism, as Herbert had once implied. Structurally and ton-ally, George Lucas was just as influenced by *Flash Gordon* and the films of Akira Kurosawa, not to mention the huge influ-ence of Joseph Campbell's Jungian theories about "the hero's journey," which also influenced Herbert's writing of *Dune.** If Joseph Campbell is right, and various monomyths tap into some kind of shared collective unconscious, then Lucas and Herbert were mining the same psychological places for story structures.

In 1984, David Lynch called it the way most people see it. "George did a fantastic thing, and he may have been influ-enced by these different things, but he took them in a super creative way, he made it go very far from the feeling of *Dune*." In other words, it's nuts to think George Lucas wasn't inspired by the aesthetics of *Dune*. But the basic aim of the story of *Star Wars* is, at least at first, the opposite of the story of *Dune*. Luke Skywalker is a poor moisture farmer who leaves the desert planet for a greater adventure. Paul Atreides is a cosmo-politan character, a guy who is literally royalty, who comes to live on a desert planet, and in a sense becomes a poor moisture farmer before becoming the king of the universe. Yes, there are some strange similarities to the familiar revelations—

---

*Yep. We've got both famous sci-fi/fantasy Campbells in this book. John Camp-bell and Joseph Campbell both influenced Herbert. The funny thing is, Frank Herbert never met editor John Campbell in person, but he did meet Joseph Campbell. On May 14, 1983, at the C. G. Jung Institute of San Francisco, Frank Herbert co-headlined an event with *Star Trek* creator Gene Roddenberry and novelist Ursula K. Le Guin. Joseph Campbell was also on the bill, and it's ru-mored, though not confirmed, that George Lucas was in the audience.

Darth Vader is the father of Luke and Leia, the same way the evil Baron Harkonnen is Jessica's father, and thus Paul and Alia's grandfather. Many have compared the Jedi to the Bene Gesserit, specifically the famous Jedi mind trick, in which you can get somebody to do something just by speaking, exactly like using the Voice in *Dune*. As Herbert knew, it was tough to take legal action with homage, especially when the work had been transformed into something else entirely. What Herbert feared was that the success of *Star Wars* was going to make it hard for a film version of *Dune* to become viable. Because after *Star Wars*, every movie version of *Dune* would be compared to *Star Wars*, which was, of course, backward.

"*Dune* was going to be *Star Wars* for grown-ups," Virginia Madsen said of her experience as part of the cast of the 1984 film. During the initial production design of that *Dune* film, David Lynch admitted that the existence of *Star Wars* proved to be a difficult problem in trying to craft something out of the pages of Herbert's books and translating that feeling to the screen, mostly because that aesthetic metamorphosis had already happened. The visual motifs of *Dune* had, as *Rolling Stone* pointed out in 1984, "already been co-opted" by *Star Wars*. "It was strange to go through [the novel *Dune*] and find this was done in *Star Wars*," Lynch admitted. "I wanted to do new things, so I had to do them differently."

Aesthetically, 1977 is the turning point for how the mainstream public perceives *Dune*. Even though *Star Wars* hitched a ride on the cloak of the sandriders of Arrakis, for the rest of the world, *Dune* was playing catch-up. In 2018, just after he had been announced as the director of the new *Dune* film,

Denis Villeneuve expressed nearly exactly the same sentiments David Lynch and Virginia Madsen had about their *Dune* thirty-four years earlier.

"Most of the main ideas of *Star Wars* are coming from *Dune*," Villeneuve said before he began pre-production. "In a way, it's *Star Wars* for adults."

Interestingly, even when the *Star Wars* franchise later went into more adult territory, you could argue, it again borrowed from *Dune*. In the climax of George Lucas's prequel trilogy, *Revenge of the Sith*, we learn that Anakin Skywalker's fall to the dark side of the Force is all because he was trapped by a vision of the future, which is very similar to how Paul Atreides's prescience forces him into a terrible and inevitable future in *Dune Messiah*. In Rian Johnson's *The Last Jedi*, Luke Skywalker has walked away from his entire life and then seems to preach against the teachings of the Jedi, much like Paul transforming into the Preacher in *Children of Dune*, after walking away from his empire. Even in J. J. Abrams's *The Rise of Skywalker*, Rey learns that Emperor Palpatine is her grandfather, and she's tempted to join the dark side. This is pretty similar to Alia's realizing Baron Harkonnen is her grandfather in *Children of Dune* and actually choosing to give in to that evil spirit that lives inside her. The darker elements of *Star Wars* almost always move toward being more like *Dune*, especially in *The Empire Strikes Back*, when it seems like Luke Skywalker can't ever win, even if he does learn the ways of the Bene Gesserit . . . or Jedi.

When I spoke to Denis Villeneuve before the release of *Dune: Part One*, the first thing he said to me was "You have a lot of *Star Wars* shit behind you." We were speaking over Zoom, and at that time, I hadn't mastered how to change my background to obscure the clutter of my writing desk area. Like many science fiction critics and historians, no matter how much shit I talk about *Star Wars*, the truth is, we all love *Star Wars*, and so, as Villeneuve pointed out, even the biggest *Dune* fans probably have a lot of *Star Wars* shit.

Villeneuve was mostly referring to a prominent Princess Leia action figure (Cloud City gear!), a relatively new lightsaber toy, and my 1980 vintage snowspeeder model from *The Empire Strikes Back*. This made him smile. "Oh, let me see that," he said. "I love that."

Frank Herbert probably wouldn't like this outcome. *Dune* will always be compared to *Star Wars*, even if *Dune* is the original *Star Wars*. But Villeneuve's childlike delight with a vintage snowspeeder model tells you everything you need to know about the legacy of *Star Wars* smuggling some spice away from *Dune*. In the backstory of *Dune*, we learn that the Bene Gesserit intentionally planted myths and legends on several planets, just in case, in the future, people like Jessica and Paul needed a handy religious story to embody. Which is exactly like the contemporary relationship between *Star Wars* and *Dune*. Today, if someone erroneously believes *Dune* is derived from *Star Wars*, that's okay. *Star Wars* has, paradoxically, prepared those new fans for the gospel of *Dune*.

This is a fact that Denis Villeneuve doesn't fear but, rather, embraces. "*The Empire Strikes Back* is always good for the soul," he tells me. "*Dune* is more like that, you know?"

The very first page of "Dune World Part 1," published in *Analog* for the December 1963 issue. This illustration depicts the planet Arrakis surrounded by two large hands, showing that control of the planet Dune is the central theme of the story. The introductory caption beneath the illustration mentions Frank Herbert's previous book, *The Dragon in the Sea*, all about submarines.

COVER ILLUSTRATION BY JOHN SCHOENHERR/*ANALOG*

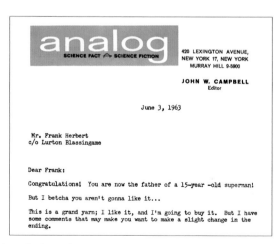

The beginning of a letter from editor John Campbell to Frank Herbert in which the three-part serial "Dune World" was formally accepted for publication in *Analog*. Campbell's introduction, referencing the "15-year-old superman," alludes to Paul Atreides and his powers of prescience. The letter is dated June 3, 1963. "Dune World Part 1" would be published five months later.

COURTESY OF CALIFORNIA STATE UNIVERSITY, FULLERTON

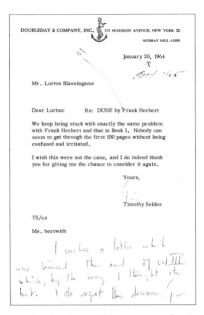

Letter from Doubleday rejecting *Dune*. This was one of at least twenty rejection letters.

COURTESY OF CALIFORNIA STATE UNIVERSITY, FULLERTON

Letter from Sterling E. Lanier to Frank Herbert, dated January 19, 1965, concerning the specifics of the first hardcover edition of *Dune*. Note: This is the official publishing moment when the novel becomes "Dune" rather than "Dune World."

COURTESY OF CALIFORNIA STATE UNIVERSITY, FULLERTON

On the left is the first edition of *Dune* in hardcover, published by Chilton in 1965. On the right is the January 1965 issue of *Analog* that contained Part 1 (of 5) of "The Prophet of Dune," a serial that completed the story that began in the previous 1963–64 *Analog* three-part serial "Dune World." The novel version of *Dune* is the combined version of all eight parts of both "Dune World" and "The Prophet of Dune." The cover art by John Schoenherr depicts Paul Atreides and his mother, Lady Jessica, in a canyon on the surface of Arrakis. This scene occurs about halfway through the novel. The Schoenherr painting, originally commissioned for *Analog*, was selected by Chilton editor Sterling E. Lanier to be reused as the cover of the novel.   COVER ILLUSTRATION BY JOHN SCHOENHERR/CHILTON, *ANALOG*

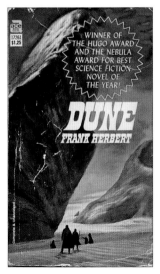

John Schoenherr's revised cover art for the first paperback edition of *Dune*, published by Ace in 1966.   COVER ILLUSTRATION BY JOHN SCHOENHERR/ACE

A prominent interview with Frank Herbert in *Vertex* magazine in October 1973. Paul Turner conducted the interview at a time in between the publication of *Dune Messiah* and *Children of Dune*. At least two failed *Dune* movie projects were ongoing at this time.

ARTICLE BY PAUL TURNER/*VERTEX*

A rare copy of all the storyboards for Alejandro Jodorowsky's take on *Dune* in the 1970s. The art for the unmade film was created by Dan O'Bannon, Chris Foss, and Jean Giraud, better known as Mœbius. This book was never sold publicly and was only created to showcase the story of the film. There were fewer than one hundred copies made.

PHOTOGRAPH BY ALAIN JOCARD/AFP
VIA GETTY IMAGES

Ron Miller's concept art for the sandworm in the 1984 David Lynch film *Dune*. The sandworms seen in the film were based on this design, and later, miniatures were constructed by Carlo Rambaldi. Miller's art depicts the sandworms with three flaps at the mouth, a design concept that survived to the final film. Of all the sandworms seen on-screen, these, perhaps, remain the most memorable.

ILLUSTRATIONS BY RON MILLER

Beverly and Frank Herbert at their home in Port Townsend on September 11, 1979, surrounded by sandworm art.

MOHAI, *SEATTLE POST-INTELLIGENCER* PHOTOGRAPH COLLECTION, 2000.107.087.11.02, PHOTOGRAPH BY PHIL H. WEBBER

Dean Stockwell, Francesca Annis, and David Lynch on the set of *Dune* in 1983.

PHOTOGRAPH BY NANCY MORAN/SYGMA VIA GETTY IMAGES

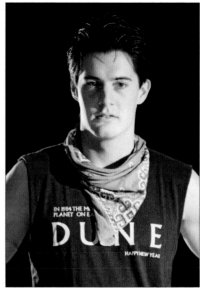

Left: Actor Kyle MacLachlan gets a piggy-back from writer Frank Herbert.

PHOTOGRAPH BY CHRISTIAN SIMONPIETRI/SYGMA VIA GETTY IMAGES

Right: Kyle MacLachlan promoting *Dune* in 1984. Note the text on the bottom of the shirt: *Happy New Year*.   PHOTOGRAPH BY PIERRE PERRIN/GAMMA-RAPHO VIA GETTY IMAGES

Frank Herbert and Theresa Shackleford at the premiere of *Dune* in Washington, DC, on December 3, 1984.

PHOTOGRAPH BY RON GALELLA, LTD./RON GALELLA COLLECTION VIA GETTY IMAGES

Julie Cox as Princess Irulan and Alec Newman as Paul Atreides in the 2000 miniseries *Frank Herbert's Dune*.   PHOTOGRAPH BY SEAN GALLUP/*NEWSMAKERS*/GETTY IMAGES

Saskia Reeves, Uwe Ochsenknecht, Julie Cox, László Imre Kish, and William Hurt promote *Frank Herbert's Dune* in 2000.   PHOTOGRAPH BY FRANZISKA KRUG/GETTY IMAGES

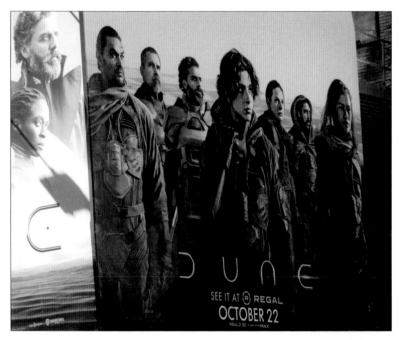

Billboard in New York City promoting the movie *Dune: Part One* in 2021, on 7th Avenue and 35th Street.

STREET PHOTOGRAPH OF BILLBOARD BY MIKE REED

Mural of Lady Jessica (Rebecca Ferguson), Duke Leto (Oscar Isaac), and Gurney Halleck (Josh Brolin) in Melbourne in 2021.

MURAL CREATED BY CONNOR McLENNAN, AMANDA NEWMAN, AND ASH COATES FOR APPARITION MEDIA. PHOTOGRAPH BY ANDREW HAYSOM

Dune Velvet

David Lynch's 1984 film and the renewed cult of *Dune*.

> There are opportunities in life for knowledge and experience. Sometimes it's necessary to take a risk.
>
> —Jeffrey Beaumont, *Blue Velvet*

There's a deleted scene from the 1984 David Lynch *Dune* film that is easily the most David Lynch thing ever. When Lady Jessica (Francesca Annis) gives birth to Alia (Alicia Witt), the newborn baby speaks to Lady Jessica. As in the novel, Alia is born with all the memories of her ancestors, so the idea was, straight out of the womb, she would turn to her mom to speak and freak her out. To make this scene as accurate as possible, Carlo Rambaldi made a puppet of the newborn version of Alia that was supposed to look exactly like what young actress Alicia Witt looked like as a baby.

"Carlo said that he had made that puppet using photos my parents had provided of me as an infant," Alicia Witt tells me in 2023, laughing. "He developed this head and face and all of it that was intended to look like mine would've looked as a newborn. When I started doing movies as a teenager, professionally, I learned quickly that was not how movies were usually made. It was such a rare and wonderful experience. For me, to work with David Lynch, in my first movie as an actress, it just set this amazing standard."

For *Dune* fans, the 1984 film set all sorts of other standards. Whether you love the film or don't, the journey of the *Dune* franchise has a historical point before this movie and a point after. It's here where *Dune* entered the zeitgeist in an entirely new way. The 1984 film made *Dune* more mainstream than ever but also accidentally reaffirmed its status as a cult phenomenon. And yet, even for the most hard-core fans, much of this *Dune* managed to reach back in time and subtly revise Frank Herbert's text, making us believe certain lines and ideas come from the book when really, some of the most memorable *Dune*-isms come from this movie.

Exactly four minutes and thirty-four seconds into David Lynch's film *Dune*, the phrase "The spice must flow" is uttered by an anonymous disembodied voice that sounds kind of like a robot. This exact phrase never appears in any of Frank Herbert's original six *Dune* novels—the last of which, *Chapterhouse: Dune*, was published in March 1985, just three months after Lynch's *Dune* hit theaters on December 14, 1984. In the original books, everyone is obviously obsessed with the spice, and there's a lot of consternation about where it's going and flowing, but that exact sequence of words was never written by Frank Herbert and was instead the result of David Lynch's screenplay.* The phrase "The spice must flow" ends the second opening narration of the 1984 movie,† following the credits and the first narration, a formal introduction from Princess Irulan (Virginia Madsen), who tells us what the spice is, what the deal is with the prophecy on Arrakis, and why a "beginning is a very delicate time." After the stirring credits, accompanied by the unforgettable theme music composed by Toto and Brian Eno, we hear about "a secret report from within the Guild," which tells us the Spacing Guild is worried about the possibility that Paul and his family could disrupt spice production because they're just too damn awesome. They dispatch a "Third Stage Guild navigator," a creepy-looking fishman mutant with tiny arms (who is not an alien), to go grill Emperor Shaddam IV (José Ferrer) in a scene where we get even more exposition. And just as the Third Stage Guild navigator lands on the planet Kaitain to give the emperor the

---

*According to David Lynch, he wrote seven drafts of the *Dune* screenplay. Early drafts were written with his collaborators on *The Elephant Man*, Chris De Vore and Eric Bergren. Lynch later said, "Dino [De Laurentiis] didn't like what we were doing," which meant he eventually wrote the final drafts alone. The phrase "The spice must flow" exists from the very first draft, spoken by the Guild navigator to the emperor in all versions. Interestingly, the phrase "The spice must flow" wasn't moved to the "secret report" voice-over until after filming began. The way "The spice must flow" appears in the movie doesn't appear in any of those seven drafts.

†The 1988 TV broadcast cut of *Dune* included a different opening narration, created specifically for that version. It omits Madsen's Princess Irulan and the secret report from the Guild, and swaps in a strange storybook intro that zooms in on Frank Herbert's novel and then describes the universe of *Dune* using various drawings depicting the characters.

business, the voice behind the "secret report" says firmly and eerily: "The spice must flow."

The voice behind the secret report isn't a character as such. If we think hard about where this narration comes from, we have to assume it belongs to a higher-ranking official from within the Spacing Guild. And since 1984, only hard-core film critics and spice heads have speculated as to who recorded this tone-setting voice-over and made the phrase "The spice must flow" into a permanent *Dune* catchphrase. Did Lynch himself record it? An unnamed voice actor? For answers, it's best to turn to the messiah, Paul Atreides himself.

"Yes, it was me," Kyle MacLachlan tells me in 2022. "It's funny. I don't remember saying 'The spice must flow,' but if it's in the secret report and it's the same voice, then yes, it must have been me." Although MacLachlan's starring role as Paul Atreides in *Dune* launched his career and changed the perception of the character forever, it turns out, he also re-defined our feelings about the spice with this strange and quirkily affecting anonymous voice-over. Once you know it's MacLachlan speaking those words, you can't unhear it. The phrase "The spice must flow" belongs to Kyle MacLachlan, now and forever.

MacLachlan was only twenty-three when he was cast as Paul, but over three decades later, his enthusiasm for the *Dune* films and books is boundless. During our lengthy interview in the fall of 2022, he searches his memory for the moment he said "The spice must flow" and then giddily slips into other memorable opening moments from the film. While reminiscing, MacLachlan busts out his impression of the Third Stage

Guild navigator saying, "Many machines on Ix."* MacLachlan laughs to himself when he does the voices of other characters—including a brief Patrick Stewart impression—geeking out on *Dune* the same way fans do with each other. In the 1984 *Dune*, the name *Muad'Dib* is a "killing word," meaning just uttering it projects power. Like Chalamet, MacLachlan has a mesmerizing voice. In the '84 *Dune*, the concept of "the Voice" is put into overdrive, thanks to Lynch's invention of the "weirding modules," sonic weapons wielded by House Atreides and, later, the Fremen.† MacLachlan's tone and candor are similar in real life. MacLachlan repeats the words and phrases from *Dune* with bemused reverie, just for the hell of it, not for conquest or power. Talking to Kyle MacLachlan reminds you that simply saying lines from *Dune* out loud is fun.

History makes it seem like MacLachlan was destined to play Paul Atreides; he'd read the book as a teenager several times before getting the part, and he was new to the environment of Mexico City, where the vast majority of David Lynch's *Dune* was filmed. Paul was new to Arrakis, and MacLachlan came from Seattle, a decent analogue for the watery planet Caladan and somewhat fitting, since Frank Herbert had spent

---

* According to Kyle MacLachlan, the voice of the Third Stage Guild navigator was that of Everett McGill, who more famously played Paul's Fremen compatriot Stilgar.

† This David Lynch concept weaponized the Voice much more literally than in any of the books. In the final scene, Paul doesn't even need the handheld weirding module; he uses the Voice to crack the floor open, which is a little like if a Jedi could destroy a building by yelling at it.

so much of his life in Washington, which Herbert later re-marked created "a kind of natural bond being from the same state." But MacLachlan is quick to remind me that his being a *Dune* fan and an actor wasn't that strange at the time: "There were literally thousands of young men—if not more—reading the book and saying, 'Yes, I am Paul.'"

Not only was the search for an actor to play Paul Atreides a massive undertaking, but there were also fans casting them-selves as Paul. In 1972, then-twenty-five-year-old science fic-tion author Alan Dean Foster wrote to the Arthur Jacobs production, saying, "I've never had an interest in performing in the cinema, I'd much rather write and teach. But when the time comes 'round for you to cast *Dune*, I'd like very much to test for the role of Paul Atreides." Four years later, Foster was hired by George Lucas to ghostwrite the novelization of *Star Wars*, which naturally became one of the biggest science fic-tion books of all time. When MacLachlan says a ton of young men in the seventies and eighties saw themselves as Paul, he's not messing around.

"Stephen Colbert said he thought he could be a fantastic Paul!" MacLachlan says with a laugh.* "I mean, he probably could have been a fantastic Paul. Different than mine. So, it was not a strange thing [that a *Dune* fan was cast as Paul]. The strange thing was that it somehow manifested itself and came to me. It found me somehow. I still really can't quite grasp how

---

*Colbert is five years younger than MacLachlan. In 1982, Colbert was acting in plays at Hampden-Sydney College in Virginia.

luck intervened to make it happen. Because I was nowhere near LA or Hollywood. I was in Seattle working in a small theater, and Seattle was one of the stops on the casting tour to find the new unknown actor to play Paul."

Although Lynch and producer Raffaella De Laurentiis—daughter of producer Dino De Laurentiis—ultimately felt a new face was right for Paul Atreides, there were other names briefly considered for the part, including Tom Cruise, Kevin Costner, Val Kilmer, Rob Lowe, and (not yet Sir) Kenneth Branagh. Rob Lowe was far enough along in the process that his meetings with Dino De Laurentiis included the notion that in a sequel he would end up turning into a sandworm "about three hundred feet long." This suggests that the plans for the Lynch/De Laurentiis *Dune* film sequels would have conflated the stories of Paul and his son, Leto II, and have had Paul become the God Emperor sandworm for the film sequels. Somewhere out there is another timeline where this all happened and Rob Lowe is famous for having his head on top of a worm body.

But in our universe, it was Kyle MacLachlan who won the role. Producer Raffaella De Laurentiis remembers that MacLachlan captured everything required of the part. "He had to be young, he had to be princely," she said. "And Kyle kind of just worked. After we saw many, many, many different people, he had that charisma." The idea of casting an unknown actor wasn't just a policy created by Raffaella De Laurentiis, it was a stipulation directly from Frank Herbert. "That's exactly what I told them to do . . . get somebody who's never been on the screen before . . . so he doesn't bring any detritus from other parts into the scenes." Herbert also wholeheartedly approved of MacLachlan as Paul, saying. "Kyle's an easy guy to like and he is extremely personable in a natural way."

In addition to getting along famously with Frank Herbert, MacLachlan and David Lynch obviously clicked, since MacLachlan went on to star in several David Lynch projects immediately after *Dune*, most memorably *Blue Velvet* (1986) and *Twin Peaks* (1990). "He was sort of like David Lynch's personal pet during the making of *Dune*," costar Sean Young—who played Chani—said. But she added that the love of Lynch was universal on the set of *Dune*. "Every single actor who worked on that movie loved David and would have done anything for him."

In every 1984 magazine article and interview related to *Dune* that was released before the film hit theaters, the tone surrounding the movie was ebullient. Herbert heaped praise on Lynch at every turn, while Dino De Laurentiis confidently claimed that this was only the beginning of a huge movie franchise, saying in May 1984, "I have no doubt there will be more." But after December 1984, this *Dune* was declared a failure, both at the box office and by the critics. *Dune* 1984 lives on as a fan favorite and the defining visual version of the story for several generations. The journey of Kyle MacLachlan from an unknown Seattle-based theater actor to the star of *Dune* not only parallels the journey of Paul in the novel but also serves as an emotional road map for how this famous 1984 version of *Dune* was made and, later, reassessed. If you view the first novel as a coming-of-age story for Paul, then the making of the 1984 film is when *Dune* lost its innocence.

The story of David Lynch's *Dune* begins, in a roundabout

way, with Ridley Scott. After Michel Seydoux's option ex-
pired, the film rights to *Dune* were acquired in 1978 by influential Hollywood power broker Dino De Laurentiis, who went
straight to Frank Herbert for a screenplay. However, Herbert's
1978 screenplay was 175 pages, which De Laurentiis considered
"unacceptable." In a 1984 joint interview with David Lynch,
Herbert even admitted his screenplay was "a dog," saying, "I
was too close to the book . . . it was too long. It lacked the
proper visual metaphors."

After rejecting Herbert's screenplay and reading *Dune*
three more times, De Laurentiis decided to pick a dynamic
filmmaker to write and direct the film. And his first choice,
based on the astounding success of *Alien*, was to hire Ridley
Scott. Unsurprisingly, this meant that Scott began collaborat-
ing with *Alien* designer H. R. Giger, who had of course previously done concept art on Jodorowsky's *Dune*. On September
27, 1979, Ridley Scott had breakfast with firebrand SF author
Harlan Ellison—who had been an early supporter of Herbert
in the sixties—and asked him to write the screenplay. Ellison
turned him down flat. Scott then picked a writing partner for
the screenplay, the novelist Rudolph Wurlitzer, who, in an
early draft of the script, created a massively controversial
change in the story of *Dune*. For Wurlitzer, the relationship
between Paul and his mother, Jessica, had "latent but very
strong Oedipal attraction," which resulted in a scene in which
Paul becomes the father and brother to Alia Atreides. Although Frank Herbert's novel *Children of Dune* suggests that
certain forces want Leto II and Ghanima to incestuously
procreate, the message of the novel and the actions of the

characters are clearly not an endorsement of incest. Whether Wurlitzer misread Paul's love of his mother or subconsciously lifted elements of Leto II and Ghanima's relationship is beside the point. While it's possible to argue that some icky subtext might exist in various familiar relationships throughout all the *Dune* books, Herbert's intention as a writer is clearly anti-incest. Accordingly, when he discovered that Wurlitzer's screenplay turned Paul and Jessica into lovers, Herbert was furious. Later drafts of the Wurlitzer-Scott *Dune* screenplay dropped this element, and despite many reports to the contrary, this controversy isn't what sunk the Ridley Scott *Dune*.

"I worked on *Dune* for over a year and a half," Scott said. "I realized *Dune* was going to take more work. A lot more work." But the reason Scott left the project in 1980 wasn't because he had anything against *Dune* or the troubled screenplay. According to Scott, his reason for giving up on *Dune* was tragic and deeply personal. "I'll tell you what really happened," Scott said in 1996. "My older brother died. Frankly, that freaked me out." Scott's older brother was Frank Scott, who died of skin cancer in 1980. For Ridley, the problem wasn't that he wanted to avoid work, but instead that the process of making *Dune* was too slow. "I needed immediate activity, needed to get my mind off my brother's death." Interestingly, producer Raffaella De Laurentiis said it was the other way around: that Scott wanted to do *Blade Runner* and have the *Dune* production wait on him. In 1984, she said: "We didn't want to wait that long, so we parted company." In 1984, it's possible that Scott wasn't being honest about his grief, or De Laurentiis was simply being polite. Either way, Scott left and put the De Laurentiis version of *Dune* on hold. As Raffaella pointed out, Ridley Scott's next project was 1982's *Blade Runner*, a film he couldn't have tackled had he been filming his version of *Dune* in 1980. Basically, two of Ridley Scott's most famous (and best?) films—*Alien* and *Blade Runner**—wouldn't have ever existed without a failed *Dune* movie happening before each. Even when *Dune* movies don't get made, the attempt creates other classic sci-fi movies by accident.

Still, by 1981, Dino De Laurentiis was a dog with a *Dune* bone and "convinced, more than ever, that the book was filmable." According to Frank Herbert, both Dino and Raffaella refused to let go of the *Dune* project because Federico De Laurentiis—Dino's son and Raffaella's brother—had been a massive fan of the novel. "Dino De Laurentiis picked up the rights because his son insisted on it," Herbert said. "Federico was killed in Alaska. In fact, Federico was at our house three or four days before he was killed." Federico, like his father and sister, was also a film producer; he died in a plane crash on July 15, 1981, while scouting locations. Dino De Laurentiis repurchased the film option to *Dune* more than once, and some of this determination can be partially ascribed to Federico's *Dune* fandom. A dedication in the 1984 *Dune* reads, "This film is dedicated to Federico De Laurentiis."

Blade Runner's relationship with *Dune* is intertwined in many other ways. Sean Young being cast as Chani for the 1984 *Dune* is a direct result of her performance as Rachael in *Blade Runner*. And of course Denis Villeneuve directed *Blade Runner 2049* (2017) before taking on the newest *Dune* in 2019.

Before the 1984 *Dune* coalesced, Dino De Laurentiis had proven his talent for making impossible science fiction and fantasy movies click—specifically, his production of the 1976 version of *King Kong*. Although most don't think much about Jeff Bridges and Jessica Lange's *King Kong* remake today, that film (directed by John Guillermin) was a box office smash in 1976. This *King Kong* was a critical hit, too. It's one of those strange remakes/reboots that was utterly successful and yet is rarely praised or revisited by anyone today. It's possible that had this *King Kong* come out in 1978, it might have been better remembered. But as it stands, this is one of those seventies blockbusters that drifts in the liminal space in the cultural consciousness as a film that just happened to exist between *Jaws* and *Star Wars*. In any case, the success of the '76 *King Kong* was at least part of the reason why Herbert believed Dino De Laurentiis was the right person for the job, saying, "Anyone who can make a giant ape should have no trouble with sandworms."

It also helped that hard-core sci-fi fans were aware that De Laurentiis was responsible for producing kitsch genre hits like 1968's *Barbarella* and 1980's *Flash Gordon*. Dino De Laurentiis was such a massive Hollywood mogul in the 1980s that Herbert's widow, Theresa Shackleford, tells me she saw him leave in the middle of dinner with President Ronald Reagan following a screening of *Dune* in December 1984. "What could have been more important than dinner with the president? That was power. I couldn't believe it."

All this bluster might make you think De Laurentiis steamrolled David Lynch into making the movie his way.

Interestingly, although Lynch is still upset about not having final cut on his *Dune*, he doesn't blame Dino De Laurentiis at all. As late as 1993, Lynch said, "Dino was very different than I expected—charming, warm and very persuasive . . . we loved each other."

The day-to-day production of the movie wasn't handled by Dino De Laurentiis, however. Instead, his daughter Raffaella became the first woman ever to produce a film with a budget of more than five million dollars. To the uninitiated, *Dune* might scan as a male-centric story, but its serious fans know that it's the female characters who hold the true power and move everything forward. This was true in real life with Raffaella De Laurentiis, a strong Bene Gesserit guiding David Lynch through the desert. "She is an astonishing person, she really is," said *Dune* production coordinator Golda Offenheim. "People will work their guts off because she's doing the same thing."

Alicia Witt, who played the young child Alia and turned eight years old while filming, also praises Raffaella De Laurentiis. In 2023, Witt tells me that De Laurentiis would not allow a certain blue eye dye to be used on extras or any cast members until she had tested it herself first. "She was the first one to test out the blue dye directly in her own eyeballs," Witt explains. "She wanted to see if it was safe. It wasn't! She was temporarily blinded. I thought that was a strong thing for someone to do. To take that risk was amazing."

Like her late brother, Raffaella felt very close to the novel. "I loved the book," she said, and firmly explained that in adapting the novel, she wanted to make sure the film captured the organic and fluid elements from the world of *Dune*. For Raffaella, her *Dune* was to be the antithesis of "big, science fiction, hardware movies." Like any true fan, Raffaella De Laurentiis knew *Dune* should be treated as art, not as a sci-fi product. "Anybody can do spaceships today," she said in 1984. "But we wanted to keep the movie true to the book and give it that mood, and for us to do that, you had to be able to care for the characters. We picked David Lynch to direct for that quality because he really cares for people."

"I went out and got a tape of *The Elephant Man*, and I got this funny gut feeling that we had finally found the guy who could do it," Herbert said in 1984. "David selects his visual metaphors with care and his treatment of suspense is magnificent."

When Lynch was first approached by Dino De Laurentiis to tackle a film version of *Dune*, he was completely ignorant of the novel. "I thought he said 'June,'" Lynch recalled, but then, after reading the book, he became enamored of doing it justice. "I was just knocked out," Lynch said. "Herbert created an internal adventure, one with a lot of emotional and physical textures. And I love textures." Later, Lynch admitted, "The most difficult thing was being true to the whole thing. . . . I couldn't reduce it to the point where the story's essence was lost. It's very dense with actions and levels of interpretation. So the rule I used to shape the script was common sense."

While it's tempting to laugh out loud at the idea that the famously idiosyncratic Lynch used "common sense" to craft *Dune*, this comment is also revealing and essential to truly appreciate what the 1984 *Dune* did for the world of science fiction cinema and the *Dune* fandom at large. It's easy and common to describe something arresting, macabre, and visually uncomfortable as "Lynchian," in the same way we all lazily refer to the erosion of public privacy as "Orwellian." But the cinematic effect of what we call "Lynchian" is simply the result of an artistic process that makes sense to David Lynch. And whether somebody likes this kind of art is sort of irrelevant, because one thing is apparent in all of Lynch's films, including *Dune:* This process works. You can call Lynch's films "weird" or "trippy," but they're not nonsensical. The hyperbolic nature of Lynch's cinematic storytelling isn't too far off from Herbert's calling his writing of *Dune* "high camp." It's wrong to think of Lynch as a camp director, but there are plenty of exaggerated and affected characters throughout his wholly unique oeuvre. Nobody does over-the-top like David Lynch, which includes *Dune*, a film in which we see Baron Harkonnen (Kenneth McMillan) eaten by a sandworm after Alia (Alicia Witt) stabs him. It's totally faithful to the novel to have Alia kill the baron. It's less faithful for the baron's body to then have a Looney Tunes–ish fate by falling into the gaping maw of a shai-hulud. The sandworm doesn't burp or anything—like the Sarlacc did when it ate Boba Fett in *Return of the Jedi*—but this moment is a good microcosm of just how far this *Dune* goes.

"There are some eccentric situations and performances in there," Kyle MacLachlan tells me with a wry smile. "But I happen to really enjoy that David created all that, you know?"

One piece of eccentric trivia interestingly serves as the perfect symbol for how Lynch worked on *Dune*. In the iconic scene in which Duke Leto rescues the workers harvesting the spice ("Damn the spice!"), Lynch himself plays one of the nameless miners, working tirelessly until the last minute to get as much spice loaded as possible before the sandworms attack. A common worker using common sense. Lynch didn't try to turn *Dune* into a non-narrative art-house film. Instead, he brought clear filmic structure to a novel that, in many ways, defied cinematic adaptation. Despite its length and detail, Herbert doesn't tell you what everything looks like, meaning all of the filmmakers behind the *Dune* films—from Lynch to John Harrison to Denis Villeneuve—ended up coming up with certain visuals on their own. Even John Schoenherr's sandworm illustration for the cover of the March 1965 issue of *Analog* was, to an extent, intuitive. The visual art of *Dune* is shaped by visual artists, working not against Herbert's prose but perhaps outside of it. In terms of cinematic art, Lynch was the first to actually pull it off, and he did that by using common sense, specifically the notion that he, as a filmmaker, would have to invent a lot of what this universe would look like on-screen. "A lot of things are left to your imagination, even in the book," Lynch said. "A lot of times [I'd] go searching for descriptions of things, but they weren't there."

Practically speaking, what David Lynch did with *Dune* was exactly what Paul and Jessica did when they encountered the Fremen. Yes, the Bene Gesserit have planted a myth here, but the Atreides family now must live it. Lynch had the book but had to bring that myth to life, a challenge that he admitted, even as the movie was about to hit theaters, was maybe impossible. Just before agreeing to take on *Dune*, Lynch had been approached by George Lucas to direct *Return of the Jedi*, which he declined in favor of *Dune*. Lucas, who, as we know, was clearly inspired by Frank Herbert, warned Lynch that trying to turn *Dune* into a movie was a mistake. "Well, [George Lucas] did say that you couldn't make the book into a movie," Lynch told *Rolling Stone* in 1984. "It's pretty true."

Even MacLachlan also expressed some dismay at just how different the script was from the novel. Paul and Chani's first child together exists nowhere in this version. And through the course of filming, the pivotal moment in which Paul defeats Jamis (Judd Omen) in a knife fight was cut from the film. This led to a strange detail that most viewers overlook. In several scenes, we see a character named Harah (Molly Wryn) with two very young boys, played by Danny Corkill and Diego Jose, in miniature stillsuits. In the final confrontation with the emperor, these kids are even seen holding the late Duke Leto's adorable pug. So who are these Fremen children? In the novel, after Paul kills Jamis in an honorable duel to the death, Jamis's sons, Orlop and Kaleff, become Paul's responsibility. Harah was Jamis's wife, but because Jamis doesn't exist in this film, she and her children are cinematically orphaned, mostly because we have no idea who they are.

The film also eliminated several supporting characters, like Lady Fenring and Count Fenring, as well as the smugglers of Arrakis. Herbert's beloved banquet scene doesn't exist in this script, and a huge subplot involving a conspiracy to frame Lady Jessica is also absent. Finally, and most prominently, this *Dune* also changed the nature of the Voice, by inventing the "weirding modules," physical weapons that fired sonic blasts.

"When I first read the script, I was disappointed," Mac-Lachlan said in 1984. "I came in saying 'I want *Dune.*'" What had initially biased him against the condensation of his favorite book wasn't just his fandom but his inexperience with screenplays in general. "It took me a little time to get used to the differences . . . scripts are like books in shorthand. Later, when I read a lot of other scripts, I realized how strong ours was and got really fired up to do it."

Despite the quixotic undertaking of turning the novel into a film, Lynch and Raffaella De Laurentiis hired an astounding team of artists to make *Dune* a cinematic reality. Lynch once again collaborated with cinematographer Freddie Francis, whom he'd worked with on *The Elephant Man.* The production designer was Anthony Masters, most famous then, and now, for the immortal aesthetic of *2001: A Space Odyssey.* Initial storyboards were drawn by Sherman Labby, who had previously created storyboards for *Blade Runner* but also for the 1956 sci-fi classic *Forbidden Planet.** The costumes, including the memorable rubber stillsuits, were designed by Bob Ringwood, who by 1989 would create Michael Keaton's batsuit for Tim Burton's *Batman.* The stillsuits were later built by Mark Siegel, who had also constructed costumes for two other big 1984 sci-fi films, *Ghostbusters* and *Star Trek III: The Search for Spock.* As Sean Young revealed, each stillsuit was created to be

---

* Raffaella De Laurentiis said, "We storyboarded it twice." This is why Sherman Labby isn't credited on the final film, because the second set of storyboards was done by Richard Malzahn.

formfitting, and every actor was subjected to having a plaster cast of their body made in Los Angeles before heading to Mexico for filming. As awesome as these costumes look, every single actor sweated pools of water out, making the suits do the opposite of what the stillsuits are supposed to do in the book: preserve every ounce of moisture. While they filmed in the Samalayuca Dunes, temperatures were often 120 degrees, meaning the stillsuits were just making everything worse. In the real-life versions of Arrakis on planet Earth, you'd never want to be wearing what Kyle MacLachlan is wearing in *Dune*, no matter how rad it looks.*

The sandworms and other creatures—including the Guild navigator—were designed by Carlo Rambaldi, who is probably best known in cinema history for giving the world the specific look of E.T. in 1982. "If you look at E.T., it looks like Carlo Rambaldi," Lynch joked. "And the same is true of the Guild navigator."

In terms of the sandworms and the visual effects—which were primarily handled by Barry Nolan—this is one part of the film's legacy that Kyle MacLachlan feels doesn't hold up as well as he'd like. Would *Dune* 1984 be better remembered if the sandworms were more badass? MacLachlan tells me that one of his favorite things about Villeneuve's *Dune* is simply that the sandworms look more realistic. "I especially enjoyed

---

*One unused costume design for this *Dune* featured a mesh window over the actor's chest. When fans posted photos of MacLachlan in this costume in 2022 on Twitter and asked why it wasn't used in the film, the actor replied, "First of all, mesh on the nipples, ouch!"

the sophistication of the special effects [in *Dune* 2021]," Mac-Lachlan explains. "We didn't have the ability to do that back then." That said, Herbert loved the way the film looked. In 1984, he praised the visuals of the film often.

"I get asked a specific question a lot of times, if the settings and the scenes I saw in David's film match my original imagination," Herbert said. "I must tell you some of them do, precisely, some of them don't and some of them are better . . . which is what you would expect of an artist such as David and Tony Masters. And I'm delighted. Why not take it and improve on it visually? As far as I'm concerned, the film is a visual feast."

In the film, Paul says ominously that "God created Arrakis to train the faithful." And the ordeal of the cast and crew in 1984's *Dune* runs parallel to the difficulty of adapting to living on Arrakis itself. Filming in Mexico City meant the production was beset with either extreme heat or, ironically, rain when nobody wanted it. Tires were burned to create black smoke for specific battle scenes, so much so that at the moment when Paul is reunited with Gurney Halleck (Patrick Stewart), MacLachlan briefly lost his voice because he'd accidentally inhaled toxic fumes.

Throughout the filming of *Dune*, in many cases, the danger to the cast members was real. This was the 1980s; none of the explosions are faked, and somewhat astoundingly, all the knife fights in *Dune* are performed by the actors themselves without stunt doubles, who were trained by martial arts expert Kiyoshi Yamazaki. What you see in the climactic duel between Paul and Feyd (played by rock-and-roll legend Sting) is, shot for shot, the actors themselves, with zero stand-ins. MacLachlan also revealed that when Paul fights the training robot toward the start of the film, that, too, included some realistic improvisational combat.

"Kiyoshi and I had choreographed a whole scene around this thing, depending upon the robot for certain moves here and there," MacLachlan said. "Well, I got into the ring and quickly found out that the robot could not be controlled quite as precisely as we'd expected. Consequently, I actually fought the robot."

One character who was supposed to get to do a lot more stabbing and knifing was young Alicia Witt as Alia Atreides. Although it is Alia who kills the baron in the film (which is the case in the novel, too), there was way more footage shot of her taking out various Harkonnen troops. "I thought it was really fun," Witt tells me. "Like, running through the desert and fake-stabbing the soldiers. A lot of it didn't end up in the film. In fact, in the movie, that famous scene where I'm standing there in the desert with the fires burning in the background, just after I've killed the baron, that was part of a bunch of other scenes filmed the night before."

Another actor who fights a lot in the 1984 *Dune* is Patrick Stewart as Gurney Halleck. Although Stewart would become world-famous to science fiction fans as Captain Jean-Luc Picard in *Star Trek: The Next Generation* in 1987, in 1983, during the filming of *Dune*, he was a late addition to the cast. So much so that Kyle MacLachlan tells me he had to explain all the *Dune* lingo to Patrick Stewart on their first day of filming. As Gurney, Kynes (Max von Sydow), Paul, and Duke Leto

(Jürgen Prochnow) headed out in an ornithopter to inspect the spice mining, MacLachlan was Stewart's personal tour guide to the planet Arrakis.

"It was one of Patrick's first films!"* MacLachlan says, referencing the fact that like MacLachlan himself, Stewart was mostly known for his theater work at that time. "Patrick was called in very late and sort of found himself in Mexico City on the set of *Dune* with me sitting in an ornithopter, talking about looking out the window and seeing giant worms. He was like, 'What the hell is going on!' So I kind of did a shorthand version of where we were and what was happening."

Stewart corroborates this story, telling me in 2022 that Kyle MacLachlan did in fact give him a *Dune* crash course on the set. "I was a late arrival in Mexico City," Stewart says. "There had been a rather difficult situation that had developed with the actor that originally was going to play my part."

The first actor cast to play Gurney was Aldo Ray, who, Sean Young later revealed, was struggling with alcohol addiction, which resulted in Ray's being "let go," as Stewart tells me. But the strangest aspect of filming *Dune* was that Stewart was double-booked at the time for a movie called *Uindii*, in the middle of production in Hamburg, Germany. Just as the Guild navigators can fold space and the Kwisatz Haderach can be in multiple places at the same time, Patrick Stewart essentially

---

*This is true-ish. While MacLachlan had done zero films before *Dune*, Stewart had done at least four movies before *Dune*, not to mention several TV appearances. His first was *Hennessy* in 1975, but in 1981, Stewart had starred in John Boorman's epic fantasy *Excalibur*.

existed in two parts of the world simultaneously to appear in *Dune*. "For about four weeks, I commuted between Europe and Mexico City," Stewart tells me with a laugh. "The whole experience was fun. Difficult, but fun. I got to be in a film with one of my heroes, Max von Sydow, and I met Kyle, who became a lifelong friend."

"Difficult, but fun" not only is a wonderful way to describe the entirety of the *Dune* books but also distills what became the legacy of the 1984 Lynch film. "At a certain point in the making of *Dune*, I think David got scared and felt like he was on a sinking ship and didn't know whether he would be able to make a great movie," Sean Young said. "And he was a little spoiled in that he'd only made great movies up till then."

Young was alluding to the various behind-the-scenes problems Lynch and Raffaella De Laurentiis had not just while making the film but also while editing it. The problems of Lynch's *Dune* can't be chalked up to just one thing. Had Lynch been given final cut on the film, it's still possible the movie would have felt incongruent. In short, if you think the 1984 *Dune* is bad, there's not really anyone to blame. As Lynch said in 1996, "It is what it is."

◄ ◄ ► ►

In the summer of 1984, Kyle MacLachlan was in New York City, looking at an immense painted image of his own face on the side of a building in Times Square. He turned to his friends and said, "That's me. That's the thing I have coming up." For nearly a year, MacLachlan had been prevented by his

Dune contract from auditioning for any other film or television projects, and so he was at "loose ends" until the film finally hit theaters in December. His friends were unimpressed by the giant image of MacLachlan as Paul. "No one cared," MacLachlan tells me with a laugh. "I was like, 'This is exciting.' But I was kind of treading water for a long time." MacLachlan tells me that he expected his life might be nothing but *Dune* movies for almost a decade. "The contract I had to sign with the De Laurentiis corporation was for five sequels," he says. "I don't know why they kept five, but they were definitely planning on *Dune Messiah* and *Children of Dune*. They were banking on the fact that the movie was going to be very successful and that I would be sought after once it came out. The whole idea was that they would have control over me to a certain degree. I had no choice but to sign because I hadn't ever done a movie, and this was my big opportunity. I ended up signing them, and of course, none of them actually were exercised. Which is probably just as well. But I was sorry about that. I was really looking forward to doing a sequel. Particularly doing *Messiah*. I think that would've been an interesting journey for Paul. But it never happened."

Because early cuts of *Dune* didn't satisfy executives at Universal, the marketing for the film wasn't what it could have been. Despite excellent coverage in niche science fiction and film publications like *Cinefantastique*, *Starlog*, and *Enterprise Incidents*, the mainstream promotion of *Dune* was severely curtailed by Universal. Harlan Ellison was even prevented from going to a press screening of the film, on the grounds that the studio wanted as few critics to see the movie before opening as possible. In the world of movie reviews, what was true in 1984 is still true in 2023: If a movie studio is preventing critics from seeing a film ahead of time, nine times out of ten, it's because the studio has lost faith in the project.

David Ansen, a film critic for *Newsweek*, notable for being one of the only critics in 1984 to give *Dune* a positive review, put it like this in 2003: "There was a big backlash against it . . . there was a lot of publicity about the movie before it opened . . . about how they were having all sorts of problems in Mexico . . . and the media kind of fed off of that. People smelled blood in the air. And there was a certain ganging up on the movie when it opened. . . . I do think a lot of my colleagues [other film critics] jumped on the bandwagon with undue viciousness." For Ellison, this bandwagon was caused by Universal itself, for not believing in the film once it was completed. "Most of what Universal did, in my view, is indefensible," Ellison said. "They had no faith in the film." Like MacLachlan's friends' being uninterested in the huge painting of him on a building, the studio itself pretended like the building had never been painted in the first place.

The legacy and reputation of this *Dune* remain mixed to this day. Unlike 1982's *Blade Runner* (one of MacLachlan's favorite films), 1984's *Dune* isn't universally regarded as a misunderstood science fiction masterpiece. While many fans (including this writer) hold the opinion that Lynch's *Dune* is a brilliant attempt and an enduring classic in the annals of science fiction cinema, there's still a caveat even among the movie's biggest fans. *Dune* 1984 is never called "perfect" or "flawless." Instead, all the praise for the film tends to come out as a backhanded compliment. Theresa Shackleford, Frank Herbert's third wife, who attended the premiere of the film with Herbert in Washington, DC, tells me that she felt the experience of watching the 1984 movie was like "watching a preview of the book." Meaning, Ellison ranted in 1985, "of the five hours *Dune* committed to film, only two hours and seventeen minutes made it to the screen." Ellison's implication that Lynch may have intended a five-hour *Dune* isn't factual. But in 1988, Lynch did express interest in putting out a cut longer than the theatrical release.

To this day, Lynch's biggest complaint about *Dune* is that his arrangement with De Laurentiis prevented him from controlling the final cut. However, most sources, including producer Raffaella De Laurentiis and Lynch himself, confirm that the fabled five-hour version was a "work print" that was screened only once during post-production and lacked any visual effects. Lynch says this was never intended to be "the final version." The 1988 TV version, produced by Universal and overseen by Raffaella De Laurentiis, was 176 minutes, putting it just under three hours, meaning there's just under 40 minutes of previously unseen footage in this cut. However, this is by no means a better or more complete version of the film. Although this version restored the pivotal fight between Paul and the Fremen warrior Jamis, in these scenes, none of the Fremen's eyes are blue, because these were deleted scenes to which visual effects hadn't been added. Most of the 1988 TV cut is like this, simply a mishmash of more scenes rather than better ones. Lynch didn't participate in this project and asked his name to be replaced with a pseudonym for it, which resulted in this version sporting the phrase "directed by Alan Smithee" in the opening credits. For those not in the film business, this is a standard nom de plume directors use when they don't want their name on a film. In this version, Lynch also used the name "Judas Booth" for his writing credit on *Dune*.

The larger point? A longer version of Lynch's *Dune* wouldn't necessarily have been better.

"When the movie came out, we were pretty hammered, critically," Kyle MacLachlan tells me. "I mean, just nobody liked it. I can't say I completely disagree. It's very dense material. It's very hard to follow. I think you had to be a fan of the book to appreciate what was happening. I mean, they actually handed out pieces of paper at the movie theaters, to help people connect the dots." In the same way Frank Herbert included a glossary of terms at the front of the first edition of *Dune*, Universal sent movie theaters similar cheat sheets to help audiences get the perceived wackiness of *Dune*.

But this single fact proves only one thing: The 1984 *Dune* came out at the wrong time. Today, nobody worries whether mainstream moviegoers can handle a bunch of complex science fiction nomenclature. We know they can. Keeping the continuity of the Marvel Cinematic Universe straight is more difficult logistically than following the plot of *Dune* and remembering everyone's name. Naturally, *Dune* has more philosophical depth and layers embedded into its story than, say, *Ant-Man*, but zany names and complex sci-fi conceits are no longer considered a barrier to entry in the twenty-first-century cinematic landscape. David Lynch's *Dune* crawled through the desert so Villeneuve's films could run. "I love that version," Timothée Chalamet said in 2021. "I watched it about two months before we started shooting. I have huge respect for Kyle's performance."

After the box office failure of *Dune*, Dino De Laurentiis funded David Lynch's next film, *Blue Velvet*, which starred Kyle MacLachlan in the lead role as Jeffrey Beaumont, a young man who returns to his small hometown and becomes involved in the bizarre twisted underbelly of the town's pervasive criminal element, specifically the psychotic Frank Booth (Dennis Hopper). Several other *Dune* cast members also appeared in *Blue Velvet*, including Dean Stockwell, Brad Dourif, and Jack Nance. For MacLachlan, it was the beginning of another kind of career, one that would result in what is probably his other most famous role, that of Special Agent Dale Cooper in Lynch's immortal series *Twin Peaks*. But none of these wonderful pieces of art could have been made without the 1984 film *Dune* coming first. Just as unmade *Dune*s benefited people like Ridley Scott, the first completed film version of *Dune* became the catalyst for David Lynch and Kyle MacLachlan's future astounding body of work. There's no world in which *Twin Peaks* is as good as it is without Lynch's meeting MacLachlan through *Dune*. So if you love *Twin Peaks*, the person everyone should probably thank is the late Frank Herbert.

"I went sailing with him once," MacLachlan tells me. "In Port Townsend, he took me on his sailboat. He was a lovely, hospitable, curious guy. Who knew he could sail? He created a desert planet, but he was just as comfortable in the water as he was in the sand."

10

Twilight of the Emperor

**The second *Dune* trilogy and
Frank Herbert's final decade.**

*The prophet is not diverted by illusions of past, present,
and future.*   —Leto II

While on tour for his fifth *Dune* book, *Heretics of Dune*, Frank Herbert asked his driver to pull over so he could buy a razor. It was the summer of 1984, about six months before the David Lynch *Dune* would hit theaters. Herbert had been rocking his giant beard since 1963, during the time the first *Dune* stories were written and published. His second wife, Beverly Herbert—whom he had been married to for thirty-eight years—had encouraged the beard, but the woman who was to become his third wife, Theresa Shackleford, did not. "Frank always thought of himself as Walt Whitman, and he admired Ernest Hemingway or the image of Ernest Hemingway," Shackleford tells me in 2022. "But I hated the beard. And so he called me and told me he shaved his beard off in the back of the car! He said, 'New life. New love.' He was a new person. Frank was never one to look back."

From 1981 until his death in 1986, the world of Frank Herbert and the saga of *Dune* changed immeasurably. During this time, Herbert published three *Dune* novels in very close succession, suffered the death of his wife Beverly, married Theresa Shackleford, and, tragically, died at the age of sixty-five from a pulmonary embolism, following a battle with pancreatic cancer. By the end of 1984's *Heretics of Dune*, the planet Arrakis was utterly decimated, with only one sandworm left alive, smuggled out by the Bene Gesserit. This meant that in 1985, Herbert's final *Dune* novel, *Chapterhouse: Dune*, became the first *Dune* novel in which the titular planet doesn't appear. Just a year before his death, Herbert destroyed Arrakis and didn't look back. And yet, although the eighties were the twilight of Frank Herbert's life, his widow doesn't remember him as bitter or cynical. To Theresa Shackleford, Herbert was full of life, right up to the end.

"He was the funniest, smartest person I've ever known," Shackleford tells me. "Every day was a celebration. He'd always find something to celebrate."

Three years before Beverly's death on February 7, 1984, and before he met Shackleford that spring, Herbert had good reason to celebrate. As 1979 passed into 1980, multiple renewals of the film option for *Dune* from Dino De Laurentiis meant the Herbert family was in the best financial shape of their lives. Nineteen seventy-six had seen the triumphant smash success of *Children of Dune*, which, although it was billed as the end of the "*Dune* trilogy," emboldened Herbert to write three more books, which can be described only as the most confidently bonkers sequels in any fiction series ever.

Other than various ghola clones of Duncan Idaho, and the now-wormified Leto II,* the fourth *Dune* novel, 1981's *God Emperor of Dune*, features exactly zero characters from previous *Dune* novels, mostly because the bulk of this novel takes place 3,500 years after the ending of *Children*. Structurally, *God Emperor of Dune* is bananas. If the first three *Dune* novels were unfairly labeled as dense or unapproachable, *God Emperor of Dune* pretty much lives up to *Dune's* "difficult" reputation. Instead of just telling readers exactly what happened to Leto after he fused with the sandworms at the end of *Children*, Frank Herbert decided to write an entire book that is metafictionally ascribed to Leto's "stolen journals." Like all of *Dune*—including the various prequels and sequels written by Brian Herbert and Kevin J. Anderson—the reader has to imagine a future date when the present tense of the novel will pass into future history and somebody, in this case historians, will curate all of this fictional text. *God Emperor* opens with a lecture from a future historian named Hadi Benotto, telling a group of colleagues that they've unearthed the lost writings of Leto II. Thankfully, the rest of the novel is not written in first person from the perspective of the main worm-man, but

---

*Herbert's original title for this book was *Sandworm of Dune*, which is a little like having the title of the book be *Dune Dune*. That said, in 2007, Brian Herbert and Kevin J. Anderson published *Sandworms of Dune*, the supposed "final" novel in the *Dune* saga.

instead sticks to the same kind of roving third-person point of view Herbert favors throughout the *Dune* books. The difference is that this book is punctuated by observations from worm-Leto, all from his "stolen journals," which, again, we have to imagine him writing with his tiny *Tyrannosaurus rex* hands, somewhere beyond the scope of the novel.

While brilliantly creative, *God Emperor of Dune* is the book where Herbert turns the *Dune* saga into what he often claimed it was about all along: a refutation of consolidated governmental power, and the danger of mixing that power with religion. Because we haven't watched Leto evolve into a deranged worm dictator in real time, the impact of *God Emperor* is more philosophical and less visceral. But even if the plotting in *God Emperor* is a bit more muddled than that of the previous three books, Herbert lands an exciting philosophical twist. Worm-Leto has created peace throughout the universe, but at the cost of freedom. Technology has stagnated across the empire, to the point where it somehow feels even more medieval than previous *Dune* books. Leto is secretly aware that all of this is bad and has set a secret plan into motion: the birth of a human who will be invisible to all prescience, who will go on to sire future humans, all of whom can control their own destinies, free from spice-induced future planning. The first person in this line of new humans is the best character in *God Emperor*, Siona Atreides.

We learn that Siona, a descendant of Ghanima, is the first human who has "prescience-cloaking" genes. In each *Dune* book, Herbert tends to float a new version of a "Chosen One," first Paul, then Leto II in *Children*, and then, in *God Emperor*,

Siona. In the next book, 1984's *Heretics of Dune*, Herbert's final Chosen One is Sheeana Brugh, who, we later learn, is a descendant of Siona and possesses the superpower of being able to tell the sandworms what to do.* In the first three novels, Herbert's themes suggest that we all suffer the fates handed down to us by our family, that pain and tragedy are, on some level, inherited. Throughout *Dune*, each Atreides "hero" tries to break this cycle, until, eventually, Siona and, fifteen hundred years later, Sheeana do operate with a degree of autonomy that characters in *Dune* never had in the previous three novels. Back in 1963, John Campbell worried that Paul's prescience was a superpower that could overcome the entire narrative. And in 1981, and again in 1984, Herbert freed the future humans of his fiction from anyone's knowing their fate through prescience. If Herbert were Kurt Vonnegut, then his killing of Leto and the empowerment of Siona would be like the moment at the end of *Breakfast of Champions* when Vonnegut releases his fictional character Kilgore Trout, allowing him to follow his own destiny.

Although Herbert's messiahs in the first two *Dune* novels were specifically male, everything after *Children*, and specifically the creation of Siona and Sheeana, suggests his belief

---

*Both Siona and her descendant Sheeana are very reminiscent of Rey (Daisy Ridley) from the *Star Wars* sequel films, starting with *The Force Awakens*. In fact, because Sheeana lives on Rakis (formerly Arrakis) at the start of *Heretics* and is unaware of her heritage, she is very much the *Dune* version of Rey. So much so, you have to wonder if Daisy Ridley could play Sheeana in some future film adaptation.

that the future was female. In the final moments of *God Emperor*, after worm-Leto has been killed, Siona explains to Duncan that her fate is invisible to any form of prescience. "I'm the new Atreides," she says, closing the novel. "The multitude is there, but I walk silently among them, and no one sees me."

"Frank believed women should be running everything," Theresa Shackleford tells me. "He worshipped women. And I think that comes across in those books."

For whatever reason, neither Siona Atreides nor Sheeana Brugh tends to make it on the list of everyone's favorite *Dune* characters. This is a small tragedy because the final three Frank Herbert–penned *Dune* novels are filled with several underrated and very interesting people who are basically invisible to fans because the vast majority of readers never make it beyond the first book, much less the third or fourth. Herbert's characters in the second *Dune* trilogy may not seem as classic or original as those who populate the first novel. But even when the characters are remixed with familiar names and attributes, Herbert still tries to do something new. Even the titular God Emperor of Dune, Leto II, is essentially a new character. In *Children of Dune*, Leto II is a child who, like his father, Paul, before him, shoulders a huge burden and takes over as ruler of the universe by the end. But in *God Emperor*, thousands of years have passed and Leto II is a giant half-sandworm mutant.

And though we get a variety of different versions of Duncan duplicates in *God Emperor*, *Heretics*, and *Chapterhouse*, each of those Duncans is, technically, a different man. If there are contemporary *Dune* movie adaptations or TV series that tackle the post-*Children* novels, Jason Momoa clearly has his work cut out for him.

It is certainly not true that *God Emperor of Dune* is the greatest of Herbert's books. But because the central character is a half-worm/half-man dictator in charge of a breeding program that leads to his own downfall, it's certainly the *Dune*-iest and straight-up weirdest of the books. For this reason, it's possible that the very best version of *God Emperor* might be the rare, almost never discussed shorter version, buried in the pages of the January 1981 issue of *Playboy*. Unlike the first three *Dune* novels, which were serialized in the science fiction magazines *Analog* and *Galaxy* prior to publication, the fourth book appeared in *Playboy* roughly four months before the hardcover novel version was published by Putnam in April 1981. But this was no ordinary book excerpt designed for a magazine. Instead of chopping up *God Emperor of Dune* into bite-size installments spread out over several issues, legendary *Playboy* fiction editor Alice K. Turner convinced Frank Herbert to do something radical: condense the entirety of the novel into seventeen large-format pages of an oversize "Holiday Anniversary" issue. With a cover dominated by Barbara Bach; an extensive interview with John Lennon and Yoko Ono—published literally the same month as Lennon's death; an essay from Stephen King on the state of horror movies; and a new short story from Ray Bradbury, it's understandable that *God Emperor of Dune*'s big debut is somewhat muted in this particular vintage *Playboy*. And yet, it is mentioned on the cover, at the bottom of the right-hand side: "The New Episode in Frank Herbert's Great 'Dune' Saga." By 1981, *Dune* was mainstream enough to make the cover of *Playboy* but also, apparently, malleable enough to present its most complex installment in highly abridged form.

Alice K. Turner acquired and edited fiction for *Playboy* from 1980 to 2000. She was an iconoclastic editor who published a variety of prominent writers in *Playboy*, including Ursula K. Le Guin, Joyce Carol Oates, David Foster Wallace, and countless others. Her attitude toward the rest of *Playboy* was famously flippant and adversarial, meaning her work as an editor was often transgressive. The publication of *God Emperor of Dune* certainly fits with Turner's style: The story appears to support a creepy worm-man who has an all-female cult worshipping him, only to reveal an ending in which that man is killed by his followers and a woman wins true freedom for all mankind. And in the shorter, breezier version of *God Emperor* that she published in *Playboy*, the paradox of the later *Dune* novels, prequels, and spinoffs is fully revealed. These books are perhaps more fun to talk about than to read.

Despite not hitting number one on the *New York Times* bestseller list, *God Emperor of Dune* was solidly reviewed and sold extremely well in hardcover. *The Cincinnati Enquirer* enthused, "Once again, Frank Herbert has given his best." Meanwhile, *The Baltimore Sun* pointed out that *God Emperor* "allows Herbert to bring much that is buried perplexingly in its precursors out into the light." This assessment is essentially correct: If you feel like you didn't fully grasp the contradictory and winding philosophy of *Dune*, then *God Emperor* is the book where Herbert makes it all much clearer, by making it way more complicated. *God Emperor* serves as both a cap to the story that began with the first novel and also a soft reboot, allowing Herbert to jump ahead even further into the future for the fifth book, *Heretics of Dune*, which takes place fifteen hundred years after *God Emperor* and ends with the destruction of Arrakis.

In 1981, Frank Herbert inked "the biggest science fiction book contract in history" for *Heretics of Dune*. But because of Beverly Herbert's failing health, this book wasn't completed until 1983. At this time, the Herberts were living in Hawaii, hoping that the weather could help the ailing Beverly. Her battle with lung cancer had been ongoing since 1974, and although several surgeries had prolonged her life, she died on February 7, 1984, in Maui, at only fifty-seven years old. The Lynch film was in post-production. *Heretics* was about to hit bookstores, and Frank Herbert's life had changed forever.

Anyone who might think Herbert's courtship and marriage to Theresa Shackleford happened quickly after the death of Beverly Herbert would be correct. But it's also important to note that Shackleford had never met Herbert until the spring of 1984 and tells me, "Frank would have never looked at me had Bev been alive." In fact, before meeting the legendary author, Shackleford had no interest in science fiction, *Dune*, or Frank Herbert at all.

"I was in LA at the time. Putnam would hire a publicist to arrange the schedule, and that would mean I would be there to get the author a glass of water or whatever," Shackleford says. "What was funny was that Dick Francis—who wrote all those great mystery novels—was coming to town at the exact same time Frank was gonna be there. And I was like, 'Oh, please let me get Dick Francis.' But Putnam told me, 'Frank is a very important author to us, and he recently lost his wife, and he's very fragile, and we want you to just be with him and treat him with kid gloves.' Evidently, after Bev died, he'd gone into seclusion for a while. This was his first foray out into the world again. They were worried about the pressure he was feeling. He and Bev were famously joined, you know?"

In the days before text messages and cell phones, book publicists anonymously met authors by casually holding a copy of the author's novel in a predetermined place. Wearing a "blue dress" and waiting in the lobby of a Beverly Hills hotel, Theresa Shackleford held a copy of *Heretics of Dune*, to let Frank Herbert know she was the person handling him for the Los Angeles leg of the book tour. But, just a few weeks prior, Shackleford had obtained CliffsNotes for *Dune* in order to give herself a crash course on the novels up to that point.

"That cracked Frank up, later," she tells me. "He didn't even know there were CliffsNotes of *Dune*. He was like, 'What did they say about me!' He thought it was hilarious. Of course, after we got together, I read all the books and loved them. But I had the benefit of being able to ask the author any questions I had."

Shackleford was twenty-nine years old when she met Herbert in that hotel lobby. For her, it wasn't love at first sight.

"I didn't think of him as somebody to date, at all," she tells me. "I know there were several women who were chomping at the bit to go out with him. But in those first two days when I was with him on that book tour, he did seem sort of fragile. I remember before we got out of the car to go to a restaurant,

I just put my hand on his shoulder and said, 'Hang in there.' I said to him, 'You've just got one more thing to get through and then you can go back to the hotel and you can rest.' And he looked at me like I had scalded him. I surely didn't think he was falling in love with me. I thought maybe I'd done something wrong by touching him. Later he would tell me that when I touched him, it did sort of sear him."

After Herbert had finished with his LA events for *Heretics of Dune*, he flew to DC to be interviewed by Larry King. But he called Shackleford long-distance to tell her he was in love with her and wanted to marry her.

"It was one of the most shocking conversations of my life," Shackleford says with a laugh. "I was a little freaked out by him at first. But I wasn't seeing anyone at the time, and we started talking on the phone. For four and five hours at a time, and those were still the days when an operator would come on the line and tell you that somebody had to pay for the call! I don't know if other people have told you this, but Frank was the most fun person to talk to. He was the most fun person to be around. He knew something about everything, but he wasn't pedantic about it. And he never made you feel inferior or lacking in any way. He's the most brilliant person by far that I've ever been around."

By the end of 1984, Herbert had moved in with Theresa Shackleford, and the two lived in Los Angeles together for the last two years of his life. They weren't married when they attended the premiere of *Dune* in Washington, DC, in December, but by 1985 they were. Herbert told Waldenbooks in 1984 that he'd shaved his beard to "rebrand," and because he was "uncomfortable" with his fans thinking of him as a kind of "bearded guru." But it seems just as possible he shaved that beard for Theresa.

Frank Herbert felt that his marriage to Theresa Shackleford had given him a new lease on life. But from 1984 until his death in 1986, he was plagued with health problems. At one point, doctors worried Herbert had Crohn's disease, but then, in 1985, Herbert was diagnosed with adenocarcinoma of the liver. To treat this cancer, Herbert underwent a radical procedure at a university in Madison, Wisconsin. His body was given a fever on purpose as part of this treatment, which caused Herbert to lose weight. Eventually, it was determined that Herbert had pancreatic cancer. Following surgery to remove that cancer, Herbert died not from the cancer itself, but from a blood clot in his lung. This pulmonary embolism is what killed him. Tellingly, in these final days, Herbert had begun to write again and had had a special new computer and keyboard set up in his bed. He died while typing.

"Pancreatic cancer was a death sentence back then," Shackleford tells me. "I'm sixty-six now. I'm older than he was now when he died. I can't believe that." Today, this kind of cancer is still hard to beat, and Shackleford suggests that what kept Herbert alive longer than many others with the same diagnosis was the radical heat treatment.

When Frank Herbert died at sixty-five years old, many newspapers carried a photo of the bearded version of the author. The man who had become reborn, the man who looked thinner and younger than he'd been in years, the hopeless romantic who was suddenly wearing jeans and living in LA, was gone. Herbert is remembered for *Dune*, and the image of him as the real-life messiah of *Dune* has endured. But the man who loved with abandon was lost to time. If Beverly Herbert was the Chani to Frank's Paul, then Theresa Shackleford is Princess Irulan. The one who was left behind, to remember and remind us that once, the messiah was just a man.

Walk Without Rhythm

The phantom menace of the new *Dune* novels and the Sci Fi Channel miniseries.

Damn sandworms, up thirteen percent . . . welp, I better find a job. —Michael Keaton as Beetlejuice (1988)

For teenagers in the 1990s, the two most famous men to have ever tangoed with sandworms were Michael Keaton and Kevin Bacon. Although neither Keaton nor Bacon has ever been attached to a *Dune* film or TV project, they starred in iconic movies sporting sandworms, both of which couldn't have existed without *Dune*. In 1988, Tim Burton's gothic tour de force *Beetlejuice*—starring Keaton in the title role—gave the world skinny, black-and-white-striped Claymation sandworms, not unlike those that artist Don Punchatz drew for the 1974 Ace paperback edition of *Dune*, on which a Fremen outstretches his arms like a rock star. In 1990, Kevin Bacon created one degree of separation between himself and *Dune* by starring in *Tremors*, a horror-comedy in which people in a small desert town in Nevada are plagued by attacks from "Graboids," miniature versions of shai-hulud, that come across as what *Dune*'s sandworms would look like if they were imagined by Oscar the Grouch.

If you add up the appearances of the Graboids in the various *Tremors* films,* the sandworms in *Beetlejuice*, and the wildly popular animated cartoon of the same name,† the total number of minutes in which ersatz, non-*Dune* sandworms are seen on-screen is easily quadruple the amount of screen time legit shai-hulud sandworms got in the 1984 Lynch film. So if you were a young person in the 1990s, and you'd never read *Dune* or watched the 1984 film on VHS, cable, or network TV, then your idea of what a monster sandworm was came exclusively from *Dune* parodies. When Fatboy Slim and Bootsy Collins recorded the dance hit "Weapon of Choice" in the year 2000 (it was released the following year), the lyric *Walk without*

---

*As of 2020, there are a staggering seven individual *Tremors* movies, not to mention the short-lived TV series *Tremors*, which, bizarrely, aired on the Sci Fi Channel from March 28, 2003, to August 8, 2003. Because *Children of Dune* first aired on March 16, 2003, on the Sci Fi Channel, it's conceivable that an innocent viewer watching various reruns on Sci Fi throughout 2003 might have believed the network was specifically obsessed with sandworms that year and broke that addiction only in December 2003, when the *Battlestar Galactica* miniseries hit.

†From 1989 to 1991, an animated children's version of *Beetlejuice* ran on ABC, and then, in late 1991, on Fox affiliates. As in the film, Beetlejuice (voiced by Stephen Ouimette) hates sandworms, but in the animated show the sandworms have their own realm called "Sandworm land." It looks exactly like how you'd imagine an early nineties cartoon rendering of a faux Arrakis. The cartoon *Beetlejuice* was so successful that it briefly aired on both ABC and Fox at the same time.

rhythm and you won't attract the worm could only really be a reference to the book versions of *Dune*, since, at that time, sandworm imposters were much more well-known than the real thing. So listen up, goth kids of the nineties and early aughts: If you believed Fatboy Slim was making a *Beetlejuice* reference in the year 2001, you're totally forgiven. It was a confusing time for sandworm lovers everywhere.

There's no question that the biggest *Dune* renaissance occurred in the twenty-first century. But that process began in 1999, arguably one of the most pivotal years in science fiction history, period. That year saw the release of *The Matrix* and the first *Star Wars* prequel film, *Episode I: The Phantom Menace*. And in October 1999, five months after George Lucas went back in time to tell the origin story of his galaxy far, far away, Brian Herbert and Kevin J. Anderson released the first *Dune* prequel, *House Atreides*.

Set thirty-eight years before the events of the first novel,[*] the story of *House Atreides* connects the *Dune* dots for various character histories. Calling it *House Atreides* is a bit of a misnomer because the book reveals the backstories of Jessica, Duncan, Emperor Shaddam IV, Duke Leto's father, and Duke Leto himself. In their quest to fill out the entire history of the *Dune* universe, Herbert and Anderson have left no grain of sand unturned, resulting in books that have been as contro-

---

[*]Interestingly, *Star Wars: The Phantom Menace* is set thirty-two years before the original film, which means in 1999, both the *Dune* and *Star Wars* franchises released game-changing prequels set three decades before their originating stories.

versial as they have been bestselling. As Frank Herbert's eldest son, Brian Herbert had been a novelist in his own right for decades before coauthoring *House Atreides* with Kevin J. Anderson. Meanwhile, Anderson was a successful science fiction writer, too, widely loved for his various *Star Wars* novels.

According to Brian Herbert, he'd initially resisted writing *Dune* continuation novels set in his father's famous fictional universe. But an editor named Ed Kramer "kept after" him. Kramer's initial concept was to coedit a one-off anthology of short *Dune* fiction, with each story written by a different science fiction author. One of the authors who was interested was Kevin J. Anderson. Around this time, Brian Herbert got a call from his estate lawyer, who informed him of the existence of two safe-deposit boxes that, according to Brian Herbert, contained "papers and old-style floppy computer disks that included comprehensive notes from an unpublished DUNE 7." As far as most people know, nobody has seen these disks and notes other than the lawyer, Anderson, and Brian Herbert. To date, none of the raw material has ever been made available to the public. This isn't to say what the younger Herbert has divulged is somehow not factual, simply that we have no other sources to confirm it. Even aspects of "Spice Planet" are contained in the Fullerton library archives. But any raw "Dune 7" notes remain within the purview of the Herbert estate, perhaps for understandable reasons.

The long and short of all of this is that these notes apparently contained a narrative smoking gun that allowed Anderson and Brian Herbert to retroactively create prequel novels, which would eventually justify a huge twist in the long-awaited concluding novels. "By the end of *Chapterhouse*, the characters had been driven into a corner, utterly beaten," Brian Herbert said. "And then the reader learned that the Honored Matres themselves were running from an even greater mysterious threat . . . a peril that was drawing close to the protagonists of the story, most of whom were Bene Gesserit reverend mothers. . . . Now Kevin and I knew for certain where Frank Herbert had been headed, and we could weave the events of our prequel into a future grand finale for the series."

So where was Frank Herbert supposedly headed with "Dune 7"? What was the "even greater mysterious threat"? According to everything that happens in these continuation books, the short answer is: evil robots.

Wait. What? If you've never once ventured into the *Dune* continuation novels by Kevin J. Anderson and Brian Herbert, it might be impossible to believe that these *Dune*s contain malevolent AI hell-bent on destroying humanity. And yet, the vague backstory for *Dune* does mention a historical event called "the Butlerian Jihad," in which humankind defeated oppressive "thinking machines." Although *Dune* famously contains no aliens and no robots, Frank Herbert did stick a kind of *Terminator*-style AI uprising into the ancient history of his universe. And the fact that he left that concept in the backstory of the first novel is telling. While a mysterious group called the "Ones of Many Faces" does exist in *Chapterhouse: Dune*, Frank Herbert stops short of outright confirming that an evil AI is out there plotting to destroy everyone. In the spinoff novels, the two leaders of this ancient thinking machine empire are called Omnius and Erasmus. Nearly everything in the Brian Herbert and Kevin J. Anderson books connects to these concepts, which is coupled with a very liberal use of gholas. When they got around to doing "Dune 7," Anderson and Herbert split it into two books, *Hunters of Dune* (2006) and *Sandworms of Dune* (2007). In the final book, nearly every single famous *Dune* character is brought back to life as a ghola, making the copious Duncan Idaho duplicates from Frank Herbert's original books seem quaint by comparison. In *Hunters* and *Sandworms*, it's not a question of if a classic character will return from the dead, it's when.

As of 2023, there are a total of sixteen *Dune* novels written by Brian Herbert and Kevin J. Anderson, of which only two—*Hunters of Dune* and *Sandworms of Dune*—are sequels to Frank Herbert's original six novels. In the grand scheme of *Dune*'s mythology, these books have done the impossible: complicate the mythology of *Dune* even more than Herbert had, but also keep the franchise alive as a series of contemporary books, which results in occasional solar flares of genius, combined with a steady stream of fan service for the diehards, who of course don't entirely agree about these books anyway.

Unlike Frank Herbert's first three *Dune* novels, these books present a stiff barrier to entry. Some novels are more approachable than others, but for the most part, the existence of all the "expanded *Dune*" books can be thought of like this: Imagine if every footnote in the book you're holding was expanded into its own essay collection. The expanded *Dune* novels favor information first and artistry and theme second. As Kristina K. Iodice put it in her 1999 review of *House Atreides* for the *Fort Worth Star-Telegram:* "The narratives are too lengthy. Only the wealth of information that clarifies points in the later novels sustains readers through some sections." John R. Alden of *The Philadelphia Inquirer* noted that readers could start with this novel before having read *Dune*, writing in his review, "[It's] successful enough to stand on its own as an epic space opera. But the real pleasure here comes from watching the authors lay out the plot threads that will converge in *Dune*."

Both these 1999 reviews of *House Atreides* are a microcosm of how to think about all sixteen of the spinoff *Dune* novels. The boundaries of *Dune* were endlessly expanded, and yet, the reader's interest in these books still leads back to the original novels every single time. The popularity of Kevin J. Anderson and Brian Herbert's *Dune* books is very similar to the popularity of the *Star Wars* prequels* insofar as everything that people like about these books reminds them of the originals, and everything that has caused fan controversies either feels in conflict with the originals or doubles down on aspects of them that felt murky to begin with. Much has been written and said about the nature of these books and whether they "really count" when it comes to *Dune* canon. But there's only one thing in them that truly made a huge and lasting impact on the entity of the saga: These books brought one of science

---

*Analogously, it's probably better to compare the expanded *Dune* books to the various post-2015 *Star Wars* films, TV shows, and endless books and comic books. George Lucas famously was in charge of the *Star Wars* prequels, whereas with the newer shows and films, he's not. And like the different Disney+ *Star Wars* shows, each *Dune* spinoff novel tends to be very connected to something fans are familiar with. Usually.

fiction's oldest (and most tired) tropes—killer robots—into the *Dune* saga, forever. The in-development HBO Max prequel TV series *Dune: The Sisterhood* is based on the 2011 prequel novel *Sisterhood of Dune*, which opens just after the end of the Butlerian Jihad. So there's a good bet that killer AI will be a part of the visual *Dune* canon for a while, even if the original novels generally sidestep this common science fiction trope.

Just one year after the publication of *Dune: House Atreides*, the writer and director of a massive new made-for-TV *Dune* miniseries seemed to present a slightly opposite viewpoint from some of the expanded *Dune* novels. John Harrison, who had worked as a first assistant director on *Day of the Dead* (1985) and was the director of *Tales from the Darkside: The Movie* (1990), would eventually transform the first three novels into two epic miniseries, 2000's *Frank Herbert's Dune* and 2003's *Frank Herbert's Children of Dune*. And in the year 2000, he made it clear that this story wasn't about killer AI at all.

"[*Dune*] is not about technology overwhelming human beings," Harrison said. "It is not about space wars . . . it's a story about the human condition." In the summer of the year 2000, just as *Tremors 3* was green-lit as a direct-to-video production, Harrison was hoping his new version of *Dune* would help shake off the sandworm posers and bring Frank Herbert's vision back to its proper place of zeitgeist dominance, with not one robot or black-and-white-striped sandworm in sight. "I wanted to approach it the same way Herbert laid it out," Harrison said in 2000. "To tell the story the way Herbert told it . . . in three nights."

Both the 2021 and 2023 *Dune* films list John Harrison as a producer. This is because he was the last person to successfully produce and direct *Dune*, which means Warner Bros. and Legendary Pictures had to make a deal relative to the screenplay and film option rights to *Dune*. In 2022, Harrison tells me that he had nothing to do with the Villeneuve versions, but from a structural point of view, his *Dune*s represent a bridge between the various earlier attempts and the high-level prestige treatment *Dune* enjoys in the 2020s. Villeneuve's approach to filming *Dune* was to make sure he was allowed to adapt the first novel with two films instead of one, an idea pioneered by the 2000 and 2003 Harrison-produced miniseries.

"After David's movie, I think people thought, 'This is not an adaptable story,'" Harrison tells me in 2022. "Nobody wanted to do it. The only way we got a chance to do it is because Richard [Rubinstein] and I pitched it as a television miniseries. And I was able to convince people that we could do this in three nights, as opposed to trying to cram this book into a two-hour, two-and-a-half-hour movie. It's just too much material. There's too much good stuff."

Directed by Harrison and shot by legendary cinematographer Vittorio Storaro—who won an Oscar for *Apocalypse Now*—the Sci Fi Channel's production of *Frank Herbert's Dune* was an original miniseries that ran from Sunday, December 3, 2000, to Tuesday, December 5, 2000. The total average viewership for the initial broadcast was roughly 4.4 million viewers. According to an analysis from *Broadcasting and Cable* published on December 10, 2000, "despite a slow start and a notoriously complicated storyline, Sci-Fi Channel's adaptation of *Dune* became the most watched program in the network's history . . . this miniseries is a decided home run."

The success of this miniseries spawned a 2003 sequel miniseries, *Children of Dune*, which adapted both *Dune Messiah* and the titular novel in one script. In a positive review in *Variety*, Laura Fries wrote, "Give exec producer Richard P. Rubinstein credit for recognizing the shortcoming of David Lynch's 1984 movie and the confounding mythology of the books: He has made *Children of Dune* decidedly more accessible even if that means more soaplike."

If we leave the knee-jerk twentieth-century mainstream drumbeat that *Dune* has "confounding mythology" to one side, Fries does accurately describe what is simultaneously wonderful and challenging about both Sci Fi Channel *Dune* miniseries. In the era just before mainstream prestige sci-fi drama, a TV movie version of *Dune* looks and feels like what you would expect from TV movies from the early aughts, a faithful-ish adaptation of the books but rendered as a very well-produced and brilliantly cast soap opera. If the Lynch film employed aspects of surreal camp to highlight the ostentatious flavor of the novel, the Sci Fi Channel versions do the same thing, but instead, the hyperbole here comes from the soapy not-quite-prestige TV style of the time. The early-aughts *Dunes* are what *Babylon 5* is relative to the reboot *Battlestar Galactica* or *The Expanse*; they created the foundation for serious and in-depth science fiction TV but lack the mainstream flavor of their successors. Because the production values of the rebooted *Battlestar Galactica* have aged slightly better, it feels like the beginning of the Sci Fi Channel's golden period, even though *Frank Herbert's Dune* and *Children of Dune* happened first.

The microcosm for this collision of intended audiences and sensibilities can be found in the original TV trailers that ran on cable ahead of the launch of the miniseries. Embarrassingly, the 2000 *Dune* was described as "a Sciniseries Event," a bizarre pun in which we're supposed to get that "Mini" has been swapped for "Scini," even though the "Sci" in "Sci Fi" is clearly pronounced "Sigh," not "Sih." While this marketing term was not cooked up by Harrison, there's something perfect in still thinking of the 2000 *Dune* as a "Sciniseries." Like *rockumentary* or any other silly nineties cable TV portmanteau, the word captures the naïve quirkiness of these *Dunes*, while it also reveals the very specific fact that these two miniseries could not have withstood the scrutiny of a mainstream theatrical release and basically weren't even trying for that kind of audience.

The only crime the Sci Fi *Dunes* have committed in the history of the flowing spice is that they were filmed and released at the wrong time. While the CGI effects of the late nineties and early 2000s have a certain charm, it's clear that *Frank Herbert's Dune* didn't have Lucasfilm's Industrial Light & Magic on their side. Spacecraft move through space with an eerie and realistic silence in this *Dune*, but today, the ships of the 1984 *Dune* seem more believable. In fact, because the visual effects feel very much of their time, both Sci Fi *Dunes* are perhaps unfairly judged. Cinematically, the Lynch film probably holds up better, but had Harrison and Storaro had access to *Phantom Menace*–level VFX, it's kind of a toss-up which version may have been better remembered.

What the Sci Fi *Dune*s lack in slick visual effects, they more than make up for in star power. *Frank Herbert's Dune* starred William Hurt, right smack-dab in the middle of his official sci-fi movie dad phase, just two years after he played a space dad in the 1998 *Lost in Space* and before his turn as a robot dad in 2001's *AI: Artificial Intelligence*. Meanwhile, *Children of Dune* starred Susan Sarandon and James McAvoy—as Wensicia Corrino and Leto II Atreides, respectively. The former, as discussed in the introduction, basically cast herself in the role, while James McAvoy was very much not the James McAvoy we think of today. These films also starred Alec Newman as Paul, Barbora Kodetová as Chani, Laura Burton as the child version of Alia, and renowned character actor Ian McNeice as the baron. In the 2000 miniseries, Saskia Reeves played Lady Jessica, but when she was unavailable for the 2003 follow-up, Alice Krige stepped in. Krige is probably most famous to sci-fi fans for her role as the Borg Queen in *Star Trek: First Contact*, in which she was the ultimate foe for Patrick Stewart, proving, once again, that *Dune* is a crossroads of all other sci-fi franchises. Joining Krige in *Children of Dune* were Jessica Brooks as Paul's daughter, Ghanima Atreides, and Daniela Amavia as Alia, the only person (to date) to portray Alia in her adult years.*

"This stuff is hard, because it's so bonkers," McAvoy told

---

* In 2023, Alicia Witt told me that she is open to playing an adult version of Alia should the new films ever get around to *Children of Dune*. Witt also said that at forty-seven, she "might be too old now," but considering Paul is always a little older in the movies than in the book, and that the miniseries made Leto and Ghanima much older, you never know.

journalist Hoai-Tran Bui in 2021. "I was in an adaptation of the second and third books. But I've read them all cover to cover, and I love those books. They're crazy. . . . I mean, the level of bonkers is unparalleled. But I love them."

If these *Dune*s had come out as Netflix shows in 2013 instead of on Sci Fi in 2000 and 2003, then it's possible they would have become the defining versions, akin to a TV version of Peter Jackson's *The Lord of the Rings*. If Villeneuve's *Dune* films had never materialized, the most faithful filmed versions of *Dune* would still be these two Sci Fi Channel miniseries. As Emmet Asher-Perrin put it in 2014, *Frank Herbert's Dune* is "the most okay version of *Dune*, ever." This might sound like a case of damning with faint praise, but prior to the 2020s, for most hard-core fans, calling a filmed version of *Dune* "okay" is a huge compliment. While the production values of both Harrison-produced miniseries haven't aged well, their ambition and scope are praiseworthy, enjoyable, and in the grand scheme of *Dune*, unique insofar as almost nothing about these adaptations scans as unfaithful. Even when character backstories and arcs are expanded drastically, these changes feel perfectly appropriate, specifically the fact that the unifying narrative voice of Princess Irulan (Julie Cox) has a hugely expanded role that drastically departs from the novel, even though it feels very faithful.

"The key to a great adaptation is creating what is called the illusion of fidelity," *Frank Herbert's Dune* co-producer Mitchell Galin said in 2000. "This is sort of how Herbert really saw this character [Irulan]. We're not really straying far afield emotionally with what he's doing with this character." In the first three *Dune* novels, Irulan is the most overstated and under-stated character simultaneously. Overstated, because her co-pious epigraphs are scattered throughout the first novel. And understated, because she simply doesn't appear in real time as much as it seems like she should, and her total romantic love of Paul is admitted offstage in *Dune Messiah*.

"My agent in London had already cast a couple of people in this and she mentioned it to me and didn't realize that I was already a big fan of the book," Julie Cox recalled in 2000. Although Irulan is not technically the narrator of *Dune*, her epigraphs do create a veneer of plausibility that what you are reading is an amalgamation of her various texts.

"In my book, the character is the narrator," Cox said. "But in the miniseries, she plays a much more active role. I like the way John [Harrison] adapted it very much, he made it stronger."

Cox's film career began in 1994, when she played the "Childlike Empress" in *The Neverending Story III*. Strangely enough, in between *Frank Herbert's Dune* (2000) and *Children of Dune* (2003), Cox starred with *Dune* veteran Patrick Stewart in a TV miniseries loosely based on *King Lear* called *King of Texas*. And although her career extends to such contemporary TV classics as *Broadchurch*, Cox's performance as Irulan in both Sci Fi *Dune*s does accurately demonstrate her immense talent. Because 2003's *Children of Dune* takes place well after Paul and Chani's children are adults, Cox takes Irulan where Herbert and other *Dune* films never could: from ambitious princess to lonely stepparent of the heirs of the known universe. "She's very intelligent . . . coquettish when she needs to be, but not for her own personal gain," Cox said in 2000. "She's Bene Gesserit trained, [so] she has a very childlike quality, but great maturity and wisdom. She'd probably be a better emperor than her father."

What goes unsaid by Cox is that the version of Irulan she played would also probably be a better emperor than Paul. There are no Marvel-style what-ifs in the *Dune* canon, but if there were, an alternate universe in which Irulan somehow becomes emperor instead of Paul would probably be the most interesting. As played by Cox, Princess Irulan is the number one reason *Dune* fans should watch both the 2000 and 2003 versions. Yes, Virginia Madsen was memorable in the Lynch version, but after her stunning (and hilarious) opening monologue, she gets only one word of spoken dialogue in the entire film, when she utters the word *father* to Shaddam IV. Florence Pugh's Irulan in *Dune: Part Two* (2023)* may become the definitive Irulan for generations of *Dune* fans for the foreseeable future, but Julie Cox made it happen first.

Like Cox's nuanced and brilliant performance as Irulan, the 2000 version of Paul Atreides is similarly underrated. Nineteen years before Timothée Chalamet became the definitive Muad'Dib of the 2020s, there was another prophet of

---

*Florence Pugh's Irulan doesn't appear in 2021's *Dune: Part One*, because that film breaks with the structure of the book by giving the opening narration to Chani (Zendaya). In the 2000 *Dune*, one scene in which Irulan appears to seduce Feyd (Matt Keeslar) is a modified version of a similar scene from the novel in which Lady Margot Fenring does the same thing. In 2023, Lady Margot is played by Léa Seydoux, the first person to do so, other than the Fenring scene Cox stole as Irulan in 2000.

Arrakis. His name is Alec Newman, and his version of Paul has nearly about the screen time of Chalamet's and MacLachlan's combined.* In the year 2000, in a time when streaming science fiction and fantasy TV didn't exist, and the so-called geek renaissance of the early aughts had yet to take hold, Alec Newman created a uniquely honest version of Paul, which, at the time, many fans considered to be the most faithful filmed version of the character. In contrast with MacLachlan's Paul, Newman dared to do what Herbert did on the page: introduce us to Paul not as a hero in training but instead as a spoiled brat. With arms folded and a pout on his face for much of the first episode of Frank Herbert's *Dune*, Newman's Paul Atreides feels like the perfect science fiction reflection of a nineties teenage sitcom character who is totally over it.

"I had the kind of foolishness of youth," Alec Newman tells me in 2022. "I had a kind of bullishness, but if I knew then what I know now, I would've been much more intimidated by it. I didn't know much about *Dune* when I was cast. But maybe that lack of a preconceived idea about what it was and how important it was to so many people was actually helpful. I might have been spooked otherwise."

Like Kyle MacLachlan, Alec Newman was in his twenties

---

*For round figures, MacLachlan's *Dune* is roughly two hours, and both of Chalamet's *Dune*s are roughly five hours combined. Newman was in both Sci Fi *Dune* miniseries, which are each four hours long. Paul isn't in *Children of Dune* as much, but Alec does dominate the first episode of that series, which puts his screen time as Paul at roughly seven hours, maybe a bit more. So until Chalamet does that promised movie version of *Dune Messiah*, Newman is still the reigning champ in terms of total number of hours as Paul.

when he began shooting his *Dune*. Because Paul is a teenager in the novel, Newman's performance leans into the adolescent flippancy, which makes him seem even younger, mostly through body language. In early scenes, Newman's Paul is slouching or has his feet up on a table. Newman tells me that of all the scenes he filmed for both his *Dune*s, those early scenes are the hardest for him to revisit.

"It's a difficult thing," Newman tells me. "In a sense, you'd almost want more than one actor to play Paul throughout all these stages, from being a teenager and then older. But John [Harrison] made a decision early on that one person would play the role. I think if you're gonna have one actor, invariably parts of the story will benefit and parts of the story will feel the weight of that decision. The benefit is you get to see one portrayal with the same idea. And particularly for us as we went onward into *Dune Messiah* and *Children*, I really felt the benefit of having played him further and further into the story that we get. And what I've heard from fans is the deeper into the story we get, the more comfortable they got being around [my] Paul Atreides."

As it turns out, being around Alec Newman's Paul is wonderful. For longtime fans, the brilliance of the Sci Fi Channel *Dune*s can be found in their endless novelty. Unlike other popular installments of huge sci-fi franchises, these two *Dune* miniseries haven't been endlessly critiqued and analyzed in the mainstream, which gives them a kind of refreshing newness when you watch them today. In a sense, the underrated qualities of the Sci Fi *Dune*s have protected them a bit from undue scrutiny, which is good for open-minded *Dune* fans, because there is much to love about these versions. Yes, these *Dunes* do wrap the world of Arrakis in a kind of late-nineties melodramatic sensibility, but again, in 2000 and 2003, prestige sci-fi TV wasn't yet a codified phenomenon. Outside of nineties *Star Trek*, *Babylon 5*, and the Sci Fi Channel's other favorite child, the burgeoning *Battlestar Galactica*, there was little on TV that you could compare to *Dune*. Two decades later, that's thankfully still the case. In the bigger story of *Dune*, these two miniseries seem like sweet love letters, passed to fans in a time when we were all a little more innocent.

The 2000 miniseries *Frank Herbert's Dune* also faithfully tackles many aspects of the first novel that other adaptations either mangle or leave on the cutting-room floor. The warmaster Gurney Halleck—played by Patrick Stewart in 1984 and Josh Brolin in 2021 and 2023[*]—is known in the novel as much for his fighting as for his tender ability to play the mandolin-esque instrument the baliset. As one of Duncan's gholas later claimed, "he could be killing you while he was singing and never miss a note." And yet, in both Lynch's film and Villeneuve's *Dune: Part One* (2021), scenes of Patrick Stewart or Josh Brolin playing the baliset were cut from the final version. In 2021, composer Hans Zimmer told me that he'd even composed specific songs for Gurney's baliset that went unused. There is some hope that Gurney will play the baliset in *Part Two*, but still.

However, in the 2000 miniseries, P. H. Moriarty's version

---

[*]In the 1970s, Jodorowsky had wanted Hervé Villechaize to play Gurney.

of Gurney does get to play the baliset. A lot. And in the same scene, as Gurney tells Paul of his hatred for the Harkonnens, he pronounces the name the preferred Herbert way, "*Hahr-ken-en*," rather than the more common Lynch way, "Hark-*koh-nen*."* This small detail represents just how all-in these two miniseries went. If something wasn't good enough for a theatrical cut of a film, that same *Dune* idea would probably be about twenty minutes long in the Sci Fi version.

The microcosm for this geeky, detail-oriented feature of these versions is how the 2000 miniseries handled Frank Herbert's favorite scene from the first novel: the famed banquet scene.† This scene does not appear in either the Lynch version or Villeneuve versions. But Herbert loved it. Although he never did a full audio recording of *Dune*, he did record selections from several of the novels in the 1970s and 1980s, specifically his beloved banquet sequence, in which Leto, Jessica, and Paul learn about their newfound home of Arrakis, all through the concealed warfare of polite dinner conversation. Ironically, although this is the only time a *Dune* adaptation has included this iconic scene, it's also the moment where the

---

* In 2021, longtime *Dune* audiobook narrator Scott Brick told me that the name Harkonnen is the "bane of [his] existence," saying, "Even after narrating over twenty *Dune* books, Lynch's pronunciation is so engraved in my brain that I still screw up sometimes when I read it aloud." For what it's worth, Herbert went on record at least once saying fans are free to say the names however they want. He just had his preferences.

† In nearly every interview Herbert conducted for the 1984 film, he mentioned the loss of the banquet scene at least once, sometimes more. He really, really loved that scene.

2000 *Dune* radically departs from the novel, in a way that paradoxically also feels hyper-faithful to Herbert's intentions. In the book, Princess Irulan narrates from afar and eventually marries Paul, initially out of political convenience. But in the 2000 miniseries, Irulan crashes the banquet scene, showing up on Arrakis in person and creating a love triangle that doesn't really exist in the books but totally should.

Today, both *Frank Herbert's Dune* and *Frank Herbert's Children of Dune* exist as a kind of novelty in between the 1984 film and the new blockbusters. And yet, in 2003, when *Children of Dune* showed us the beginnings of James McAvoy merging with the sandtrout in order to become part sandworm, part Fremen, and all God Emperor, this was the final word on a filmed version of Frank Herbert's saga. To date, nobody has gotten as far into adapting the original novels as John Harrison, and it remains to be seen whether anyone ever will. These miniseries were ambitious and very much a product of the early 2000s. But without their walking awkwardly, without rhythm, through the landscape of cable TV in the early aughts, there's no way the contemporary film versions of *Dune* could exist.

"I say this with all humility," John Harrison tells me. "But I think that our miniseries was so successful that it actually made the industry say, 'Oh, maybe we can do this as a film again.'"

The Slow Blade
Penetrates the Shield

**The Denis Villeneuve *Dune* film series
and the new spice renaissance.**

To me, reading *Dune* is like a paradise.

—Denis Villeneuve

I n early 2019, in a French wine cellar, Timothée Chalamet learned to fight with a knife like it was a stick. In the 2021 film *Dune: Part One*, the House Atreides knife-fighting style is based on the single-stick combat form balintawak, which comes from the ancient Filipino martial art kali. Because his prep for the Wes Anderson film *The French Dispatch* overlapped with his filming of *Dune: Part One*, Chalamet says he started learning balintawak in a wine cellar in Angoulême, France. "That's where I started my prep," Chalamet tells me in 2021, and later reveals that the scenes in which he fights Gurney (Josh Brolin) were the first things he shot for *Dune*. As Chalamet was learning to fight, he was also learning to become the character of Paul Atreides, meaning, exactly sixteen minutes into the film, when Paul and Gurney spar, we're witnessing both the fictional birth and the real birth of the modern Muad'Dib. Tellingly, according to stunt coordinator Roger Yuan, the trick to this kinetic action is that in rehearsal, he told Chalamet and Brolin to "do everything in slow motion."

This single concept explains not only why Denis Villeneuve's 2021 *Dune* was so successful but also why *Dune* as a phenomenon is so enduring. At the beginning of the twenty-first century, *Dune* has proven more relevant and more powerful than it ever was in the 1960s. Its recent reemergence as a major force in pop culture isn't just a slow burn, it's a patient one. In the 2021 film, Reverend Mother Gaius Helen Mohiam tells Jessica, "Our plans are measured in centuries." In our world, the emergence of *Dune* as one of the most important cinematic and literary stories can be measured in six decades. What only readers of science fiction magazines knew in 1963 is now common knowledge in 2023. *Dune* has proven the value of art that takes a long view and is made with care and patience. As Chalamet said: "*Dune* was written sixty years ago, but its themes hold up today. . . . [It's] a warning against the exploitation of the environment, a warning against colonialism, a warning against technology."

At first blush, close-quarters knife fights might scan as anachronistic and bizarre. In a far-future world of starships and lasguns, why do members of royal houses still fight with knives? The answer is both specific and revealing of a much larger philosophy in *Dune*, and is perhaps its most penetrating concept. Because everyone has access to what is essentially a personal force field* called a "shield," the use of guns isn't common, because they don't work on shields. But these shields are penetrable in one specific way: If a knife is slipped in, very slowly, the shield won't protect you. In all cinematic versions of *Dune*, in the first novel, and even in 1963's "Dune World," Gurney says the same thing: "The slow blade penetrates the shield." The Bene Gesserit Litany Against Fear, which begins with "Fear is the mind-killer," might be the most famous phrase associated with *Dune*, other than, perhaps, "The spice must flow." But "The slow blade penetrates the shield" is the microcosm for all of *Dune* all at once. The narrative is packed with conflict and danger, but the notion of slowness as an asset is as profound as it is unique.

Because of this technological quirk, the feudal world of *Dune* has high-stakes knife fights, which, by the time the story exists, are commonplace. In the 2021 *Dune*, well after his sparring with Gurney, when Paul is forced to fight the Fremen warrior Jamis (Babs Olusanmokun), Jessica (Rebecca Ferguson) tells Stilgar (Javier Bardem) "Paul has never killed" anyone

---

*A huge amount of technology in *Dune* is powered by "Holtzman fields," a type of catch-all sci-fi energy that explains not only shield tech but a good portion of space travel, too. Although the spice allows Guild navigators to see the complex ways in which space can be folded, the spice itself does not allow them to fold space. Although the 1984 film implies space travel exists because of the spice, it's simply that the spice prescience allows for navigation, not travel itself. The space travel comes from Holtzman tech.

before.* But, in the novel, Paul has also never fought anyone with a blade without the aid of a shield. Using a shield in the open desert will only attract a worm, so nobody on Arrakis bothers with shields unless they're in the city. As *Dune* begins, we're shown that the shields can be beaten through a combination of patience and old technology, and then, later, when Paul and Jessica join the Fremen, that same technology is rendered moot and dangerous.

Dune isn't entirely anti-technology in general, but as NASA system analyst Zachary Pirtle points out, the story of *Dune* philosophically bridges two types of social anxieties, because "[*Dune*] represents a nuanced worldview between social construction and technological determinism." In other words, our lives are either spent as a reaction against technology or are not-so-secretly shaped by technology constantly. For Chalamet, there's no crystal ball prediction inherent in any of this, but he does tell me that all the tech in *Dune* is a "projection" of how our twenty-first-century concerns might deal with technology. "I think that's what makes people fans of it," he tells me. "It escalates an entire universe of world-building. It's not just the heroes' arcs, but the intimate relationship you have with the world-building itself."

This insight is part of the reason why Chalamet is such a convincing Paul Atreides. In real life, he's grounded and doesn't

---

*In both novel and film, Paul does help his mother kill Harkonnens in the ornithopter, which of course happens before the knife fight with Jamis. This is why in the novel Jessica says, "Paul has never killed a man with a naked blade." Very specific!

make the conversation about only himself, but rather, the circumstances surrounding him and his character. In the film, as in the novel, Paul tells Gurney (Josh Brolin) he's "not in the mood" for shield practice. But it's hard to imagine Chalamet being similarly flippant or entitled. He lets you imagine what it would be like if you were there instead of him, a quality that translates onto the screen. "I feel like I'm here to show that to wear your heart on your sleeve is okay," he told *Time* in 2021. Crediting the success of the 2021 *Dune* to a twenty-something young actor wearing his heart on his sleeve, in opposition to soulless technology, might be a bit reductive. But it's also not inaccurate. The 2021 *Dune* film feels like an artistic reaction against breathless, rapid-fire cinema. In a sense, it's the anti-Marvel, which is interesting because one of Chalamet's personal rules for his own career follows the advice he received from an anonymous source: "No hard drugs and no superhero movies." The 2021 *Dune* isn't actively telling audiences to throw away their phones or delete every single social media app, but tellingly, one well-meaning reviewer (who shall remain nameless) told me in the fall of 2021 that he didn't believe *Dune* would truly break into the mainstream because "there aren't any meme-able moments."

Certain corners of the internet have proved there are moments that are great for memes, even if you have to work a little harder to get the joke. Unlike, say, one of the *Guardians of the Galaxy* films, or even the newer *Star Wars* movies, the 2021 *Dune* has few sci-fi "money shots." There's no climactic lightsaber battle or death-defying starship rescue. Anything that feels larger than life is presented matter-of-factly. When

Duke Leto (Oscar Isaac), Gurney, Paul, and Liet-Kynes (Sharon Duncan-Brewster) first encounter a sandworm, we barely see the entire creature. *Dune*'s massiveness is too massive to fully depict. The suggestion of its largeness makes the scope seem bigger, but only when you take in the entire film. The 2021 *Dune* works only as a culminating experience. Chalamet tells me he thinks of it as "a high-level indie," suggesting that yes, as a blockbuster, *Dune* is actively the opposite of other blockbusters. In a world of dwindling attention spans, *Dune* begins with the premise that movie audiences can be calmer and absorb epic stories more gradually.

That said, it's not like the 2021 *Dune* is an indie movie or a black box theater experience. The budget for *Dune: Part One* was $165 million. This puts it behind *Avengers: Endgame* (2019), which had a $356 million budget, and also behind the other big blockbuster of 2021, the Bond film *No Time to Die*, which had a $250 million budget. Next to those two movies, *Dune* seems humbler, but compared to the 1977 *Star Wars*'s $11 million budget ($40 million adjusted for inflation), *Dune* is still very much a twenty-first-century film, and both the 2021 film and the 2023 sequel did use plenty of cutting-edge technology to make this organic human story possible. Still, even when you zoom in closely to look at the VFX process, *Dune* is different from its peers. From the knife fights to the sand, little is faked in this movie.

Movie buffs know that big sci-fi epics often rely on green screen technology or AR walls to create fantastic environments, creatures, or vehicles, which are then inserted after the fact during the editing process. But *Dune* didn't use any green screens.* Not one. Instead, production designer Patrice Vermette substituted various fabrics, each painted to "mimic what the set would ultimately look like." VFX were later inserted in post-production over this fabric.

According to Vermette, this process created a more organic feeling than green screens, a "technique [that] would dictate where the light would be coming from, and the obstacles that the light would hit." So, although *Dune* is a technologically complicated movie from a filmmaking perspective, even within those arenas, the spirit of the book comes through and creates techniques that are more grounded and more human. Slow blades penetrating shields, or beautiful fabrics instead of green screens. Chalamet tells me that he enjoyed "spending time" with all the props, because each object felt "real" and allowed him to inhabit the world of *Dune*.

Despite relying on an abundance of technology to convince audiences of this world, the visual effects of *Dune* never overpower. "I like to try and make things as invisible as possible," visual effects supervisor Paul Lambert said. "We were never in a position where we shot something and had to add something else in the background and were like, 'We'll just fix it in post-production.' We always knew there was going to be a very specific structure or element behind the actors at all points, so we could make decisions based on that certainty." Denis Villeneuve's tactile and textured approach results in a film that Theresa Shackleford tells me would have delighted

---

*There were, however, two blue screens used. But only two!

her late husband. "Frank would have absolutely loved it," she tells me. "That's exactly the kind of movie he wanted. The way it looked was perfect."

In 2021, Denis Villeneuve tells me that he began to make *Dune* by starting with fidelity to Herbert's text. "From the beginning, I said to the crew, to [the] studio, to the actors: 'The bible is the book. We will, as much as possible, stay as close as possible to the book.' I want people who love the book to feel like we put a camera in their minds."

And yet, as with all truisms within *Dune*, the statement from Villeneuve belies a contradiction. While *Dune: Part One* and its 2023 sequel, *Dune: Part Two*, are very faithful to the structure and meaning of Herbert's text, the first film also makes massive changes. And yet, like the 2000 John Harrison film before it, the 2021 *Dune*'s changes feel aligned with the spirit of Herbert's first novel, even if the result reframes the narrative. While both the 1984 and 2000 versions strove to justify the nature of Princess Irulan as the after-the-fact narrator of the story, Villeneuve shifts the opening monologue to Chani (Zendaya), which means the story of Arrakis begins from the point of view of the people who live there. Speaking for the Fremen, Chani muses that the departure of the Harkonnens isn't necessarily a good thing. "Why did the emperor choose this path?" she wonders. "And who will our next oppressors be?"

This single decision reflects the entire sensibility of how Villeneuve crafted his version of *Dune*. Chani doesn't narrate the opening of the novel, meaning a hard-core fan would quibble with this change. But by taking the opening narrative away from the aristocracy (Irulan) and giving the start of the story to the voice of the Fremen, the endpoint of the story is hinted at for viewers who aren't die-hard readers.

"When you adapt, it's an act of vandalism. I had to make certain decisions," Villeneuve tells me. "It would be so easy to make a *Dune* movie only for hard-core fans. My goal was to please the hard-core fans, that they feel the spirit, the poetry, and the atmosphere of the book—but to make sure that someone who had never heard about *Dune* would also have fun and understand the story. I had to make sure that everyone would be on board right at the beginning."

Villeneuve knew the decision to begin the film from Chani's point of view was bold, but this choice is connected to a longer game. The slowness of Villeneuve's *Dune* is best exemplified by the simple fact that it's not one movie but, rather, two. As early as 2018, he made it clear that "the goal is to make two films, maybe more." In 2019, speaking to *Vanity Fair*, Villeneuve said, "I would not agree to make this adaptation of the book with one single movie."

Lauded for films like *Sicario* (2015) and *Arrival* (2016), Denis Villeneuve was specifically selected by Mary Parent, a senior producer at Legendary Pictures. Parent had acquired the film rights from Rubinstein (from the Sci Fi days) in 2011, following a long process in which director Peter Berg had been previously hired by Paramount to direct a possible *Dune* film back in 2008. According to a hilarious story from John Hodgman, who talked to Berg on a plane ride, "Basically, Peter Berg's take on *Dune* was that he was going to focus on the adventure and the warfare and a little bit less of the psychosexual stuff. . . . I don't want to put words in Peter Berg's mouth, but he was like, 'I'm going to make this a guy's movie, not a weird guy's movie.' And so I was like, 'Well, good luck to you.'" Essentially, the fact that we got the Denis Villeneuve *Dune* in 2021, and not the Peter Berg version a decade earlier, is clearly for the best. At least one other source claimed that Berg had not read the entire novel well into writing the unused screenplay.

In partnership with Legendary and Warner Bros., Mary Parent believed in Villeneuve's vision for *Dune* and encouraged him to develop the screenplay attuned to that vision. Overall, the screenplay was written by Jon Spaihts, Eric Roth, and Villeneuve himself. After the 2017 box office failure of Villeneuve's *Blade Runner 2049*, the director worried he would be "banned from the filmmaker community." But Legendary and Mary Parent believed in Villeneuve, and so the push for a new cinematic *Dune* universe continued.

Historically, it's fascinating that *Blade Runner*, once again, preceded *Dune*. In 1982, after Ridley Scott turned down *Dune* and directed (the original) *Blade Runner* instead, it, too, bombed at the box office. Then Lynch's 1984 *Dune* also bombed at the box office. The difference here is that in 2021, *Dune: Part One* was a box office success, while Villeneuve's 2017 *Blade Runner* sequel was not. In the twenty-first century, the *Dune* curse has been broken, while the *Blade Runner* curse—at least in terms of mainstream success—sadly remains pervasive. Still, Villeneuve could not have made *Dune* without having made *Blade Runner 2049* first, in the same way that

Ridley Scott needed the failed Jodorowsky *Dune* to make *Blade Runner*. All of this might make you wonder if Philip K. Dick—the author of *Do Androids Dream of Electric Sheep?*, upon which *Blade Runner* was based—actually knew and liked Frank Herbert.

The answer, it turns out, is a resounding yes.

In 1974, Dick said of Herbert: "Never model yourself after any [science fiction] writer. Except Frank Herbert. He is, in my mind, a great writer. But even more, a great and kind human being, with a twinkling, genial worldly wisdom you should pay attention to, and which you may never see the like of again. . . . I like him. Hell, I love him."

The love of Herbert's writing was also deeply personal for Villeneuve, a kind of love that is less about films and more about honoring what his teenage self would have wanted. "With *Blade Runner*, I had to be respectful of Ridley Scott's masterpiece," he said in 2021. "[With *Dune*,] it's totally different. I'm dealing with the pressure of the dreams I had as a teenager . . . that teenager in me is totalitarian and I had to please those dreams. That was the biggest challenge."

One of the possible reasons that Villeneuve decided to split *Dune* into two films instead of one might be connected to the way he originally read the books as a teenager. In the summer of 2021, Villeneuve tells me that his first version of *Dune* was the 1980 French paperback translation, with a cover from Wojciech Siudmak. The image of a man against the desert, with startling blue eyes, hooked Villeneuve right away. "When you're a kid, the covers can really make an impact. The artists that were drawing them were so talented that even though I had never heard of *Dune*, I was drawn to that title and the simplicity. I was always attracted to the desert."

Because Villeneuve is French Canadian, his first *Dune* was a French translation from Robert Laffont, which, interestingly, in 1980 did split the first book up into two volumes. That year, Villeneuve would have turned thirteen years old, the prime age to be converted into a huge *Dune* fan.

"I instantly fell in love with it for several reasons," Villeneuve tells me. "The way Paul is trying to find his identity while finding his home in another culture, with the Fremen. I was fascinated by the way they need to survive and adapt. . . . I have always been in love with biology, the science of life, of nature. The way Frank Herbert used biology was insanely beautiful. To me, reading *Dune* is like a paradise. The book stayed with me all these years."

Because *Dune: Part One* gets us only roughly halfway through the first novel, introducing Chani earlier—and not just through Paul's future visions—is one way in which Villeneuve's take on *Dune* is less faithful to the original novel but perhaps more faithful to Villeneuve's teenage impressions of it. Either way, this structure results in one of the most interesting features of Villeneuve's *Dune* movie saga. While other film versions have been desperate to introduce characters like Shaddam IV and Feyd much earlier than they appear in the novel, Villeneuve didn't even bother casting those actors for *Dune: Part One* and instead elevated the part of Chani, because, ultimately, her partnership with Paul defines the overall story in a way that is essential to make the sequel work.

"I kind of scratched the surface," Zendaya said in 2021, though Villeneuve and fans knew her part would be huge in *Dune: Part Two*.

By holding back in revealing several key players in the saga, Villeneuve has proven he understands something about making a *Dune* movie that perhaps nobody else has. Maybe it wasn't a mistake that Herbert didn't fully reveal Irulan, Feyd, and the emperor until much later in the story. Maybe holding those characters back is exactly why the first half of the novel is so affecting. We truly do see the story unfold from the perspective of the Atreides, with a few jaunts over to the depravity of House Harkonnen. Villeneuve's *Dune* saga is the same. Although the emperor is referenced often, we don't see Shaddam IV in the flesh once in *Dune: Part One*, because, realistically, none of the characters would ever have a meeting with him. Just like Villeneuve barely lets us see the sandworm in the 2021 *Dune*, he also keeps Feyd, Irulan, Lady Fenring, and the emperor offstage.

Of course, all those characters are in *Dune: Part Two*. The dark archenemy of Paul, Feyd-Rautha, is played by Austin Butler in *Dune: Part Two*, Léa Seydoux plays Lady Margot Fenring, and Florence Pugh will take on the complex and all-important part of Princess Irulan. But it's the casting of Irulan's father, Emperor Shaddam IV, that is perhaps the most interesting, and the spookiest, thing about *Dune: Part Two*. Twenty-three years after he danced to Fatboy Slim's *Dune*-inspired "Weapon of Choice," Christopher Walken is playing the emperor of the known universe. Of course, the only one of these new *Dune: Part Two* actors who will make it into

Villeneuve's proposed third film—an adaptation of *Dune Messiah*—is Pugh's Irulan, and maybe Seydoux's Fenring, depending on how much her role is expanded. Either way, Villeneuve's *Dune* films are poised to become the *Lord of the Rings* of the 2020s, echoing Arthur C. Clarke's claim that he could only compare *Dune* to *The Lord of the Rings*.

Against its $165 million budget, *Dune: Part One* made $400 million at the box office worldwide. Only $100 million of that was in the United States, however, mostly because Warner Bros. decided to release the movie straight to subscribers on HBO Max on the same day it hit theaters. To some, this COVID-era policy threatened to possibly destroy the ability for *Dune* to make money conventionally, which thus might have doomed the entire new franchise before it even got started. In an utterly iconoclastic rock star move, Villeneuve penned a scathing op-ed against Warner Bros. for the decision to release *Dune* straight to streaming, arguing, "Warner Bros.' decision means *Dune* won't have the chance to perform financially in order to be viable and piracy will ultimately triumph. Warner Bros. might just have killed the *Dune* franchise."

Luckily, Villeneuve was only partially right. Obviously, the fact that *Dune* was available to stream at home, combined with reluctance by some to return to in-person events in 2021, did hurt the US box office results. But the global box office more than made up for it. *Dune* was also nominated for ten Academy Awards and went on to win six. For the first time—perhaps ever—the idea of *Dune* connected equally with both mainstream and hard-core fans alike. Villeneuve did the impossible: He made everyone happy.

The triumph of *Dune* in the twenty-first century reveals the dual nature of the phenomenon. It exists as two things: a blockbuster, mainstream adventure with killer knife fights, but also a patient and meditative treatise about life, the universe, and everything, in which one of the most important themes is that if you want to win, you need to learn how to slow down. The knife fights and other action end up looking lightning fast on the screen. But everything we see in the new *Dune*s was created through an astounding amount of patience, and, crucially, love.

The Sleeper Must Awaken

The future of the *Dune* franchise, and *Dune* as an ecological guide for the future.

> Our goal is to become activists. We must rely on our own actions more than on words. And these are just words.
>
> —Frank Herbert

an *Dune* change the world? Can a novel that involves old-timey knife fights and giant space worms convince people to get serious about climate change? Is it possible the book could encourage more religious tolerance and understanding? The answer to these questions might be a cautious yes. Because although *Dune* did not truly begin its life as a political or ecological text, it's impossible to ignore those themes in it today. Between 1965 and now, *Dune* transformed from a curious science fiction book released by an automotive repair manual publisher to a book that seemed to be a repair manual for the entire planet.

On April 22, 1970, in Fairmount Park in Philadelphia, Frank Herbert spoke to thirty thousand people in celebration of the very first Earth Day. He told the gathered crowd he wanted everyone there to "begin a love affair with our planet," and to that end, he hoped that they would all join him in never again buying a new car. He firmly believed that if people boycotted the purchase of new internal combustion engines, the automotive industry would eventually be forced to make more efficient cars or create clean-energy fuel alternatives. "Getting rid of internal combustion will be no permanent solution. But it will give us breathing room."

At the time, Herbert was also concerned about overpopulation as well as pollution. Some of the ways he phrased his arguments may seem dated. But it's also striking how mainstream most of his views are today. The public perception of *Dune* as an ecological science fiction novel is perhaps the most important factor in its immortality. And while Herbert himself was a bit preachy, his novel isn't. And that's how the magic happens.

Herbert's self-styling as an environmental activist didn't happen in 1965, when the hardcover was published by Chilton, and it didn't happen in 1966, when the first paperback version was published by Ace.* Instead, the public transformation of *Dune* from an underground science fiction novel to an

---

* *Dune*'s reputation as being a "long book" started when the publisher Ace acquired the paperback rights in 1966. The Chilton hardcover was 412 pages. But the typesetting required for the Ace paperback (also dated 1965 in mass-market first editions) pushed the book to 544 pages. By 2010, the Ace mass-market paperback edition was 883 pages. As explained previously, none of these different editions contains different text from the others, just a different number of words per page.

essential ecological text read and analyzed by environmental activists happened in 1968, three full years after the book hit bookshelves.

"I refuse to be put in the position of telling my grandchildren: 'Sorry, there's no more world for you. We used it all up,'" Frank Herbert said in 1970, in the nonfiction book *New World or No World*. "It was for this reason that I wrote in the midsixties what I hoped would be an environmental awareness handbook. The book is called *Dune*, a title chosen with the deliberate intent that it echo the sound of 'doom.'"

The notion that Herbert wrote *Dune* specifically because he hoped it would be an "environmental awareness handbook" is almost certainly revisionist. But that doesn't make *Dune*'s political and environmental commentary incorrect. Even the earliest versions of "Dune World" contain ecological themes simply because of the way Arrakis works. Herbert later said that on Arrakis, both water and spice are analogues for oil, and of course, for "water itself." The idea that Arrakis wasn't always a desert wasteland is suggested vaguely in the first novel, but what Herbert's later novels—specifically 1976's *Children of Dune*—do is to reveal a kind of inverted problem. Because of the rapidity of forced climate change on Arrakis, the most integral part of the wildlife—the sandworms—is pushed to near extinction. What is subtle in the first novel is made perfectly clear in the sequels.

Herbert even tips his hand to his own revisionism because he mentions Pardot Kynes—a character you're excused from forgetting because this person doesn't really appear in the actual story of *Dune*. Most of Pardot's story and his quotes come from the first appendix in *Dune*, "The Ecology of *Dune*," which gives us the backstory of Pardot Kynes, the father of Liet-Kynes, the imperial planetologist who more famously accompanies Leto, Paul, and Gurney during their first inspection of the spice mining and later gives his life to save Paul and Jessica in the desert. As Liet-Kynes lies dying, he recalls a quote from his father: "The highest function of ecology is the understanding of consequences."

"I put these words into his mouth," Herbert said in 1970, speaking of both Liet-Kynes and Liet's father, Pardot.

Because the science fiction community inconsistently embraced Herbert in the late sixties, one could say that he found his true community with environmentalists. In 1968, within the pages of *The Whole Earth Catalog*, biologist and editor Stewart Brand forever changed the perception and importance of *Dune*. *The Whole Earth Catalog* was a publication conceived by Brand as a way of giving forward-thinking environmentalists and progressives "access to tools" for rethinking everything about the way humankind saw Earth. In the introduction to the first catalog, Brand wrote that hardships caused "by government and big businesses" led to a movement where "a realm of personal power is developing—power of the individual to conduct his own education." To that end, Brand created *The Whole Earth Catalog* with the following stated purpose: "*The Whole Earth Catalog* functions as an evaluation and access device. With it, the user should know better what is worth getting and where and how to do the getting."

On page 42 of this catalog, *Dune* was listed with the following description: "A more recent Hugo Award winner than

Stranger in a Strange Land, Dune is rich, re-readable fantasy with a clear portrayal of the fierce environment it takes to cohere a community. It's been enjoying currency in Berkeley and saltier communities such as Libre. The metaphor is ecology. The theme revolution."

One of Brand's big criteria for anything listed in *The Whole Earth Catalog* was that it could "not already [be] common knowledge." By 1970, when Frank Herbert was invited to speak at the first Earth Day, it's safe to say that *Dune*'s ecological themes were common knowledge. But in 1968, that hadn't happened yet. These two years rewrote the reputation of *Dune*, for the better. And this seemingly influenced Herbert to take his sequels in directions more in line with his ecological views and less aligned with what a smaller science fiction readership might have wanted.

In crafting the first *Dune*, Herbert created a science fiction novel that was palatable to old-school science fiction readers while attempting something new: establishing world-building that had far-reaching implications about the environmental struggle of our own planet. Herbert might not have sold *Dune* to *Analog* or Chilton or Ace as an ecological book, but once prominent environmentalists picked up on what he was laying down, his true colors were shown. It's tricky to believe that Herbert really picked the title *Dune* because it reflected the word *doom*, mostly because the process through which he started writing the book doesn't seem to support that. But even later in his life, Herbert seemed to walk the environmentalist's walk that he outlined in *New World or No World*.

A decade and a half after the publication of this book, both his son Brian and his widow, Theresa Shackleford, confirmed that Frank Herbert loved riding around in limos and always flew first class if he could help it. And yet, by all accounts, he never broke his promise in 1970. It would seem that to his dying day, Frank Herbert never, not once, bought a new car.

But if the environmental legacy of *Dune* is clear, its political messaging is less on the nose. For various critics and scholars, the political messages of *Dune* are not all one way. Is it a story that elevates minorities and, along with the Fremen, truly punches up?

In 1984, Francesca Annis, Lady Jessica in the David Lynch *Dune*, said that she read the entire story of *Dune* in a conservative light. "I can't relate to the story politically," she said. "The book just doesn't say much about ordinary people. As far as its values are concerned, it's just one group of powerful people triumphing over other powerful people. In that way, it's a very right-wing story."

You can kind of squint and see where Annis is coming from, especially through the lens of the 1984 film. Close readings of *Dune* reveal the subversion Frank Herbert inserted into this "white savior narrative," and as prominent *Dune* scholar Haris Durrani has pointed out, even in his subversion of it, Herbert still "reinscribes the white savior narrative." From this point of view, Paul and his family are like missionaries, coming to "tame" a native people, steal their culture via Bene Gesserit manipulation, and then create a new power base that is arguably just as bad, if not worse. Again, Zendaya's Chani says at the beginning of the 2021 film, "Who will our new oppressors be?"

"If Herbert wanted to make it clear that he was subverting the hero's journey in the first novel, he could have done a better job," historian Alec Nevala-Lee tells me. "It's clearer in *Messiah*, but it's easy to read the first novel the 'wrong' way." But Durrani isn't so sure. For him, *Dune* isn't a white savior narrative at all and is somewhat secretly a one-of-a-kind twentieth-century science fiction novel that speaks to Muslim ideas.

"It's an attempt to explore Muslim ideas and different Muslim cultures in a way that I think is unique," Durrani tells me. "There was something unique about what Herbert was doing, bringing his unique viewpoint to thinking about the future of Islam and other Muslim cultures." The evidence Durrani cites relative to the Muslimness of *Dune* is somewhat obvious for any reader with an Arabic or Muslim background. In the first book, Paul is sometimes referred to as "the Mahdi," which in Arabic refers to a spiritual leader who will unify and save the people, generally just before the entire world ends. For Durrani, this idea blurs the "white savior trope" because you can easily imagine a version of Paul who isn't white but is still a fallible and dangerous leader.

"Is he white?" Durrani says with a laugh. "I mean, you could imagine a version of Paul who wasn't white. I certainly think Gurney Halleck is a nonwhite character. Herbert probably intended Paul to be white, but he's also drawing on histories of North Africa and the reference to the 'Mahdi,' who is not white. I think what's interesting is that even if Paul is a nonwhite character, he's still a colonial character. Herbert is playing with ideas of internal colonization."

As Durrani outlines in his essay "*Dune*'s Not a White Savior Narrative. But It's Complicated," the agency of the indigenous people of Arrakis (the Fremen) "appears downplayed," mostly because of "the narrative focus on the Atreides and Bene Gesserit." But from his reading of the text and Herbert's various comments over the years, Durrani says that all the colonial themes in *Dune* are strictly anti-colonial, even when the "heroes" are depicted as such. "I read the focus on leaders as critical, not hagiographical. . . . Herbert saw the series as about communities, not individuals." While talking to me in 2022, Durrani tells me that the endpoint of the series, in *Chapterhouse: Dune*, features a slate of heroes and protagonists who are specifically not the pseudo–Anglo-Christian characters of House Atreides in the first book. "I think it is significant that the whole series ends with basically a rabbi, a Fremen, a Sufi saint, and basically some guy who's representative of Afghanistan," Durrani says. "I don't know if Herbert was successful, but he wanted to do both: You could read this as just a traditional sci-fi story of this heroic journey. And he wanted the sense of people who are playing into that narrative. But it's a hard line to walk."

Dune may or may not convincingly subvert the white savior tropes, but it does push back against other clichés in coming-of-age stories and hero's journeys. Nobody refuses the call to adventure in *Dune*. And Paul's parents aren't distant and mythical like nearly all the parents in *Star Wars*. In fact, the story of the first *Dune* is as much the story of a mother as it is of a son. Imagine Luke Skywalker growing up with Padmé guiding him, while also fighting her own battles, and you've got an approximate feeling of just how radical *Dune* is within the pantheon of other sci-fi adventure epics. Even Leto II's transformation into the God Emperor isn't a black-and-white Darth Vader morality tale. *Dune* doesn't wag its finger at bad decisions. It reminds us that everything has consequences.

"Herbert thought of science fiction . . . as a form of myth," biographer William F. Touponce wrote in 1988. "But he did not see myth as an absolute. Myth and Jungian archetypes were simply another discourse that he set out to master and that he incorporated into the dialogical open-endedness of his *Dune* series."

Now, contrast this kind of thinking with *Star Wars.* Everyone is told over and over that the reason that saga is so popular is that George Lucas stuck so close to the archetypes that people couldn't help but love it. *Dune* is the opposite of *Star Wars* in this way; Herbert uses archetypes like the "hero's journey" as what Touponce calls a "strategy" to "get people emotionally involved in his stories." Touponce points out that with the publication of *Messiah* and *Children of Dune*, some more traditional, Campbell-era SF readers felt like Herbert had betrayed them. And maybe he had. Whether it was slightly retroactive or not, Herbert used the hero's journey as a framework, but unlike Lucas, he didn't adhere to it. *Dune* rejects the archetypes it creates, which gives the story more flexibility. This is why the saga continues to organically expand well beyond what Herbert wrote.

After Villeneuve's *Dune: Part Two* is out on home video and streaming sometime in 2024, the immediate future of *Dune* is probably the story of the Bene Gesserit. Created by

Diane Ademu-John along with showrunner Alison Schapker, the in-development HBO TV series *Dune: The Sisterhood* has been pitched as the story of the origin of the Bene Gesserit roughly ten thousand years before the events of the first novel. This series is loosely based on Brian Herbert and Kevin J. Anderson's 2011 novel *The Sisterhood of Dune*, which charts the rise of various organizations in the *Dune*-iverse, including the Spacing Guild and the human computers known as Mentats. As the 2020s march on, the future legacy of *Dune* will possibly leave the story of Paul Atreides in the dust. Although there is a huge degree of uncertainly around the future of the *Sisterhood* series, one stated premise would follow two sisters, Valya and Tula Harkonnen, as they struggle to establish the Bene Gesserit order amid the reign of Empress Natalya reign of Empress Natalya (Indira Varma).

The last name of the two protagonists—Harkonnen— should raise some eyebrows, too. In the distant past, the dreaded enemy of House Atreides wasn't necessarily all evil, demonstrating that the unfolding story of *Dune* continues to defy easy classification. The idea of a sci-fi prequel series revealing its two main characters are part of a family that has largely been portrayed as villains would be like if there was ever a Sherlock Holmes prequel set in the 1400s, in which a heroic captain named Moriarty battled for truth and justice on the high seas. The specific place that *Dune: The Sisterhood* will hold in the long history of the flowing spice is, at this time, unknowable. In fact, because Diane Ademu-John left the project in 2022, it's unclear if the series will materialize as it was originally pitched. But the basic setup of the show has the potential to make *The Sisterhood* the most transgressive *Dune* story yet and, if the show enjoys *Game of Thrones*–level enthusiasm, push the chronicles of Arrakis even further into the mainstream. Maybe.

The timing of *Dune*'s twenty-first-century renaissance isn't just a coincidence. It's true that *Dune* has benefited from the gradual mainstreaming of sci-fi and fantasy in the early twenty-first century, but, because the phenomenon of these novels and books has always stood separate and apart from sci-fi trends, the emergence of *Dune* as a dominant pop culture force now is explicable for bigger reasons. In *New World or No World*, Herbert equated apathy regarding environmental activism with trying to rouse a "heavy sleeper." But he also believed that people could change: "We can shake the sleepers— gently and persistently, saying 'time to get up.'"

The history of *Dune*'s making is a history of contradictions and paradoxes. And, crucially, how we can emerge from that chaos better and wiser. In a lovely and famous *Dune* scene, Duke Leto tells Paul that "without change, something sleeps inside us and seldom awakens. The sleeper must awaken." Although often attributed to Herbert's book, these exact lines come from the 1984 film, not the novel version of *Dune*, proving that interpretations and, yes, revisions of *Dune* have the power to reshape our thinking and our hearts.

Later, in both the 1984 *Dune* and the novel, Paul speaks of his awakening, when he becomes the person he believes he's meant to be. *Dune*'s meaning to millions and its longevity are specifically connected to this kind of thinking: We can ignore the ills of the world, but not forever. At some point, everyone will have to wake up. On the final page of *New World or No World*, Herbert writes a single question, wondering if all the storytelling and real talk are sinking in. He asks damningly, and quite simply: "What are you doing?"

The "what" he refers to is somewhat obvious. Are you actively doing something positive in your community? Are you acting generously? Are you doing something about the horrible power structures that keep people down? Herbert may have found his fame and fortune through *Dune*, but his creation endures not because it lets us escape and ride a sandworm and get super-high on an awesome space drug, but because it makes us feel guilty.

From racial and gender inequity, to class divide and poverty, to dishonesty and corruption in politics, Herbert believed that communities can turn back the slow tide of oppression. The hyperbole in *Dune* helps to illustrate the ways in which those revolts might happen and the ways in which those revolts might go wrong. Misinformation motivates many of the horrible events throughout *Dune*, especially when ideological demagogues allow their followers (or voters) to believe they are above the law.

"At the very core of *Dune* is a warning," Denis Villeneuve tells me in 2021. "Anyone who is trying to blend religion and politics—that is a dangerous cocktail. When someone behaves like a messiah, you have to be careful."

Frank Herbert's heart was always in the right place, from the real sand dunes of Oregon to the spice fields of Arrakis.

His intentions don't mean that *Dune* is perfect or without problematic elements. And yet, unlike so many touchstones of twentieth-century literature, *Dune* is unique because its weaknesses are also its strengths. It's a story that dares to make us hate the heroes and search inside ourselves for ways in which we, too, have made the same well-meaning mistakes. It challenges us to think outside of our own day-to-day experiences and imagine a world in which just one drop of water is more precious than gold. It pushes us to rethink our emotional strategies for dealing with disappointment, failure, and most of all, fear.

As Paul's mother teaches him, the Bene Gesserit Litany Against Fear is the first and last line of mental defense. The battles fought in *Dune* occur across various planets and employ all sorts of ingenious weapons. And yet, throughout all the book, film, and television *Dune*s, the internal human struggle not to give in to fear is paramount. We know that honorary Bene Gesserit Yoda correctly linked fear with all sorts of other horrible outcomes, but *Star Wars* suggested that a connection with a magical energy field was required to beat back that fear. The Bene Gesserit teaches that the battle can be won within your own mind. Tamping down fear doesn't work. Ignoring it or allowing it to morph into rage can lead to "total obliteration."

Instead, all of us, every day, have to face our fear. In the world of the twenty-first century, the fears we face are seemingly growing and more relentless than ever before. The mental health of each person in the world is like a dam holding back the tide of chaos. And *Dune* helps. A little. As Herbert said in

1970, "these are only words," but he also taught us that fear truly is the mind-killer and that the battle for a better world begins inside each person.

"In horrible times, people tend to turn to musicals or science fiction," Rebecca Ferguson, Lady Jessica herself, tells me. "Personally, I think the world of *Dune* is so profound and so layered that I hope it's the kind of thing more of us can turn to. If people do need to escape, do need to feel comfort, I think this brand of science fiction, this kind of reflective art, is buoying and transformative. I hope it helps people. I truly do."

Ferguson didn't need to use the Voice to make this ring true. The love of *Dune* in all its forms is about both things: escape from fear and awakening from a slumber of the mind.

Dune allows us to live in the future, love the artistic intricacy of that future, and then realize, with sobering clarity, that we can't allow things to end up like that. *Dune* teaches us to face our fears, to recognize there are plans within plans, and to accept that not every victory is always what it seems. It also makes us look in the mirror and wonder who we are. Like Alia, Leto, and Ghanima, it sometimes feels as though we all have the memories of our ancestors lurking in our minds. The horrible things we've done as a species as well as the triumphs are all there, running through our consciousness at the same time. *Dune* says there is no way to turn away from the mixed bag of human history. There's no easy fix for the horrible ways history has unfolded or the ways in which it may repeat itself. Herbert ended his last novel, *Chapterhouse: Dune*, with a leap into an unknown part of space, a future that was suddenly unwritten. "We're in an unidentifiable ship in an unidentifiable universe," Duncan Idaho says. "Isn't that what we wanted?"

The mystery of the future of humanity is similar. We can't yet imagine the way in which we get to the future, and we can't really picture what the universe will look like when the future unfolds. But it is what we want: to survive and to change. *Dune* says that change is possible. It's not always all good, but it's not all bad, either. "The best thing humans have going for them is each other," Frank Herbert said. We don't have to be owned by our fear. Because in the end, we can look at ourselves honestly, at this moment, and ask, without fear, "What are you doing?"

Spice Up Your Life

Just one more dune to go.
Nope. You said that three dunes ago.

—Lone Starr and Barf in *Spaceballs*

I n the summer of 2022, I'm reading a book to my five-year-old daughter, and buried in the pages is a sandworm of Arrakis. To be clear, this isn't the 1984 kids' book *The Dune Storybook*, adapted by the legendary sci-fi author Joan D. Vinge. Nor is it one of the *Dune* coloring books from the same era, nor is it a comic book adaptation, or 1978's beautiful *The Illustrated Dune*, festooned with John Schoenherr's striking artwork. I am also not reading aloud from the original *Dune* novel, either. My daughter can handle me reading *The Hobbit* out loud, but *Dune* for a little kid would be pretty extreme and utterly inappropriate. And yet, there it is, a sandworm in her book, and she knows it's a sandworm, and she knows what a sandworm does. After identifying the sandworm and mentioning that if you "hang around sandworms you get blue eyes," my daughter says confidently, "Sandworms are cute, aren't they, Dad?"

The book we're reading is *The Octonauts and the Growing Goldfish*. Although the cartoon TV version of *The Octonauts* is more famous, the equally wonderful book series came first, written and illustrated by Vicki Wong and Michael Murphy. In this specific 2014 storybook (which does not have a TV adaptation), the stalwart crew of anthropomorphized animals is tasked with assisting a rapidly growing prehistoric fish who has accidentally drifted into a too-small pond. We learn that where he really belongs is in a massive undersea cavern with other monstrously huge sea creatures. And on one page, as the journey down takes us through the earth, where other massive critters dwell, there is, very plainly, a hooded figure, with iridescent blue eyes, navigating a smiling sandworm. All versions of *The Octonauts* contain sly Easter eggs and references to all sorts of science fiction media, including, but not limited to, *Star Trek*, *Doctor Who*, *The Lord of the Rings*, and *Thunderbirds*. But this sandworm Easter egg can be caught only by parents, or kids with parents who talk about *Dune* all the time. My daughter is right in saying the sandworm is cute, because it is very adorable in this illustration. It's so cute, in fact, that it would be innocuous if you didn't know what it was. And therein lies the secret of *Dune*. Even when you don't know it's there, it's right in front of you.

It's tempting to say that the staying power of *Dune* is all because of every single thing that's been discussed in these pages. Its social commentary, on subjects from religion to ecology, is clear, and not only that but highly original, too. It

changed the course of the way books were published and the
way science fiction was read, and it proved that "unfilmable"
books can eventually be filmed. It's a nexus for conversations about feminism, classism, racism, and the constant fight
against fascism. The first novel is also, occasionally, a wonderful treatise on parenting. Paul doesn't need to be an orphan
to have a huge adventure, and his parents don't need to be
secretly evil to be interesting and compelling characters. Despite its coming-of-age elements at the start, *Dune* reminds
us that adventures continue well into adulthood and that people who become caregivers—from Lady Jessica to Irulan and
beyond—don't stop being interesting just because they are in
charge of young people.

And yet, for all the deep diving into the sand to sort out
the relevance of *Dune*, the trick to its staying power might be
simpler than these profundities. The cute sandworm buried in
the pages of a children's book gestures at something more
than just a subject for literary and academic study. It's more
basic than that. *Dune* is really, really fun.

In 1984, *National Lampoon* published a 221-page parody
novel by the humorist Ellis Weiner titled *Doon*. The book is
slightly longer than *Dune Messiah* and about the length of
some of Frank Herbert's other non-*Dune* SF novels, like *Whipping Star* or *The Heaven Makers*. It's about as profound as
Spaceballs but occasionally carries some wit that approaches
the brilliance of Douglas Adams. It's difficult to maintain a
spoof for an entire novel, but what makes *Doon* so funny is the
way that Weiner really pays homage to Herbert's style in a way
that only a true fan could. Toward the end of the book (which

is mostly about controlling a galaxy-wide supply of beer and riding some pretzels), the character of "Pall" repeats the Litany Against Fun, saying, "I must not have fun. Fun is the time-killer . . . when fun is gone there will be nothing. Only I will remain. I, and my will to win. Damn, I'm good."

What Weiner proves of course is that *Dune* is very fun and that it's sometimes easy to make it not fun because it seems so serious. Again, we're reminded of Herbert's jarring assertion that *Dune* was written in a style of "high camp," a style of narrative that pushes back against easy answers and binary societal viewpoints. The Bene Gesserit Litany Against Fear is obviously an amazing and immortal philosophy, but the parody version of it in *Doon* helps to reinforce its brilliance by mocking some of the earnestness. This seems appropriate, simply because every single account of Frank Herbert—from his son Brian's wonderful memoir to what I learned firsthand from Theresa Shackleford—tends to paint a similar picture. Frank Herbert laughed a lot, loved corny jokes, and despite being put on the spot constantly to explain the deeper meaning of *Dune*, also didn't take himself too seriously. He rejected the idea that his fans saw him as a guru, which was a subject that was very important to him. But within all of that, the serious artist was also having a lot of fun, too. In April 1984, in the foreword to *Heretics of Dune*, Frank Herbert wrote: "There's an unwritten compact between you and the reader. If someone enters a bookstore and sets down hard-earned money (and energy) for your book, you owe that person some entertainment and as much more as you can give."

If adults are interested only in telling other adults about

why climate change is important or why fascism is bad, there is plenty of nonfiction out there to help them. Frank Herbert edited *New World or No World*, but that's out of print and *Dune* isn't. Good humans want to learn things, do better, and discover various things they didn't know about the nature of life. But if we're being honest, Herbert didn't need to invent sandworms to make that point. *Dune*'s omnipresence in various aspects of culture can't be attributed only to its serious tone and urgent, socially relevant messages. At a certain point, the goofiness of riding a massive sandworm is just flat-out awesome. Or, if you're a five-year-old, cute.

◄ ◄ ► ►

In 2021, right around the time I started working on this book, Matt Caron released an absolutely perfect and hilarious video for Nerdist that crammed in pretty much every single pop culture reference to *Dune* found in other TV shows and films. Some are shockingly obscure. *Scooby-Doo! Mystery Incorporated* pays homage to the opening of the David Lynch film, while in the 2019 final episode of the HBO comedy *Silicon Valley*, Monica (Amanda Crew) tells Dinesh (Kumail Nanjiani), "I know who fucking Frank Herbert is." But my favorite reference that Caron put into this video is the moment from a 1993 *Simpsons* episode in which Lisa Simpson eats extra-spicy food and suddenly declares, "I can see through time!" Fast-forward to December 2022, and I'm having a coffee with Matt Caron in Portland, Maine, and he's telling me how much he loves all the various games that have been created from

Dune. This strikes me as funny, mostly because if we viewed *Dune* as a conventional game, there would be no way to win without losing. Having a *Dune* coloring book makes about as much sense as having a *Dune* board game or, for that matter, *Dune* action figures. Of course, all of these things exist, and the various versions of both tabletop games for *Dune* and video games based on the franchise are varying degrees of fun, depending on your investment into the world of Arrakis to begin with.

What's fascinating about thinking about games based on *Dune* is the implicit nature of why we play games: fun. While writing this book, I tracked down a version of the 1992 *Dune* computer game, which was created by Cryo Interactive Entertainment and released by Virgin Interactive Entertainment. I periodically played this game while I was writing *The Spice Must Flow*, often to touch base with a part of *Dune* that would have appealed to me as a much younger person: pixelated sci-fi graphics juxtaposed with challenging gameplay and stakes that are utterly unclear. This game is hard to understand, hard to win, time-consuming, and totally addictive. If we're only thinking about the emotional truth of *Dune*, there may not be a better adaptation than this on the planet. Interestingly, this game came out at a time when there were basically no new *Dune* things in the world and there was no real demand for the franchise at all. But if you grew up in the era of these kinds of early '90s computer games, it's perfect. You control a version of Paul who looks just enough like Kyle MacLachlan to make this feel like it's set in the Lynch *Dune* universe, because even in 1992, nostalgia for the '80s was strong. The game allows you to take your ornithopter out to various sietches to recruit Fremen to your cause, although most of them aren't really sure about you yet. If you stay out in the desert too long, you will starve to death, and the computer shows your skin rotting away, pixel by pixel, until you're just a skeleton. Then you can start over.

Here's the funniest part. In order to save your game in the 1992 PC version of *Dune*, you have to go into a room and "look in a mirror." This is when you see yourself, looking like a 1992 knockoff Kyle MacLachlan. In order to save your progress in the game of *Dune*, the game requires you to look in the mirror deeply. When I first realized this was how you had to save your progress, by participating in a kind of false digital reflection, I laughed out loud. Nothing could be more *Dune*-ish than this. A novel of self-reflection and adventure adapted into a video game that requires you to literally look in the mirror in order to walk away from the game. I tried to imagine a bookmark that's also a mirror, and how hilariously jarring that would be if you had to stare into your own eyes before saving your place in a book you were reading. Particularly if that book was the 1965 novel *Dune*.

I suppose you could play this *Dune* video game without looking in the mirror and without saving your spot. But that doesn't mean it would stop existing, or that you couldn't hypothetically beat the game on the first try. As I write these words, I've just read an article in my local paper that tells me that discarded Christmas trees will be used on a local beach in Portland, Maine, in order to keep the sand dunes in place. This 2023 newspaper article doesn't mention that this process is similar to what inspired Frank Herbert's *Dune*. It's possible the journalist who wrote the piece didn't even know that detail. And yet, the connection is there. *Dune* fills in so many spaces in our lives and creates wonder while it does so. The journey of the spice from the 1950s until now doesn't require you to understand or even remember what has happened. The Bene Gesserit know that even they won't live to see the results of their plans. *Dune* will be around for much longer than any of us. Because as long as children can recognize a sandworm and see one thing, while adults see something else, the Golden Path will continue to unfold, hopefully, forever.

ACHNOWLEDGMENTS

This book would not have been possible without the support of my agents, Christopher Hermelin and Ryan Harbage, the Guild navigators who helped me see just far enough into the future to make this book happen.

For the second time, I've been very lucky to work with the brilliant Jill Schwartzman, an editor who is part Mentat and part Bene Gesserit: capable of instant and correct analysis, but also always playing the long game. Thank you, Jill, for your patience, insight, and humor.

Also, thanks to Charlotte Peters for providing suggestions for this book's structure, which proved to be revelatory and transformative.

A big thanks to everyone I interviewed for this book. Many of you did not have to generously give your time, but you did, and I'm so grateful. So, huge thanks to Kyle MacLachlan, Timothée Chalamet, Alec Newman, Alicia Witt, Patrick Stewart, John Harrison, Alec Nevala-Lee, Kara Kennedy, Rebecca Ferguson, Denis Villeneuve, Hans Zimmer, Emmet Asher-Perrin, Haris Durrani, Frank Pavich, and Bill Ransom.

Special thanks here to Theresa Shackleford, who forever changed the way I thought about Frank Herbert and gave this book the heart it needed.

Important thanks to Mike Cecchini at Den of Geek, who asked me to write a cover story about *Dune* back in the summer of 2021, which led directly to my thinking about doing an entire book. Special thanks to Patrisia Prestinary for taking my phone call and tracking down the letters from the Fullerton Library that made the research for this book come alive.

Shout-outs to my regular collaborators and editors in my non-book writing, who all continue to support me professionally and make me a better writer in so many incalculable ways: Tyghe Trimble, Lizzy Francis, Matt Berical, Julia Holmes, Tyler Santora, Jake Kleinman, Hoai-Tran Bui, Mark Hill, and Adrienne Westenfeld.

While writing this book, I discussed or joked about it, or briefly blew off steam, with several wonderful writer friends. A writer needs creative friends, and I'm lucky to have some of the greatest on the planet. So, thanks to Lena Valencia, Ryan Spencer, Leigh Stein, Anthony Ha, Stefan Block, Phuc Tran, Colin Cheney, Sarah Braunstein, Lev Grossman, Chris Lough, Caseen Gaines, and Karen Russell. Special thanks to Brian Shuff for always being down to listen to me rant and always catching my Oasis references.

Huge thanks to my old friend Zach Pirtle, the smartest *Dune* aficionado on the planet. Your notes were essential to making this book better, and I don't think I would have even written it if I had not met you way back when we were both pre-born abominations.

Thanks to the *Dune* fan community, who have been very supportive of this project, including Mark Bennett, Daniel Rohrbach, and the always wonderful Secrets of Dune.

Thanks to Justin Lemieux, Katy Lemieux, and the whole Lemieux clan for your friendship and support. I can't wait to see this book on the shelves of Talking Animals.

Also, a huge thank-you to the local businesses who tolerate me as a fixture, hunched over my laptop in a spice trance: Thaddeus St. John, Doug Watts and the crew at 93 Main, and James LaPlante at SoPoCo Works.

Special thanks to Marie Plouffe and everyone at the South Portland Public Library.

Big high fives to my local bookstores in Portland, Maine, specifically Beth at Nonesuch Books, the whole crew at Print, the good folks at Longfellow Books, the cool kids at Bull Moose, and everyone at Sherman's. And of course, this book could not exist and would not exist without Michelle Souliere at Green Hand Bookshop. Michelle, I hope you love this book as much as I love your shop, though that may not be possible.

Huge love to Kellie, C.J., Charlie, and Harper. And thanks a million to Simon Navarro for making me the person I am today.

Finally, thanks to my daughter, Randell, for reminding me to live in the moment. I love you so much and am so proud of you every single day.

And to Mary. My wife. My best friend. The only person I trust with eternity. I love you now and forever. History will remember you as the best mother, wife, poet, and artist on the planet.

SOURCE NOTES

Author's Note: Some phone conversations with Timothée Chalamet, Rebecca Ferguson, and Denis Villeneuve were initially conducted in July 2021 by the author for the Den of Geek cover story "Visions of *Dune*," published in October 2021. Some quotes derived from those interviews appear throughout this book in entirely different contexts, and many quotes from those interviews were not included in "Visions of *Dune*." Thus, all of the quotes appear uniquely in this book, and some for the first time. Otherwise, all other interviews conducted for this book are completely unique to these pages.

Prologue: Use the Voice, Paul

Interviews with Timothée Chalamet, Rebecca Ferguson, Bill Ransom, John Harrison, and Denis Villeneuve, conducted by the author.

Dr. Willis E. McNelly, *The Dune Encyclopedia* (Berkley, 1984).

Tanya Lapointe, *The Art and Soul of Dune* (Insight Editions, 2020).

Bill Ransom, "Introduction," in *The Jesus Incident* (Wordfire Press, 2012).

"*Dune* Cast Q&A with Stephen Colbert," Nerdist, September 9, 2020, https://www.youtube.com/watch?v=SjLijCWt76o.

Letter from John Campbell to Lurton Blassingame, October 15, 1968. From the Willis E. McNelly Science Fiction Collection: Frank Herbert Papers, Fullerton Library, California State University, Fullerton.

Letter from John Campbell to Frank Herbert, June 3, 1963. From the Willis E. McNelly Science Fiction Collection: Frank Herbert Papers, Fullerton Library, California State University, Fullerton.

Alec Nevala-Lee, *Astounding: John W. Campbell, Isaac Asimov, Robert A. Heinlein, L. Ron Hubbard, and the Golden Age of Science Fiction* (Dey Street, 2019).

Tape recording of Willis McNelly interviewing Frank Herbert and Beverly Herbert on February 3, 1969, transcript, https://libraryguides.fullerton.edu/ld.php?content_id=16165047.

Harlan Ellison, *Harlan Ellison's Watching* (Underwood-Miller, 1989).

Paul M. Sammon, "My Year on Arrakis," *Cinefantastique*, September 1984.

Dune: A Recorded Interview (interview with Frank Herbert and David Lynch), cassette, Waldentapes, 1984.

William F. Touponce, *Frank Herbert* (Twayne Publishers, 1988).

Chapter 1: Frank Herbert's Beard

Interview with Bill Ransom, conducted by the author.

Frank Herbert, *Dune* (Chilton Books, 1965, et al.)

Brian Herbert, *Dreamer of Dune: The Biography of Frank Herbert* (Tor, 2003).

Brian Herbert and Kevin J. Anderson, *The Road to Dune* (Tor, 2005).

William F. Touponce, *Frank Herbert* (Twayne Publishers, 1988).

Kurt Vonnegut, *Mother Night* (Fawcett Publications/Gold Medal Books, 1962, et al.)

Frank Herbert, "Survival of the Cunning," *Esquire*, March 1, 1945, https://classic.esquire.com/article/1945/3/1/survival-of-the-cunning.

Denis Fischer, "Frank Herbert Author of *Dune*," *Enterprise Incidents Special: Dune*, October 1984.

Chris Hodenfield, "Daring *Dune*," *Rolling Stone*, December 6, 1984.

Daniel Immerwahr, "Heresies of *Dune*," *Los Angeles Review of Books*, November 19, 2020, https://lareviewofbooks.org/article/heresies-of-dune/.

Tape recording of Willis McNelly interviewing Frank Herbert and Beverly Herbert on February 3, 1969, transcript, https://libraryguides.fullerton.edu/ld.php?content_id=16165047.

Dune: A Recorded Interview (interview with Frank Herbert and David Lynch), cassette, Waldentapes, 1984.

Frank Herbert, "When I Was Writing *Dune*," in *Heretics of Dune* (Putnam, 1984).

Chapter 2: Fear Is the Mind-Killer

Interviews with Hans Zimmer, Kara Kennedy, Alicia Witt, Emmet Asher-Perrin, and Theresa Shackleford, conducted by the author.

Frank Herbert, "Afterword," in *Chapterhouse: Dune* (Putnam, 1985).

Frank Herbert, *Dune* (Chilton Books, 1965, et al.).

"Possible Futures," Blu-ray/DVD special feature for *Dune* (2021; Warner Bros./Warner Bros. Home Video, 2022).

Tape recording of Willis McNelly interviewing Frank Herbert and Beverly Herbert on February 3, 1969, transcript, https://libraryguides .fullerton.edu/ ld.php? content_ id= 16165047.

Brian Herbert, *Dreamer of Dune: The Biography of Frank Herbert* (Tor, 2003).

Pat Stone, "Frank Herbert: Science Fiction Author," *Mother Earth News*, May 1, 1981, https://www.motherearthnews.com/sustainable-living /nature-and-environment/frank-herbert-science-fiction-author -zmaz81mjzraw/.

Kathrine Beck, "Herbert, Frank Patrick (1920–1986)," HistoryLink.org, June 9, 2021, https://www.historylink.org/File/21248.

Brian Herbert and Kevin J. Anderson, *The Road to Dune* (Tor, 2005).

Frank Herbert, "First Draft, Handwritten notes for Chapter 1 of 'Spice Planet.'" From the Willis E. McNelly Science Fiction Collection: Frank Herbert Papers, Fullerton Library, California State University, Fullerton, https://libraryguides.fullerton.edu/ld.php?content_id= 16206333.

Donald A. Wollheim, *The Universe Makers* (Harper & Row, 1971).

Chapter 3: Magazine Worms

Interview with Alec Nevala-Lee, conducted by the author.

Letter from John Campbell to Frank Herbert, June 3, 1963. From the Willis E. McNelly Science Fiction Collection: Frank Herbert Papers, Fullerton Library, California State University, Fullerton.

Paul Turner, "Vertex Interviews Frank Herbert," *Vertex: The Magazine of Science Fiction*, October 1973.

Letter from Lurton Blassingame to Frank Herbert, May 26, 1959.

Letter from Frank Herbert to John Campbell, June 12, 1959.

Frank Herbert, *The Dragon in the Sea/Under Pressure* (Doubleday, Smith and Street, 1956, et al.).

Frank Herbert, "Dune World," parts 1–3, *Analog*, December 1963–February 1964.

Frank Herbert, "The Prophet of Dune," parts 1–5, *Analog*, January 1965–May 1965.

Denis Fischer, "Frank Herbert Author of *Dune*," *Enterprise Incidents Special: Dune*, October 1984.

Cory Doctorow, "Read: Jeannette Ng's Campbell Award acceptance speech . . . ," Boing Boing, August 20, 2019, https://boingboing.net/2019/08/20/needed-saying.html.

Harlan Ellison, "Thirty-Two Soothsayers," in *Dangerous Visions* (Berkley, 1967).

Letter from Mark L. Schibel to John Campbell, January 6, 1964.

Letter from Frank Herbert to Mark L. Schibel, January 29, 1964.

Letter from P. M. Strain to John Campbell, January 15, 1964.

Letter from Frank Herbert to P. M. Strain, January 29, 1964.

Letter from Russell S. Grove Jr. to Frank Herbert, April 10, 1965.

Thomas Clareson, *Understanding Contemporary American Science Fiction: The Formative Period, 1926–1970* (University of South Carolina Press, 1990).

Chapter 4: Novel Repair Manual

Paul M. Sammon, "Commentary Track," *Dune* (1984; Arrow Video, 2021), Blu-ray.

Lauren Panepinto, "Book Cover Trends Thru Time (Via *Dune*)," Muddy Colors, September 10, 2020, https://www.muddycolors.com/2020/09/book-cover-trends-thru-time/.

Frank Herbert, *The Dune Audio Collection: Performed by Frank Herbert* (Caedmon Audio/HarperCollins, 1977, 1978, 1979, 1994, 2007).

Karin Christina Ryding, "The Arabic of *Dune*," in *Language in Place*, edited by Daniela Francesca Virdis, Elisabetta Zurru, and Ernestine Lahey (John Benjamins Publishing Company, 2021).

Letter from Timothy Seldes to Lurton Blassingame, July 12, 1963.

Letter from Timothy Seldes to Lurton Blassingame, August 28, 1963.

Letter from Sterling E. Lanier to Frank Herbert, January 19, 1965.

Letter from Timothy Seldes to Lurton Blassingame, January 20, 1965.

Letter from Sterling E. Lanier to Frank Herbert, March 15, 1965.

Letter from Lurton Blassingame to Frank Herbert, August 24, 1965.

Letter from Frank Herbert to Lurton Blassingame, August 27, 1965.

Mark Zaloudek, "Successful Author Was Also a Sculptor," *Herald Tribune*, August 7, 2007.

Chapter 5: My Own Private Duncan Idaho

Interviews with Timothée Chalamet, Haris Durrani, Alec Nevala-Lee, and Jason Momoa, conducted by the author.

"Julie Cox Interview from *Frank Herbert's Dune*," SciFi.com, 2000. Archived by Dune Info, January 1, 2011, https://www.youtube.com/watch?v=buBbDTtHNHo.

Olivia Pym, "The Real-Life Heroics of Jason Momoa," GQ (UK), August 8, 2022, https://www.gq-magazine.co.uk/culture/article/jason-momoa-interview-dune-3.

Brian Herbert, introduction to *Dune Messiah*, by Frank Herbert (DreamStar Inc., 2008).

Letter from John Campbell to Lurton Blassingame, October 15, 1968. From the Willis E. McNelly Science Fiction Collection: Frank Herbert Papers, Fullerton Library, California State University, Fullerton.

Susan Sontag, "Notes on Camp," in *Against Interpretation* (Farrar, Straus and Giroux, 1966).

Chapter 6: Golden Paths Not Taken

Interview with Frank Pavich, conducted by the author.

Jodorowsky's Dune, directed by Frank Pavich, Sony Pictures Classics/High Line Pictures/Camera One, 2013.

Pierre Boulle, *Planet of the Apes/La planète des singes* (Éditions Julliard et al., 1963).

Joe Ford and Bob Greenhut, *Dune* screen treatment, March 1972 (Arthur Jacobs/APJ).

Rospo Pallenberg, *Dune* screenplay, January 23, 1973 (Arthur Jacobs/APJ).

Alejandro Jodorowsky, "Lettre ouverte a Frank Herbert" (Open letter to Frank Herbert), *L'écran fantastique*, October 1984.

Emmet Asher-Perrin, "Jodorowsky's *Dune* Didn't Get Made for a Reason," Tor.com, May 2, 2017.

"Alejandro Jodorowsky Speaks Out After El Museo del Barrio Calls Off Retrospective," *Artforum*, January 31, 2019.

Canan Balan, "Healer, Rapist and Cult," 5Harfliler, November 2, 2021, https://www.5harfliler.com/healer-rapist-and-cult/.

Chapter 7: I Am the Sandworm

Frank Herbert, *Children of Dune* (Putnam, 1976).

David G. Hartwell, *Age of Wonders: Exploring the World of Science Fiction* (Tor, 1984, 1996).

Paul Turner, "Vertex Interviews Frank Herbert," *Vertex: The Magazine of Science Fiction*, October 1973.

Chapter 8: Spice Wars

Interviews with Denis Villeneuve and Kyle MacLachlan, conducted by the author.

"Virginia Madsen on *Dune* Casting," *Kevin Pollak's Chat Show*, September 11, 2016, https://www.youtube.com/watch?v=2l_UJzn7L7A.

Joe Bergren, "What *Dune* Author Frank Herbert Said About the 1984 David Lynch Adaptation," ET Online, October 22, 2021, https://www.etonline.com/what-dune-author-frank-herbert-said-about-the-1984-david-lynch-adaptation-flashback-174069.

Chris Hodenfield, "Daring *Dune*," *Rolling Stone*, December 6, 1984.

Chapter 9: *Dune* Velvet

Interviews with Kyle MacLachlan, Patrick Stewart, and Alicia Witt, conducted by the author.

Denis Fischer, "Frank Herbert, Author of *Dune*," *Enterprise Incidents Special: Dune*, October 1984.

Ed Naha, *The Making of Dune* (Berkley, 1984).

Chris Hodenfield, "Daring *Dune*," *Rolling Stone*, December 6, 1984.

Paul M. Sammon, *Future Noir: The Making of Blade Runner* (Harper, 1996).

Paul M. Sammon, "My Year on Arrakis," *Cinefantastique*, September 1984.

Chris Rodley and David Lynch, *Lynch on Lynch* (Faber and Faber, 2005).

Impressions of Dune, directed by Tim Qualtrough and Jarrod Harlow (2003), documentary special feature included with *Dune*, directed by David Lynch (1984; Arrow Video, 2021), Blu-ray.

"Timothée Chalamet on Lynch's *Dune*," comments from Venice International Film Festival press conference, September 3, 2021, archived by Dune Info, https://www.youtube.com/watch?v=TJL2ul-RXGI.

"Production Notes," special feature included with *Dune*, directed by David Lynch (1984; 2017), DVD.

Dune: Special Edition, directed by David Lynch (1984; Arrow Video, 2021), Blu-ray.

Chapter 10: Twilight of the Emperor

Interviews with Theresa Shackleford and Bill Ransom, conducted by the author.

Frank Herbert, *God Emperor of Dune* (Putnam, 1981).

Frank Herbert, "God Emperor of Dune," *Playboy*, January 1981.

Comments from Philip K. Dick republished in "THE HIDDEN HISTORY OF VCON 2: Part Three" by The Graeme, *WCSFAzine*, August 2008, https://efanzines.com/WCSFA/WCSFAzine08.pdf.

Chapter 11: Walk Without Rhythm

Interviews with Alec Newman and John Harrison, conducted by the author.

James Van Hise, *The Secrets of Frank Herbert's Dune* (I Books, 2000).

The Secrets of Frank Herbert's Dune, directed by Michael D. Messina (New Amsterdam Entertainment, 2000), DVD.

"Behind-the-Scenes Featurette," *Frank Herbert's Dune*, directed by John Harrison (Artisan, 2000), DVD.

Deborah D. McAdams, "*Dune* Does It for Sci Fi," NextTV, December 10, 2000, https://www.nexttv.com/news/dune-does-it-sci-fi-95665.

Hoai-Tran Bui, "James McAvoy, Son of *Dune*, Has Advice for His Father, *Dune* Star Timothée Chalamet," SlashFilm, October 19, 2021, https://www.slashfilm.com/617323/james-mcavoy-son-of-dune-has-advice-for-his-father-dune-star-timothee-chalamet/.

Chapter 12: The Slow Blade Penetrates the Shield

Interviews with Timothée Chalamet, Rebecca Ferguson, Denis Villeneuve, Theresa Shackleford, and Hans Zimmer, conducted by the author.

Tanya Lapointe, *The Art and Soul of Dune* (Insight Editions, 2020).

"The Training Room," special feature included with *Dune: Part One* (2021), directed by Denis Villeneuve (2021; Warner Bros., 2022), Blu-ray.

"Possible Futures," special feature included with *Dune Part One* (2021), directed by Denis Villeneuve (2021; Warner Bros., 2022), Blu-ray.

Zachary Pirtle, "Humans, Machines, and an Ethics for Technology in *Dune*," in *Dune and Philosophy*, edited by Kevin S. Decker (Wiley Blackwell, 2022).

Rick Marshall, "How *Dune*'s Visual Effects Made an Unfilmable Epic Possible," Digital Trends, March 23, 2022, https://www.digitaltrends.com/movies/dune-visual-effects-paul-lambert-vfx-interview/.

Anthony Breznican, "Behold *Dune*," *Vanity Fair*, April 14, 2020, https://www.vanityfair.com/hollywood/2020/04/behold-dune-an-exclusive-look-at-timothee-chalamet-zendaya-oscar-isaac.

Marcus Gabriel, "Roger Yuan Reveals His Role in *Dune* Movie Sequel," DuneNewsNet, March 12, 2021, https://dunenewsnet.com/2021/03/roger-yuan-reveals-dune-movie-sequel-role/.

Jeff Spry, "*Dune* Wins 6 Oscars at Academy Awards," Space.com, March 28, 2022, https://www.space.com/dune-wins-6-oscars-academy-awards-2022.

Zack Sharf, "Villeneuve Says 'It's a Miracle' He Survived 'Blade Runner 2049': 'At Least I Wasn't Banned' from Directing," IndieWire,

October 7, 2021, https://www.indiewire.com/2021/10/denis-ville-neuve-blade-runner-2049-ban-directing-1234669852/.

Jessica Howard, "John Hodgman Says There Was Almost a 'Dune' Film Adaptation Written by Him and Directed by Peter Berg," Uproxx, October 26, 2021, https://uproxx.com/movies/john-hodgman-peter-berg-dune/.

Joseph Knoop, "Here's How *Dune* Managed to Avoid Using Green Screen," IGN, November 15, 2021, https://www.ign.com/articles/dune-green-screen-fabric.

Sam Lansky, "Timothée Chalamet Wants You to Wear Your Heart on Your Sleeve," *Time*, October 11, 2021, https://time.com/6103203/timothee-chalamet-profile/.

Scott Mendelson, "As 'Dune' Passes $400 Million, Can 'Dune Part Two' Rewrite Box Office History?," *Forbes*, February 15, 2022, https://www.forbes.com/sites/scottmendelson/2022/02/15/dune-alita-chalamet-zendaya-box-office-history-400m/?sh=742631325ddb.

Helen O'Hara, "Zendaya on *Dune*: 'Chani Is a Fighter,'" Empire, August 25, 2021, https://www.empireonline.com/movies/features/zendaya-dune-interview-chani-is-a-fighter/.

Chapter 13: The Sleeper Must Awaken

Interviews with Timothée Chalamet, Rebecca Ferguson, and Haris Durrani, conducted by the author.

Frank Herbert, ed., *New World or No World* (Ace, 1970).

Alexandra Straub and Rebecca Kaplan, "Philadelphia Earth Week, Fifty Years On," Science History Institute, April 21, 2020.

Stewart Brand, *The Whole Earth Catalog*, fall 1968, https://monoskop.org/images/0/09/Brand_Stewart_Whole_Earth_Catalog_Fall_1968.pdf.

Epilogue: Spice Up Your Life

Meomi, *The Octonauts and the Growing Goldfish* (HarperCollins, 2014).

Ellis Weiner, *National Lampoon's Doon* (Pocket Books, 1984).

Frank Herbert, *Chapterhouse: Dune* (Putnam, 1985).

INDEX

Ryan Britt is the author of *Phasers on Stun!* and *Luke Sky-walker Can't Read*. Lev Grossman has said about him, "Ryan Britt is one of nerd culture's most brilliant and most essential commentators." His writing has appeared in *Esquire, Vulture, Vice*, SyFy Wire, Den of Geek, Inverse, the *New York Times*, and Fatherly, where he is a senior editor.